Emerging Literacy

Emerging Literacy: Preschool, Kindergarten, and Primary Grades

Edited by

LLOYD O. OLLILA and MARGIE I. MAYFIELD
University of Victoria

ALLYN AND BACON
Boston   London   Toronto   Sydney   Tokyo   Singapore

Series Editor: Sean W. Wakely
Series Editorial Assistant: Carol L. Chernaik
Production Administrator: Annette Joseph
Production Coordinator: Holly Crawford
Editorial-Production Service: Carlyle Carter
Cover Administrator: Linda K. Dickinson
Cover Designer: Suzanne Harbison
Manufacturing Buyer: Megan Cochran

Library of Congress Cataloging-in-Publication Data

Emerging literacy : preschool, kindergarten, and primary grades /
  edited by Lloyd O. Ollila, Margie I. Mayfield.
     p.   cm.
    Includes index.
    ISBN 0-205-13216-2
    1. Language arts (Preschool) 2. Language arts (Primary)
I. Ollila, Lloyd O. II. Mayfield, Margie.
LB1140.5.L3E44   1991   91-21029
372.6 — dc20   CIP

Printed in the United States of America

10 9 8 7 6 5 4 3 2 1   96 95 94 93 92 91

Photo credits: Page 5, Will Malcolm; pages 52, 57, 61, 65, 66, 67, 68, 258, Alison
Preece; pages 108, 114, 116, 120, Kathy Ollila; pages 143, 144, 146, 222, Joanne Nurss;
pages 176, 181, 220, Margie I. Mayfield; page 219, Lloyd O. Ollila.

Text credit: Page 129, Review of spelling research and programme ideas by Mary Tarasoff.

To write a text on the emerging literacy of children is — unavoidably — a quiet accounting of the emergence of our own literacy. This work reflects the love, patience, and teaching of parents and family, many elementary and high school teachers, college instructors, and colleagues. Some are long gone, and some we will share time with again. This work attests to their efforts, not just our own. We acknowledge them with these words of gratitude.

Brief Contents

Contents

Chapter Six   ·   *Language and Literacy for the Limited English
Proficient Child   137*

By Ruth A. Hough and Joanne R. Nurss

Chapter Nine · *Evaluation of Language and Literacy   229*
By Joanne R. Nurss

Chapter Ten · *Parents and Teachers: Partners in Emerging Literacy   253*
By Margie I. Mayfield and Lloyd O. Ollila

Preface

Emerging Literacy: Preschool, Kindergarten, and Primary Grades is a basic text intended to serve university and college students enrolled in preschool, kindergarten, and primary education programs and to provide a guide for teachers and administrators who are already working in school systems. Much of the information provided in the text can also be useful in childcare and Head Start programs and in courses for parents and parent groups.

It was our perception of the need for a text on guiding literacy development for children ages three through nine that resulted in our writing this book. We have focused on emerging literacy in both the preschool and kindergarten years as well as the early primary grades. We have emphasized continuity in guiding teachers in the development of literacy in young children. With this focus clearly in mind, we therefore tried to meet the following needs and purposes for language education, which were identified by our own experiences and those of our students:

1. We examined emerging literacy in the home, in the school, and from the young child's point of view. This research regards literacy as a multidimensional activity with cognitive, linguistic, social, and psychological aspects. The applications of this research are described and discussed throughout this book.

2. The book is not only based on current research findings. We explain basic principles of literacy instruction and describe proven classroom practices used to foster developmental continuity for children ages three through nine. We provide many specific examples of classroom organizations, schedules, methods, materials, and learning principles.

3. We address all areas of the language arts and give ideas on how to integrate the various language processes. We also give examples of how language and literacy can be integrated across the curriculum.

4. We believe that children who have a print-rich emerging literacy environment at home and in preschool, kindergarten, and primary school will have an excellent start in developing into highly competent language users. Children with a strong foundation in literacy will be more apt to develop positive attitudes toward literacy and language and find enjoyment in these activities throughout their lives. The reader should be aware, however, that there are

many approaches to helping children develop language and literacy. There is no one best way for all children. Therefore this book includes a variety of viewpoints expressed by the different chapter authors about principles of instruction, methods, techniques, and materials.

We wish to thank especially the many people who have assisted us in the preparation of this book. We are grateful to John D. Beach, University of Nevada–Reno, and Jeanne Shay Schumm, University of Miami, who reviewed the manuscript and offered invaluable suggestions. Our thanks to our colleagues and students who reviewed early drafts of the manuscript, to Kathy Ollila for her help in reviewing and editing, to Sean Wakely of Allyn and Bacon for his encouragement and assistance, and to Carlyle Carter for her careful copyediting and comments.

L.O.O.
M.I.M.

CHAPTER ONE

Emerging Literacy

Advance Organizer

In this chapter, we define *emerging literacy* as the natural, gradual development of a young child's listening, speaking, reading, and writing abilities. In the first section, we expand this definition by describing its characteristics. Then we continue with a discussion of what emerging literacy is not. Problems in defining this term may arise, since variants of the concepts have in the past produced multiple definitions. This will be discussed broadly throughout the chapter. The well-documented research basis of the emergence of literacy is summarized. In the second half of this chapter, we describe the interrelatedness of the language arts, how these areas reinforce one another, and the role of emerging literacy in the early childhood program. Classroom examples are provided. The chapter concludes with statements from professional organizations on developmentally appropriate practices for emerging literacy teaching and learning.

Objectives

After studying this chapter, the reader should be able to —

- define emerging literacy in his or her own terms;
- make two lists: one that identifies the key characteristics of emerging literacy and one that identifies things that emerging literacy is not;
- explain why emerging literacy is difficult to define;
- give a few examples of the research basis for emerging literacy;
- explain how the four language arts are interrelated, including how they reinforce each other;
- describe the role of emerging literacy in the early childhood program and cite specific examples of literacy experiences throughout a typical day;

Graphic Organizer

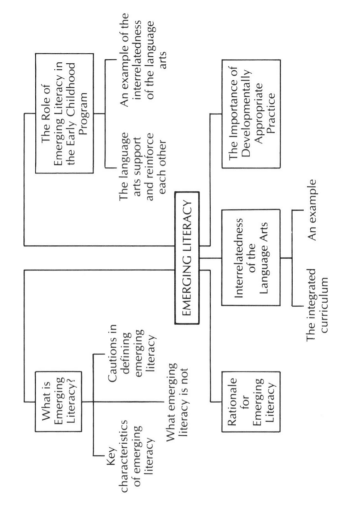

EMERGING LITERACY

The Role of Emerging Literacy in the Early Childhood Program

- The language arts support and reinforce each other
- An example of the interrelatedness of the language arts

What is Emerging Literacy?

- Key characteristics of emerging literacy
- Cautions in defining emerging literacy
- What emerging literacy is not

Rationale for Emerging Literacy

Interrelatedness of the Language Arts

- The integrated curriculum
- An example

The Importance of Developmentally Appropriate Practice

- discuss the use of an integrated curriculum and provide an example for a classroom situation;
- explain the importance of developmentally appropriate practices as they relate to emerging literacy.

What Is Emerging Literacy?

Max is 4 years old. His mother thinks he's marvelous. Yesterday, she found him curled up on the sofa with Snuffy, his favorite teddy bear, "reading" Snuffy *The Pokey Little Puppy.* It wasn't important that he didn't get all the words right. In fact, she knew he had memorized most of the story. Just two months earlier, he learned to print his name, and now he writes it on everything. Max has watched her write letters to relatives, and he wrote one to Grandma. He announced he was going to write her about his new puppy. The letter had misshaped letters, wavy lines, scribbles, and drawings, but it was signed Max and he was very proud of it. So were his mother and father as they listened attentively while he read them his letter. Thinking back to his infancy and toddler years, his mother could see signs that Max was going to excel. She talked and read to him daily in those years. Even as a baby, he seemed to really enjoy those conversations. He picked up new words easily as his mother talked with him while she went about her daily routine. She would sing little songs and nursery rhymes, and soon Max would join right in with her. He and his sister, Maria, were always building things with legos and little logs or making sand cakes and racing tracks in the sandbox with the neighbors. His mother could hear them chattering happily as they played. Even when Max was alone, she could often hear him talking to himself, playing different characters with his stuffed animals. His mother knows he is going to do well in school.

Max is what educators term a child emerging in literacy. Although more advanced in literacy than many others his age, he is naturally and gradually developing his listening, speaking, reading, and writing abilities. Max's development in these areas started long before formal instruction in school begins. He naturally developed language as an infant as he watched and listened to his parents and began to realize that certain cries produced certain reactions in his parents. Soon he was copying his parents' speech, attempting new sound, trying to make language work for him. He was constantly seeking meaning from his surroundings as he watched and talked with his mother, saw snow falling in very cold weather, and observed his sister Maria playing with stuffed animals. To understand these observations, he related them to earlier observations or enlisted the help of his family or others to explain these happenings.

As with the spoken language, Max became aware of print gradually and naturally. He observed his mother and father writing lists, cards, letters, recipes, telephone numbers, or reading newspapers, books, and magazines. Max sought meaning from this print, just as he did from other happenings in his world. Slowly he began to understand the value and function of speaking, listening, reading, and writing. He enjoyed the warm cozy feeling of sitting on his father's lap listening to the good stories that his father read every night before bedtime. Sometimes alone or through interaction with others, he began to engage in exploration of language and print, writing letters, reading to his teddy, discussing sandbox road building with Maria. This process of discovery and exploration is the essence of the emergence of literacy. Max moved naturally into literacy: when he was born, his parents did not deliberately develop a long-range plan of lessons in listening, speaking, reading, and writing. In fact, Max's mother and father didn't realize they were really teaching Max, and they would probably be rather pleasantly surprised if someone pointed out the many seemingly incidental ways they were helping Max to be literate.

Key Characteristics of Emerging Literacy

The emergence of literacy can be described in a number of ways. The following characteristics should help the reader develop a broader perspective on this aspect of a child's development. These characteristics will be further expanded upon throughout this book.

Emerging literacy includes an awareness of print and writing and other uses of language.   Children beginning to be empowered by literacy are learning how to communicate their wants and to see how print functions. They develop a sense of story (i.e., that stories have beginnings, middles, and ends) from being read to by adults and older siblings. They are aware of and are able to use print on food boxes, road signs, logos, and TV. They can manipulate language to communicate their wants and desires.

Emerging literacy is multidimensional and complex.   It involves not only the learning of cognitive skills, but also has linguistic, social, and psychological aspects. Literacy growth depends on children's interaction and active participation socially, linguistically, and cognitively with their environment — especially the people in their world.

Emerging literacy is child-driven.   Literacy grows from the child's continuous learning about and active participation in listening, speaking, reading, and writing. Children set their own pace as they are exposed to and become interested in language and print, explore and play with language, and discover and extend meaning and function. Adults may interact with children and set the stage by providing a literacy-rich environment of talk and discussion, books, posters, writing paper, and felt markers. Emphasis should be placed on providing a learning environment that allows children to become willing and active participants in literacy learning. Literacy is a continuous, developmental process beginning during the earliest years prior to entering school and lasting throughout life.

Growth in literacy varies from child to child.   All children do not grow in literacy at the same rate or with the same progression of experiences. For example, some children come from homes rich in language and print, where parents value books and provide their children with many chances to experience, explore, and play with language activities. Other children come from environments with little print and where literacy activities are not valued highly or used frequently. Children who have fewer opportunities to interact and explore print or language may take longer to become proficient in literacy skills.

Emerging literacy includes speaking, listening, reading, and writing, which are all interrelated.   Each area is developed and reinforced by experiences with the others.

Adults play a major role in helping children develop literacy.   They demonstrate the functions and usefulness of language and print materials in their daily lives and in their interactions with their children, as well as capitalize and expand on their children's existing literacy skills.

Reading a good book to a friend

What Emerging Literacy Is Not

Another way to describe emerging literacy is to describe what it is *not*. The concept of emerging literacy differs in many ways from traditional views of children's development of literacy skills (Clay, 1975).

The emergence of literacy is a broader and more inclusive concept than reading readiness. With emerging literacy, reading and writing are considered closely related processes. The traditional, formal reading readiness programs, with emphasis on perceptual-motor skills and abstract, isolated aspects of print, have no place in this perspective of helping children obtain power over literacy. Neither do methods of instruction where skills are introduced earlier and earlier, developing first reading then writing with generous helpings of drill and practice to ensure that young children do learn to read and write. In emerging literacy, the emphasis shifts from teaching reading and writing skills to facilitating children's learning by their active involvement in language and print activities. It should be recognized, however, that an emerging literacy focus is not anti-skill. Young children do not have to demonstrate acquisition of basic skills or isolated subskills before they can engage in and develop speaking, listening, reading, and writing behaviors. Strickland and Morrow (1989) expand on this issue:

> *Teachers who view literacy as a natural part of children's ongoing development tend to view skills as interconnecting parts of a whole. They are concerned with helping children develop strategies for learning to read and write. They know that as children acquire strategies they automatically acquire skills. (p. 82)*

Cautions in Defining Emerging Literacy

There are a number of problems in developing a clear picture of what emerging literacy is. Generalities abound, but it just doesn't work to make global conclusions that apply to all children. Each child is different, and literacy issues are complex and multidimensional. For instance, which aspects of literacy can be learned informally and which must be taught directly? Many types of experiences go into helping children develop literacy, but some may be more valuable than others for certain children. There is also no universal timeline when children begin to demonstrate their learning or when all children can be expected to know specific information about reading and writing. Teachers and schools have the responsibility to provide activities and materials that foster, encourage, and stimulate the literacy development of each child.

Rationale for Emerging Literacy

For much of this century, school practices upheld the idea that formal reading instruction began in grade 1. Children were given systematic, sequential reading readiness training to prepare them for reading. This consisted frequently of a workbook-based program of sequenced perceptual and motor-skill activities.

Writing lessons consisting of helping children learn to print were also taught in grade 1, but the teaching of functional and creative writing was left for later grades.

Researchers who have observed and recorded how children become literate are presenting information that calls for changing these practices in schools. Studies of early readers revealed that a number of children learned to read and write prior to coming to school. These children came from homes where there were many opportunities to be read to and to watch adults and older siblings read and write. Many of these children were interested in learning to write first and then began to read (Clark, 1976; Durkin, 1966). They wanted to write functional cards and letters for a specific audience (Bissex, 1980; Lamme & Childers, 1983). Clay (1975) also examined children's first writing and found that children begin to be literate well before formal work in reading and writing is done at schools.

Other researchers have supported this view and found that many preschoolers had a surprisingly remarkable knowledge of print and had developed some print conventions on their own (Ferriero and Teberosky 1982; Harste, Burke, and Woodward, 1982). These young children had developed a variety of strategies for obtaining meaning from print. Many of these children grew naturally in reading and writing influenced by their own interests and curiosity rather than by parental pressure or direct formal instruction (Bissex, 1980; Harste, Burke, & Woodward, 1982; Taylor 1983).

In helping children grow in literacy, the importance of reading to young children has often been highlighted (Fordor, 1966). Not only do children need to be read to, but they also need ample time to respond orally to the story (Goodman, 1984).

The idea that literacy grows continuously and naturally from real-life situations that use writing and reading to accomplish tasks has been reported in a number of observational research studies (Taylor, 1983; Teale, 1986). For instance, a child observes his father reading directions on how to put together a train set. Literacy events or activities are also seen in preschool. For instance, following a discussion on the care and feeding of Harry the classroom's pet hamster, the teacher asks the children to think of some things she can put down on paper so Harry will receive good care during the year when each child has a turn to help take care of the hamster. The teacher records the children's instructions on chart paper. She writes Michael's concern, "Harry needs new water every day," and then reads it to the children, pointing to the words as she goes along. Children's literacy development is fostered through integration of literacy across the early childhood curriculum by emphasizing the interrelatedness of listening, speaking, reading, and writing.

Interrelatedness of the Language Arts

One goal of preschool, kindergarten, and primary education is to foster children's early literacy development. This means helping children to become capable speakers, listeners, readers, and writers. The four language arts—listening, speaking, reading, and writing—are crucial for communication. The purpose of helping young children develop their competencies in the language arts is to foster their ability and desire to communicate.

Thinking and language are common features of listening, speaking, reading, and writing. These four areas involve the use of cognitive processes to gather, interpret, understand, and use information for the purpose of communicating thoughts and ideas. Children need to have the words to be able to describe what they have seen, what they need, what they want to share with their friends, how they feel, and so forth.

The Language Arts Support and Reinforce Each Other

In the influential report, *Becoming a Nation of Readers,* by the Commission on Reading, it was stated that "all of the uses of language—listening, speaking, reading, and writing—are interrelated and mutually supportive. It follows, therefore, that school activities that foster one of the language arts inevitably will benefit the others as well" (Anderson, Hiebert, Scott, & Wilkinson, 1985, p. 79).

Research studies have confirmed this mutually supportive and beneficial relationship among the language arts. In a classic longitudinal study of children's language development from kindergarten through grade 12, Loban (1976) found that children who were highly rated in language proficiency by teachers scored high on measures of oral language use, listening, reading, and writing. Children who scored lower in one of these areas tended to score lower in other areas as well. Reviews of the literature and research by Hammill and McNutt (1980) and Wagner (1985) have also concluded that there are strong relationships among the four language arts. It therefore makes sense to utilize the interrelatedness of the language arts and the mutual reinforcement of these language arts in our provision of literacy experiences for young children. According to Noyce and Christie (1989), "language arts integration is indeed the wave of the future" (p. 1).

Examples of the Interrelatedness of the Language Arts

The interrelatedness of the language arts can be seen in the typical sharing time that is part of the day in most preschool, kindergarten, and primary classrooms. The following is an example of one such sharing time:

The 24 children in Ms. Anderson's class enter the classroom on Monday morning eager to share their news about important things that have happened in their lives over the weekend. As soon as the children are settled in a circle on the carpet, many hands are raised by children eager to share their news. Jennifer tells the children that her dog had six puppies on Saturday and that they are all black ones. Carlos reports that his grandmother has come all the way from Costa Rica for a visit and is going to stay until after Christmas. Andrew says that he went to visit his grandparents on Sunday and they went in the family's new car. Mary describes the cake she and her aunt baked for her brother's birthday party. Other children share their news as well.

After the children have had an opportunity to ask questions of each sharer and/or comment on the news, Ms. Anderson asks the children to dictate one sentence that summarizes that individual child's news. She writes each sentence on a chart. At the end of sharing time, she reads aloud all the sentences with the help of the children.

As can be seen in the above description of one typical sharing time, the four language arts are not separate but interrelated. In sharing and discussing their news, the children used speaking and listening. In writing down the children's sentences and then reading these with the group, Ms. Anderson was helping to develop the children's reading and writing. Speaking, listening, reading, and writing were all used to communicate, record, and recall the children's ideas. They were all used together throughout the sharing time.

In the daily schedule of many primary classrooms, there is usually a large block labeled *language arts*. Teachers recognize the interrelatedness of the language arts and the importance of considering the language arts as an integrated whole rather than as a series of isolated activities. Although tasks such as "listening for the main idea" or "inferential comprehension" are usually not written on the schedule, these may be among the language arts objectives during a particular day. The block of time labeled language arts in a teacher's plan book typically includes many different areas. For example, in Mr. Kolaczewski's second-grade class, one such block included the following language arts activities:

- sharing time;
- reading the daily message from the chalkboard and listening to the teacher describe what the class would be doing that day;
- writing in individual journals;
- reading from basal readers and/or trade books with a reading partner (paired reading);
- discussing which character in the story they liked best and why;
- writing summaries of what they had read;
- working in small groups with the teacher on activities for practicing specific decoding or contextual analysis skills;
- listening to one group dramatize a favorite part of the story they had read;
- choral reading of a poem related to one of the stories.

Although each of these activities was planned by the teacher to help meet the specific objectives he had identified for each of the children in the class, language arts was organized holistically. Most early childhood teachers do this rather than try to separate out the language arts into the four areas. This is not to say that teachers do not or should not have specific goals and objectives for each child in each of the language arts areas. When appropriate, they should teach lessons to develop specific language arts skills needed by the children.

There are many other examples of classroom activities throughout the school day that demonstrate this interrelatedness of the language arts. Try to think of some more examples from early childhood classes that you have observed.

The Role of Emerging Literacy in the Early Childhood Program

Traditionally, literacy has played an important role in early childhood programs. Think back to the old days when the elementary school curriculum consisted of the three Rs (reading, 'riting, and 'rithmetic), and you realize that two of these were language arts. Today's emphasis on literacy in early childhood programs reflects our recognition and knowledge of the importance of young children developing communication skills during this formative period in their lives. This is not a new idea. A textbook on teaching children from 2–8 years old published more than 50 years ago stated:

> *Elementary schools the world over devote a large proportion of their time to the language arts: literature, oral and written expression, and the technique of reading. Not only are the language activities of immediate significance to the child in and of themselves, but the command of language also is fundamental to the progress of his [or her] general education. (Forest, 1935, p. 175)*

The general purpose of literacy learning and teaching is to further develop, enhance, refine, and encourage children's abilities and desires to communicate. If you observe a typical day in an early childhood program, you will note that the majority of the children's day is spent communicating. Literacy is not confined to only one or two parts of the children's school day. For example, the day may begin with a sharing time and end with the teacher reading and discussing a story with the children. In between, there are many formal and informal opportunities for literacy experiences and development.

In addition to planned literacy activities, there are numerous incidental opportunities for children to use language throughout the day. For example, during snack time and recess children use language for communicating their wishes and thoughts. They also use and practice their language skills when chatting to the class guinea pig, asking for help to find some materials needed for a project, asking questions about plants while measuring the bean plant each child is growing as part of a science experiment, describing what they saw on the way to school or did at home last night, planning the class fieldtrip to the museum, discussing as a group how they can do a better job of sharing with their classmates, talking with other children when playing games outside at recess, and so forth. There are literally countless times during the day when young children are using the language arts. As Chenfeld (1987) has stated: "Every minute of your school day is saturated with language arts" (p. 91). Language and literacy truly do occur throughout the child's day and across the early childhood curriculum. Language and literacy opportunities exist at home, in school, and on the playground.

The Integrated Curriculum

Because the language arts are not confined to one period and cannot be separated from each other or from the total program, many preschool, kindergarten, and early primary teachers integrate language arts and other curriculum areas. A recent comprehensive statement on developmentally appropriate practice in early childhood programs by the National Association for the Education of Young Children stated that: "Children's learning does not occur in narrowly defined subject areas; their development and learning are integrated. Any activity that stimulates one dimension of development and learning affects other dimensions as well" (Bredekamp, 1987, p. 3).

An Example of Integration

This integration of the curriculum can be seen in a fieldtrip to the fire station by a class of preschool children. The topic of fire fighters is typically part of a larger unit of study on community helpers (social studies). Before taking the children to visit the fire station, Ms. Garcia and Mr. Norton have their class list things they know — or think they know — about fire fighters (social studies, speaking, and listening). The children are then asked to brainstorm questions about what they would like to know about fire fighters (social studies, speaking, and listening). These questions are written on a piece of chart paper for future reference (writing and reading). The children are asked to think about ways they could find the answers to their questions (problem solving). One of their suggestions to ask a fire fighter some of their questions results in a walk to the local fire station.

On the way, several of the children comment on the spring plants sprouting up (science). At the corner of a street, the teachers review with the children the proper procedure for crossing a street (safety). At the fire station, the children listen to the fire fighters talk about what they do (social studies and listening). The children then ask the fire fighters their questions (speaking and listening). Before they leave, the fire fighters remind the children of the dangers of playing with matches (safety).

When the children return to the preschool, the teachers and children discuss what they saw and what the fire fighters told them (listening and speaking). Ms. Garcia gets out their chart of questions and reads them to the children one at a time (reading and listening). The children then determine if that question has been answered to their satisfaction or whether they need more information (speaking, listening, and problem solving). The children then dictate a thank-you letter to the fire fighters, which Mr. Norton writes down on a large piece of paper; he then rereads it to the children and asks if they wish to add anything else (speaking, listening, reading, and writing). When the children are satisfied with the letter, each one draws a picture of his or her favorite part of the visit to the fire station (art). Some children ask the teachers to write captions describing their pictures; others write their names (speaking and writing). The pictures are then assembled into a book format and are read with the children (reading and book handling). The book and the thank-you letter are later delivered to the fire station by one of the children's parents.

Throughout the next few weeks, the children refer back to their fieldtrip during sharing time (language arts), pretend to be fire fighters in the dress-up corner (dramatic play and language), build a fire station in the block corner (perceptual motor skills and cooperative play), look at picture books about fire fighters in the library corner (reading), and pretend to be fire fighters during music and movement (music and gross motor skills). The above description demonstrates that one topic in one area of the early childhood curriculum can be a springboard for the development of activities across the early childhood curriculum and that most of these activities involve literacy.

The Importance of Developmentally Appropriate Practice

A common theme in the following chapters, where the emergence of literacy will be discussed in more depth, is that the starting point for planning early literacy experiences is each individual child. Not all children are at the same developmental level. Not all 3-year-olds or 6-year-olds or even all 26-year-olds are alike. The challenge for the individual teacher is to provide a program that is developmentally appropriate for each child. The importance of developmentally appropriate early childhood curriculum is reflected in the *New' Policy Guidelines for Reading* published by the National Council of Teachers of English, which states:

> *Teachers should plan a reading curriculum which is broad enough to accommodate every student's growth, flexible enough to adapt to individual and cultural characteristic of pupils, specific enough to assure growth in language and thinking, and supportive enough to guarantee student success. (Harste, 1989, p. 49)*

The recent changes in how we perceive the teaching and learning of early literacy in preschool, kindergarten, and primary grades, as described earlier in this chapter, have resulted in professional groups reexamining teaching in light of what is developmentally appropriate practice in the early childhood years. We think it is important to call to your attention two statements on developmentally appropriate practice for emerging literacy teaching and learning. The first is an excerpt from the National Association for the Education of Young Children (see Box 1-1).

The second statement targets early literacy practices in the prefirst grade. It has relevance, however, for the early primary grades as well. (See Box 1-2.)

The major implications of these two statements for the early childhood teacher in terms of early literacy and young children are that there are developmentally appropriate practices for the education of young children which include the integration of the curriculum, the use of appropriate materials and methods, the planning of a wide variety of activities, the use of appropriate evaluation techniques, and the use of resources from the school, home, and community. All of these points will be discussed in detail in the following chapters.

BOX 1-1 • *Developmentally Appropriate Practice in Early Childhood Programs*

APPROPRIATE PRACTICE

Teaching Strategies

- Adults encourage children's developing language by speaking clearly and frequently to individual children and listening to their response. Adults respond quickly and appropriately to children's verbal initiatives. They recognize that talking may be more important than listening for 3-year-olds. Adults patiently answer children's questions ("Why?" "How come?") and recognize that 3-year-olds often ask questions they know the answers to in order to open a discussion or practice giving answers themselves. Adults know that children are rapidly acquiring language, experimenting with verbal sounds, and beginning to use language to solve problems and learn concepts.
- Adults provide any experiences and opportunities to extend children's language and musical abilities. Adults read books to one child or a small group; recite simple poems, nursery rhymes and finger plays; encourage children to sing songs and listen to recordings; facilitate children's play of circle and movement games like London Bridge, Farmer in the Dell, and Ring Around the Rosie; provide simple rhythm instruments; listen to stories that children tell or write down stories they dictate; and enjoy 3-year-olds' sense of humor.

Language Development and Literacy

- Children are provided many opportunities to see how reading and writing are useful before they are instructed in letter names, sounds, and word identification. Basic skills develop when they are meaningful to children. An abundance of these types of activities is provided to develop language and literacy through meaningful experience: listening to and reading stories and poems; taking field trips; dictating stories; seeing classroom charts and other print in use; participating in dramatic play and other experiences requiring communication; talking informally with other children and adults; and experimenting with writing by drawing, copying, and inventing their own spelling.

Integrated Curriculum

- The goals of the language and literacy program are for children to expand their ability to communicate orally and through reading and writing, and to enjoy these activities. Technical skills or subskills are taught as needed to accomplish the larger goals, not as the goal itself. Teachers provide generous amounts of time and a variety of interesting activities for children to develop language, writing, spelling, and reading ability. Some children read aloud daily to the teacher, another child, or a small group of children, while others do so weekly. Subskills such as learning letters, phonics, and word recognition are taught as needed to individual children and small groups through enjoyable games and activities. Teachers use the teacher's edition of the basal reader series as a guide to plan projects and hands-on activities relevant to what is read and to structure learning situations. Teachers accept children's invented spelling with minimal reliance on teacher-prescribed spelling lists. Teachers also teach literacy as the need arises when working on science, social studies, and other content areas.

INAPPROPRIATE PRACTICE

Teaching Strategies

- Adults attempt to maintain quiet in the classroom and punish children who talk too much. Adults speak to the whole group most of the time and only speak to individual children to admonish or discipline them. Adults ridicule children's asking of rhetorical questions by saying, "Oh, you know that."

Continued

BOX 1-1 • *Continued*

- Adults limit language and music activities because children sometimes become too silly or loud, OR they include story time and music time only as a whole group activity and require children to participate. Adults discipline children for using silly or nonsense language.

Language Development and Literacy

- Reading and writing instruction stresses isolated skill development such as recognizing single letters, reciting the alphabet, singing the alphabet song, coloring within predefined lines, or being instructed in correct formation of letters on a printed line.

Integrated Curriculum

- The goal of the reading program is for each child to pass the standardized tests given throughout the year at or near grade level. Reading is taught as the acquisition of skills and subskills. Teachers teach reading only as a discrete subject. When teaching other subjects, they do not feel they are teaching reading. A sign of excellent teaching is considered to be silence in the classroom and so conversation is allowed infrequently during select times. Language, writing, and spelling instruction are focused on workbooks. Writing is taught as grammar and penmanship. The focus of the reading program is the basal reader, used only in reading groups, and accompanying workbooks and worksheets. The teacher's role is to prepare and implement the reading lesson in the teacher's guidebook for each group each day and to see that other children have enough seatwork to keep them busy throughout the reading group time. Phonics instruction stresses learning rules rather than developing understanding of systematic relationships between letters and sounds. Children are required to complete worksheets or to complete the basal reader although they are capable of reading at a higher level. Everyone knows which children are in the slowest reading group. Children's writing efforts are rejected if correct spelling and standard English are not used.

Source: Sue Bredekamp (Ed.). (1987). *Developmentally Appropriate Practice in Early Childhood Programs Serving Children from Birth through Age 8.* Washington, D.C. Copyright by the National Association for the Education of Young Children.

BOX 1-2 • *Literacy Development and Pre-First Grade*

Objectives for a Pre-first Grade Reading Program

Literacy learning begins in infancy. Reading and writing experience at school should permit children to build upon their already existing knowledge of oral and written language. Learning should take place in a supportive environment where children can build a positive attitude toward themselves and toward language and literacy. For optimal learning, teachers should involve children actively in many meaningful, functional language experiences, including *speaking, listening, writing*, and *reading*. Teachers of young children should be prepared in ways that acknowledge differences in language and cultural backgrounds and emphasize reading as an integral part of the language arts as well as of the total curriculum.

Recommendations

1. Build instruction on what the child already knows about oral language, reading and writing. Focus on meaningful experiences and meaningful language rather than merely on isolated skill development.

2. Respect the language the child brings to school, and use it as a base for language and literacy activities.
3. Ensure feelings of success for all children, helping them see themselves as people who can enjoy exploring oral and written language.
4. Provide reading experiences as an integrated part of the broader communication process, which includes speaking, listening and writing, as well as other communications systems such as art, math and music.
5. Encourage children's first attempts at writing without concern for the proper formation of letters or correct conventional spelling.
6. Encourage risk-taking in first attempts at reading and writing and accept what appear to be errors as part of children's natural patterns of growth and development.
7. Use materials for instruction that are familiar, such as well-known stories, because they provide the child with a sense of control and confidence.
8. Present a model for students to emulate. In the classroom, teachers should use language appropriately, listen and respond to children's talk, and engage in their own reading and writing.
9. Take time regularly to read to children from a wide variety of poetry, fiction and non-fiction.
10. Provide time regularly for children's independent reading and writing.
11. Foster children's affective and cognitive development by providing opportunities to communicate what they know, think and feel.
12. Use evaluative procedures that are developmentally and culturally appropriate for the children being assessed. The selection of evaluative measures should be based on the objectives of the instructional program and should consider each child's total development and its effect on reading performance.
13. Make parents aware of the reasons for a total language program at school and provide them with ideas for activities to carry out at home.
14. Alert parents to the limitations of formal assessments and standardized tests of pre-first graders' reading and writing skills.
15. Encourage children to be active participants in the learning process rather than passive recipients of knowledge, by using activities that allow for experimentation with talking, listening, writing and reading.

Source: This is a joint statement by six professional organizations: Association for Childhood Education International, Association for Supervision and Curriculum Development, International Reading Association, National Association for the Education of Young Children, National Association of Elementary Principals, and National Council of Teachers of English. Reprinted with permission of the International Reading Association.

References

Anderson, R. C., Hiebert, E. H., Scott, J. A., & Wilkinson, I. A. G. (1985). *Becoming a nation of readers: The report of the Commission on Reading.* Washington, DC: The National Institute of Education.

Bissex, G. L. (1980). *Gnys at work: A child learns to read and write.* Cambridge, MA: Harvard University Press.

Bredekamp, S. (Ed.). (1987). *Developmentally appropriate practice in early childhood programs serving children from birth through age 8.* Washington, DC: National Association for the Education of Young Children.

Chenfeld, M. B. (1987). *Teaching language arts creatively* (2nd ed.). San Diego: Harcourt Brace Jovanovich.

Clark, M. M. (1976). *Young fluent readers.* London: Heinemann.

Clay, M. (1975). *What did I write?* Auckland, New Zealand: Heinemann Educational Books.

Durkin, D. (1966). *Children who read early.* New York: Teachers College Press.

Ferreiro, E., & Teberosky, A. (1982). *Literacy before schooling.* Exeter, NH: Heinemann Educational Books.

Fodor, M. (1966). *The effect of systematic reading of stories on the language development of culturally deprived children.* Unpublished doctoral dissertation, Cornell University, Ithaca, NY.

Forest, I. (1935). *The school for the child from two to eight.* Boston: Ginn and Company.

Goodman, Y. (1984). The development of initial literacy. In H. Goelman, A. A. Oberg, & F. Smith (Eds.), *Awakening to literacy* (pp. 102–109). Exeter, NH: Heinemann Educational Books.

Hammill, D. D., & McNutt, G. (1980). Language abilities and reading: A review of the literature on their relationship. *Language Arts, 80(*5), 269–277.

Harste, J. C. (1989). *New policy guidelines for reading: Connecting research and practice.* Urbana, IL: National Council of Teachers of English.

Harste, J. C., Burke, C., & Woodward, V. (1982). Children's language and world: Initial encounters with print. In J. Langer & T. Smith-Burke (Eds.), *Reader meets author, bridging the gap* (pp. 105–131). Newark, DE: International Reading Association.

International Reading Association. (n.d.). *Literacy development and the prefirst grade.* Newark, DE: International Reading Association.

Lamme, L. L., & Childers, N. (1983). The composing processes of three young children. *Research in the Teaching of English, 17*(1), 31–50.

Loban, W. (1976). *Language development: Kindergarten through grade twelve.* Urbana, IL: National Council of Teachers of English.

Noyce, R. M., & Christie, J. F. (1989). *Integrating reading and writing instruction in grades K-8.* Boston: Allyn & Bacon.

Strickland, D. S., & Morrow, L. M. (1989). Developing skills: An emergent literacy perspective. *The Reading Teacher, 43(*1), 82–83.

Taylor, D. (1983). *Family literacy.* Portsmouth, NH: Heinemann Educational Books.

Teale, W. H. (1986). Home background and young children's literacy learning. In W. H. Teale & E. Sulzby (Eds.), *Emergent literacy: Writing and reading (*pp. 173–206). Norwood, NJ: Ablex Publishing.

Wagner, B. J. (1985). Integrating the language arts. *Language Arts, 62(*5), 557–560.

CHAPTER TWO

Psychological Principles for Literacy Instruction

Advance Organizer

In this chapter, we present principles that are important for literacy instruction. The chapter begins with an explanation of why beginning students need to understand the underlying nature and purpose of reading and writing and why it is important for them to understand the language of instruction and the conventions of print. Since English is an alphabetic language, we next discuss the need for learning the principles of word recognition. One way to learn word recognition skills is through spelling and writing. There is also a discussion of how reading and writing work interactively. Highly literate people can recognize words and write with a minimum of attention and effort because the tasks have become automatic. Then we explain how to help students develop language skills to the automatic level. There is also an explanation of how teachers can determine if students are automatic at word recognition. Finally, we discuss how teachers can help students understand what they read.

Objectives

After studying this chapter, the reader should be able to—

- define the *cognitive clarity principle* and explain why it is important in reading and writing;

- understand what is meant by the *language of instruction* and the *conventions of print;*

- list the words and print conventions that should be introduced to beginning readers and writers and describe how to teach these concepts to the students;

- explain what is meant by the *alphabetic principle* and why it is impor-

Graphic Organizer

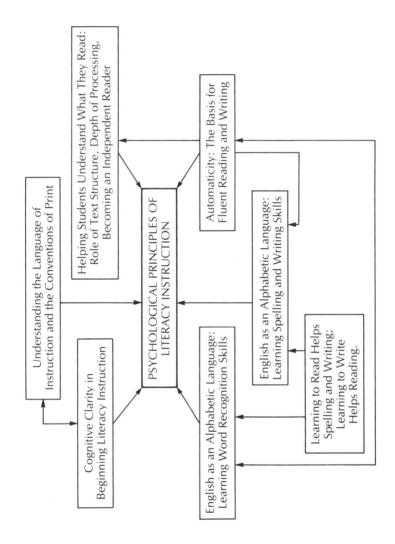

PSYCHOLOGICAL PRINCIPLES OF LITERACY INSTRUCTION

Understanding the Language of Instruction and the Conventions of Print

Helping Students Understand What They Read: Role of Text Structure, Depth of Processing, Becoming an Independent Reader

Automaticity: The Basis for Fluent Reading and Writing

Cognitive Clarity in Beginning Literacy Instruction

English as an Alphabetic Language: Learning Spelling and Writing Skills

English as an Alphabetic Language: Learning Word Recognition Skills

Learning to Read Helps Spelling and Writing; Learning to Write Helps Reading.

tant to teach students how to map print symbols to spoken and written language;

- explain the advantages and disadvantages of *alphabetic* and *logographic* writing systems;
- explain what is meant by *automaticity,* why it is important to be automatic at reading and spelling, and how one tests for automaticity in reading;
- understand what is meant by a *story grammar* and explain how story grammar can help in reading and writing;
- describe three ways to help students understand what they read;
- explain why constructing a cognitive map helps comprehension;
- draw the model of learning from memory and explain the role of attention in each of the stages.

Introduction

The focus of this chapter is on the psychological principles for helping students become literate. There are relatively few principles, and the principles often generalize to both reading and writing. These principles are all-purpose tools that can be used in a variety of situations, whereas the details of teaching are far less generalizable.

There are a few problems involved in listing these important principles, which encompass the knowledge and skills a student must have in order to become literate. Listing the principles will create a structure that resembles a scope and sequence chart for literacy. While the principles have sufficient theoretical and empirical support to justify their inclusion, unfortunately where they are sequenced in this chapter and when they are introduced in a curriculum rests on less firm ground. For example, virtually everyone would agree that in order to become fluent in reading, one needs to know print-to-sound correspondence in order to begin to decode words. Learning letter-to-sound correspondences is part of what we call *phonics.* But when does the teacher introduce phonics — early in the sequence, (perhaps in the first month or two), at the end of the first year, or not at all? So we see that while this principle states that in order to become an independent reader capable of recognizing words without the teacher's help, the student must know print-to-sound correspondences, it is open to debate when to sequence these skills into the curriculum and how to teach them.

Another problem with listing principles for attaining print literacy is the danger of listing too many. To avoid the possibility of including principles with low priority, the listing will be limited to those that most educators recognize as being very important in establishing literacy.

The Cognitive Clarity Principle

Principle   Students should understand what they are being asked to do and why it is important. With regard to reading and writing, they should understand that reading and writing are methods of communication.

John Downing (1973, p. 76), one of the foremost scholars to have studied the cognitive clarity principle, described how he became interested in the topic after he read Jessie Reid's study of Scottish children's thoughts about reading. Reid's aim was to explore the children's general level of concept formation with regard to reading and writing. She first interviewed 7 boys and 3 girls after they had been in school for 2 months, then for 5 months, and finally for 9 months. She discovered to her surprise that the students showed a general lack of understanding of what reading was going to be like, of what activities and processes characterize reading, and the purpose and use of it. Downing replicated Reid's study in England and wrote:

The replicated interviews produced remarkably similar findings to those Reid had published 4 years earlier. Some of the questions led to responses that clearly showed that these 5-year-old beginners were indeed in a state of cognitive confusion regarding the purpose and nature of the written language and how or why one should learn to use it in reading. (p. 78)

From his research Downing concluded that many beginning readers are in a state of cognitive confusion regarding the underlying nature of these skills. Some children, for example, were unaware that they could read to themselves. Some had no concept of the function of the words on a page, nor did they understand that writing and reading are conducted from left to right and from the top of the page down. When students are in a state of confusion, they have difficulty learning and following directions.

How the Language-Experience Method Reduces Cognitive Confusion

To overcome this state of cognitive confusion that many young students have about reading and writing, teachers can use the *language-experience technique* to help students understand the underlying principle that reading and writing are methods for communication. To use this technique, the teacher may arrange for all the students in the class to share a common experience, such as a visit to a local store, a fire station, or a farm. After the visit, the students dictate a group story based on the visit. While the students dictate, the teacher writes the story on a large sheet of butcher paper, which is pasted on the board using manuscript writing and a thick felt pen. The students observe while the teacher writes what they say. An example of a story might be "Today we visited a farm. The barn was big and red. We sat on the tractor." Then after the short story is written, the students read it together.

In order to help students read the story the teacher should tell them that they are going to learn to read the story they just dictated. First, the teacher reads the opening sentence and points to each word as it is spoken, then the students read the sentence in unison and again the teacher points to each word as it is read. This procedure is repeated sentence by sentence.

Of course, one reading of a story will not be sufficient to ensure that the students can read it, so the procedure will have to be repeated. Now, however, the teacher can call on individual students to read the story while pointing to the words. After the students have gained some skill reading the sentences, the teacher can take a pair of scissors and cut individual words out of the paper and use them as flashcards. The students can practice reading the words on the flashcards. Flashcards can be held by the teacher, or the students can have their own set of cards and practice reading the words with each other, one student acting as the teacher and the other as the student. Then the student pairs can reverse roles. The teacher could also have these beginning readers match words on a card to words in the text. This procedure of dictate, write, read, and reread should be repeated using other stories for a week or two while the students get practice dictating and reading. The sequence of learning is whole-to-part, from the whole story to sentences to phrases and (if the teacher did some work on ordering sentences) individual words on strips and cards.

There is a great deal to learn using this simple technique. The students get experience observing the role of the writer and the reader. When the students reread a story they wrote several days earlier, they are experiencing how the written word transcends time and place. They also see how writing is done from the top of the page to the bottom, from left to right, and with spaces between the words. The concept of what is a *word* is foreign to many children. Most students who are beginning readers cannot determine how many words are in the following spoken sentence, "I want a cup of water." Children often think of this sentence as "iwannacupawater" as though it were a long run-on superword. What the language-experience technique does is demonstrate that what sounds like a superword can be segmented into separate individual words. It also shows the students how words are written with spaces between each one.

Since the subtleties of the underlying meaning of writing and reading may escape many children, the teacher should discuss with them questions such as, "What does a writer do? What does a reader do? Why is it important to be able to read and write?" The students should also be helped to understand how writing and reading are different from speaking and listening. Activities that include discussions about the purpose of reading and writing and taking an active role in the language-experience reading technique will help students shift from a state of cognitive confusion to one of cognitive clarity about reading and writing.

Why the Language-Experience Method Should Be Used Only for a Limited Time

As excellent as the language-experience method is for teaching the concept of reading, it has a troublesome side effect if used for too long. Students who use the method learn to read using a look-say approach. The *look-say approach* is a way to teach beginning reading starting with whole units of language, such as words, phrases, or sentences. When the look-say approach is used with beginning readers, the principle of least effort operates. That is, students will choose the easiest strategy to attain the desired goal, and in this case the goal is to be able to read the words on the page. Unfortunately, the easiest route to the goal utilizes a strategy that works in the short run, but in the long run the strategy creates a confusing situation.

While the look-say approach (Samuels and Jeffrey, 1966) has advantages such as ease and speed of learning to read the words, it also has a disadvantage in that it encourages students to use a strategy where they use first-letter cues, or last-letter cues, or word-length cues in order to recognize the words. It also encourages students to use language and context clues as well as background knowledge. For example, in the following sentence, "Farmer Brown milked the cow," the first or the last letter of each word could serve as the recognition cue and all the other letters in the word could be ignored. For many beginning readers, the sentence could have been written as "Fxxxxx Bxxxx mxxxxx txx cxx." Or, for those students who use the last letter as the cue the sentence could have been written as "xxxxxr xxxxn xxxxxd xxe xxw."

Students who are introduced to reading with the language-experience method can learn about 20–30 words with little difficulty, and this is the reason to use this method. As more words are introduced, different words begin to share the same first or last letters or the words have the same number of letters and the faulty strategy begins to break down.

Even though the look-say approach leads to confusion if used for too long, its positive effects, if used to teach the underlying principles of reading and writing, outweigh the potential negative side effects. Before very long, if the students are to become independent readers, they must learn the alphabetic principle that governs our writing system. The students must learn that the sounds of spoken language are represented by the letters in words, and it is the combination of context, the structure of language, and the sounds in the word that help in word recognition.

The Language of Instruction and the Conventions of Print

Principle   *Students need to understand the language of instruction and the conventions of print.*

Why Students Need to Know the Language of Instruction and the Conventions of Print

If fish were to become research scientists, probably, the last thing they would discover would be water, because the fish are so thoroughly immersed in their watery environment that they are blind to it. Like fish who are blind to their environment, we also get so immersed in our own environment that we may fail to notice significant aspects of how we communicate with others. The verbal environment is one part of our communication environment that we often fail to notice. We use words so freely that we usually assume that common, simple words are understood by all, and often this assumption is incorrect (Samuels, 1988).

Examples of Specific Verbal Concepts and Print Conventions that Should Be Taught

As teachers, we usually assume that our students understand what appears to be easy-to-understand instructions. But in fact, young students may not understand our instructions at all. To illustrate how students may fail to understand simple instructions I would like to relate an incident that occurred years ago. A remedial reading teacher I knew invited me to observe her fifth-grade class of poor readers. During the lesson that I was observing the teacher said to a reading group, "This is a story about how pilots carried mail in the early days of flying. Read the first four paragraphs to find out how the pilots were able to know where they were as they flew their planes." The first four paragraphs were all on a single page. I watched as the students read silently. A few of the students seemed to indicate almost immediately that they had the answer, but most of the students read on for several pages. Watching the students read several pages made me wonder if they knew what a paragraph was. When the lesson was over I asked the teacher if I could ask the students a few questions.

I had all the students turn to a page they had not read and I asked them to count how many paragraphs were on the page. Next, I had them count how many sentences were in a paragraph on the page, and finally I had them count the number of words in a particular sentence.

To the surprise of the teacher there were fifth graders in her class who did not know the meaning of basic instructional terms like *paragraph, sentence,* and *word.* The teacher's comments were right on the mark when she said, "No wonder they are having difficulty learning to read. They do not understand the words I use when I give them instructions."

The fact that many students fail to understand instructional terminology, such as *word, sentence,* and *paragraph,* is not surprising. Unlike concrete nouns, such as *book* and *paper,* which are easily identified by the child, many instructional terms, such as *word* or *paragraph,* are abstract and are not so easily identified by the students. Because of their abstract nature, these instructional terms require direct explanation.

There are many other terms that students will eventually need to understand, such as *period, question mark, alphabet, lowercase, letter, colon, quotation marks, consonant, vowel, story,* and *poetry.* And as students advance through the grades, additional terms such as *table of contents, index, glossary,* and *digraph* will need explanation. Teachers must become aware of the technical terms they use and explain the meaning of these terms in a way young children can understand.

Interest in what children know about the language of instruction and the conventions of print was sparked by a study by Meltzer and Herse (1969). They conducted several experiments on the boundaries of written words as seen by first graders. The researchers had the children use a pair of scissors to cut written words off a sentence printed on a card. After observing where children cut the words, Meltzer and Herse concluded that many of the students had no clear understanding of the concept of *word.* Downing's comments (1973) on the Meltzer and Herse study are most enlightening:

> *This fits the explanation given here for children's difficulty in conceptualizing the word as a unit of spoken language—it depends on the spoken language to which he or she has been exposed. The human utterances he or she customarily hears are not sequenced into words. There are no spaces of time between the spoken words. Hence, it is not surprising that children do not understand this concept. All too often teachers assume that the purpose of literacy and the meaning of the linguistic concepts they use in talking about reading and writing are just as obvious to their young pupils as they are to them. (p. 80)*

Closely linked to the language of instruction are what may be thought of as the conventions of print. As experienced readers and writers, we take so many print conventions for granted that it is easy to overlook the fact that the meanings of these conventions have to be taught. For example, students need to know that a word in printed form is simply a letter or group of letters surrounded by space. Sentences are groups of words beginning with a capital letter and ending with either a period, a question mark, or an exclamation point; while paragraphs are represented by an indentation and a word that starts with a capital letter. Other print conventions that a student eventually should learn include italics, side heads, marginal glosses, parentheses, and quotation marks. Students need to learn how conversation and the shifts from speaker to speaker are represented by quotation marks.

It is clear that one source of difficulty that many students may have in learning how to read results from their lack of knowledge of the language of instruction and the conventions of print. In order to help students learn, teachers must become aware of the underlying concepts used in reading instruction and teach these directly to their students. Also, teachers should explain the significance of the print conventions found in books. Obviously, a natural place to teach print conventions is during writing activities. When students understand the language of instruction and the conventions of print, some of the barriers to literacy will be removed.

The Alphabetic Principle: The Basis for Reading and Spelling

Principle   Students need to learn the alphabetic system, which is the basis of our written code, in order to be able to become independent readers and writers. For reading, they need to know how to map printed letters in words on to the sounds of our language. For spelling, they need to know how to map the sounds of our language on to letters when writing.

A Brief History of Writing

If we take a global and historical look at reading, we will discover that literate societies do not all read and write the same way. When reading English, we process print from left to right, while in Hebrew reading is done from right to left. At the present time, word boundaries are shown in print by spaces, but early alphabetic writing had no boundaries between words. Lack of word boundaries made reading difficult because the reader had difficulty knowing where one word ended and the next began.

The first literate cultures did not have an alphabet but relied instead on pictures to convey meaning. North American Indian pictographic writing exemplifies a written code that is so realistic that there is direct mapping from symbol to meaning. In order to understand the ideas conveyed, one needs only to study the pictographs.

In time, the highly realistic and easy-to-read pictographs gave way to abstract symbols to convey thought. For example, the Chinese have an ancient writing system that can be traced back 7,000 years to incisions etched on pottery (Samuels, 1985). These are found in a neolithic village in Bampo, Xian Province. By looking at changes in writing in Bampo, cultural anthropologists have noted how the writing changed from realistic to abstract across successive generations. The early neolithic Chinese written symbols were easy to read because they represented realistically concrete objects and hence could convey meaning directly. While there is an advantage to having realistic symbols, it limits the ideas that can be expressed to those that are concrete. In order to communicate abstract ideas, such as those relating to love, religion, and politics, abstract symbols had to be used, which is what Chinese scholars eventually began to do. After a while, however, there was a tendency to make all symbols abstract and less realistic, so that today the Chinese writing system uses abstract symbols called *logographs* because they represent ideas, not sounds. A method of writing where symbols such as letters represent the basic sound units of a language is called an *alphabetic system*. Languages such as English, French, Russian, and Swedish use an alphabetic code. There are some formidable problems connected with the use of a logographic writing system. First, the Chinese dictionary has about 47,000 logographs, of which about 3,000 are in common use. These 3,000 characters constitute the basic vocabulary necessary for becoming literate. For beginning readers, learning to discriminate 3,000 different symbols, many of which look alike, represents a tremendous visual discrimination and memory task. Second, writing Chinese is also complicated since there are not many words containing fewer than 5 strokes and most contain 11–12 strokes. Also, since each of the 3,000 basic symbols is different, imagine the difficulty of developing a compact typewriter or word-processing program that can be used with some degree of speed and accuracy.

The invention of a writing system in which a written symbol represented a sound in the spoken language came about 2,500 years ago by the Phoenicians who lived on the Eastern Mediterranean in what is now called Lebanon. The invention of a writing system based on representing the sounds of spoken language through letters stands as one of the greatest human inventions of all time. The ancient Greeks and Phoenicians were trading partners, and the writing system invented by the Phoenicians was later adopted by the Greeks. Words like *phonics* and *phonetics* reflect the Phoenician invention of a writing system based on speech sounds rather than ideas. Mathews (1966) states:

> *Once a system for alphabetic writing is adjusted for any language, reading what is written becomes simple. A native user of such a language, already well practiced in its sounds, can learn to read it in a very short time. And he or she can write as soon as he or she has learned to make the letters or symbols in a legible manner. (p. 8)*

Why the Alphabet Is One of the Greatest Inventions of All Time

An alphabetic writing system has several important advantages over a Chinese logographic system. For example, instead of having to memorize thousands of different symbols, as is done with a logographic system, the student of English need only learn the letter-sound correspondences for the 26 letters of the alphabet plus the vowel and consonant digraphs (e.g., *sch* ool, *ch* eese, st *ea* k). There are about 47 phonemes used in English that must be represented by 26 letters. Once the student has learned how to map letters and letter combinations into sounds and has learned the strategy of sound blending to form words, the student has one strategy for becoming an independent reader. To complement this strategy for recognizing words, the student should also learn to use sentence and story context and background experience. Background experience and knowledge is so powerful that in some instances we can identify words just through the context as in "The flag is red, white, and _____," or "The jeweler cut the green _____."

How Reading and Writing Reinforce Each Other

Combining instruction in reading and writing is a very promising approach currently in vogue. With this approach, students are taught how to map printed letters into sounds (reading) and how to map basic sounds of our language into letters (spelling). Integrating the language arts holds great promise in teaching students the alphabetic system, which underlies written communication. When students are encouraged to communicate their ideas and stories in writing and when they are encouraged to read what they have written to others, the process provides an opportunity for discussing and becoming aware of the elements necessary for written literacy.

What is interesting about this "new" approach of integrating reading and writing is that it has been used before as an educational practice. Like the pendulum that swings back and forth, certain educational practices, such as the integrated reading and writing method, have gone through periods where the method is used, abandoned, and then used again. For example, in the early 1800s, the most common way to teach reading in the United States was through an approach that combined spelling and reading (Mulcahy and Samuels, 1987). During this period many of the words introduced through spelling were used in reading and vice versa. Thus, spelling and reading activities reinforced each other.

While the combined reading and spelling method had a sound basis, the way it was practiced during reading instruction had a harmful side effect. When students read orally, they were required to spell each word before pronouncing it. Obviously, this spell-then-pronounce-word method interfered with comprehension and pushed leading educators of the mid-1800s, such as Horace Mann, to advocate separating spelling and reading. Instead of having students spell each word before pronouncing it, they recommended using the look-say, whole-word method. For a considerable period of time the spell-say advocates and the look-say advocates clashed, but Huey in 1908 reported that the whole-word method had become the dominant method.

A second factor that continued to separate the teaching of reading and writing was the development in the 1940s of a new approach to writing basal readers. Edward Thorndike and Irving Lorge, two highly influential psychologists, were critical of the way basal readers were written. They thought that the words used in the first books of reading instruction should be useful. By useful, they meant that the words should be ones that appear frequently in the stories the students read outside of the classroom.

By stressing the usefulness of vocabulary, obviously Thorndike and Lorge (1944) were interested in achieving transfer of training from the classroom to reading outside the classroom when the teacher was not present to help the student. Thorndike and Lorge decided that not only should the earliest words encountered in the basal readers be ones that were common in written English but, in order to help the student learn the words, there should be a lot of repetition of these common words. In order to achieve this goal of usefulness of words introduced in these readers and primers, they had to control the vocabulary. Consequently, they first had to do word frequency counts of how often different words appeared in print. This was a monumental task, and after years of research they finally had a word frequency tally of 20,000 words.

With the word frequency counts available, basal readers were written using controlled vocabulary. In the first reading instruction books given to beginning readers an attempt was made to control the vocabulary so that only words of the highest frequency were used, and these were repeated often enough so that students could learn them. As the students advanced to higher grades, words of lower frequency were included. While this approach to writing a basal reader is logical, there was a problem. Many of the high-frequency words had low spelling-to-sound correspondence, and the rules of phonics did not always apply very well (e.g., *have, come*). Consequently, the best way to learn these high frequency words for which phonics rules did not work well was as sight vocabulary using the look-say approach. A *sight word* is one that is recognized immediately as a whole word without analysis.

And so, for about 50 years from the early 1900s until the mid-1950s, the whole-word method prevailed, and reading and writing were taught as two separate subjects. By the 1950s, a number of critics began to publish their findings about the shortcomings of the look-say approach. Rudolph Flesch (1955) was critical of the whole-word method because it ignored the alphabetic principle upon which our writing system is based, and students were taught to read as though they were learning a logographic code. He found that many students who learned to read with the look-say method had difficulty with independent reading when they encountered new words. Then, Jean Chall (1967) examined the research literature that compared the basal reader look-say approach with a phonics-decoding approach and concluded that the decoding emphasis led to better word recognition. In their First-Grade Studies, Bond and Dykstra (1967) compared a variety of approaches to reading instruction and found that an early decoding emphasis led to skill in word recognition. The findings in favor of a skills-based approach to reading led to a minor shift in reading such that basal readers began to introduce students to phonics and decoding as part of an overall program. But still reading, spelling, and writing were usually taught separately.

By the 1980s, with the emphasis given by whole-language advocates to the integration of language arts, we began to see the pendulum swing back once again to the integration of reading, spelling, and writing. By integrating spelling, reading, and writing, the young student can learn the alphabetic system, which has two aspects. The first aspect is that spoken language can be segmented into smaller units. The ability to segment speech into smaller basic units is a skill that not all students can do with ease, and there is evidence that students who have difficulty hearing the separate sounds in words often have difficulty learning to read (Vellutino, 1979). The second aspect of the alphabetic system is learning to map speech sounds with letters.

Learning to decode words in an alphabetic language such as English has been described as a mapping problem in which the student must learn to match the 47 phonemes, or basic sounds of our language, with the appropriate letters or letter combinations. In order to do this, the student must develop auditory perceptual skills so as to be able to hear the separate sounds in a word. Evidence that children can segment the spoken words into smaller units is shown by their ability to tell which words begin with the same sound as *ball* (*bat, boy, big*); by their ability to rhyme words (*house, mouse, louse*); and by their ability to delete a sound in a word to form a new word. For example, they should be able to tell what the new word is if the initial /*m*/ sound in *meat* or the final /*f*/ sound in *beef* is deleted.

While educators agree that to become a good reader the students must learn decoding skills, how to teach decoding skills is open to considerable debate. One part of the debate is over what size of visual unit to use in beginning reading instruction — whether the visual unit should be the whole word or a unit smaller than the word, such as a letter or combination of letters. Another aspect of the debate is whether to teach decoding skills directly or indirectly. For example, using the direct approach the teacher might plan beforehand to teach a group of students how to use sentence context to recognize a word. With the indirect approach, a student in a group may show that he or she does not know how to use context. The teacher, using a particular student's weakness as a cue, may then plan to introduce the skill at a later reading lesson. Finally, the debate also includes concerns about whether decoding skills should be taught in isolation or in context.

The solution to the problem of how to teach decoding skills is provided if we keep in mind that an important goal of instruction is for the student to read independently with comprehension. Teaching specific decoding skills or vocabulary as a reading lesson means that there will need to be a transfer of training from the lesson to the real reading task. Research on problem solving and transfer of training shows that transfer is less broad than we once imagined. It appears that students who are taught phonics and other decoding skills in isolation will probably have difficulty integrating these skills when reading meaningful material in context. Conversely, many students who are taught to read holistically with minimal instruction in decoding will probably have difficulty with word recognition, which is a necessary condition for comprehension (Evans and Carr, 1955).

Weaver and Shonkoff (1978) claim that the best way to teach word recognition and decoding skills is to use a combined subskill and holistic approach. In fact, they claim that the principle of a combined approach is good pedagogy across a variety of skills. They write:

In learning to play tennis, a very complex activity, students are taught components of the skill. They learn footwork, how to grip the racket, how to hit backhand and forehand shots, how to serve, and so on. And most of these components are broken down further into even smaller steps for teaching purposes. Although the instructor may often demonstrate the whole skill, mere demonstration is never the only means of teaching. The students practice the components and play the game at all stages. This kind of tennis instruction is similar to the sort of reading instruction that we are proposing. (p. 6)

Automaticity: An Essential Aspect of Skilled Reading and Writing

Principle   To become a good reader and writer the student must become automatic at many of the lower-order skills.

Why Accuracy without Automaticity Is Inadequate

Automaticity simply means that through practice a complex skill can be performed with little attention. It also means that through practice two tasks, such as word recognition and comprehension, can be performed simultaneously, whereas during the beginning stage the word recognition and comprehension tasks have to be performed separately.

From an instructional view point, is it good enough if a student has learned word recognition strategies to the point where the words in the text are recognized accurately, but the recognition process is slow, and considerable effort is required? The answer is that more than word recognition accuracy or "saying the words" is required for skilled reading. Skilled reading requires that two basic reading tasks have to be done simultaneously. Skilled readers must be able to recognize the words in the text and they must be able to comprehend what they read. In order to perform both the decoding and the comprehension tasks simultaneously, word recognition must be automatic. Word recognition is considered a lower-order skill, while comprehension is a higher-order skill.

Examples of Skilled Automatic Performance

To illustrate why automaticity is important in tasks such as reading and writing, we will use learning to drive a stick-shift automobile as a point of comparison. When the driver of a stick-shift automobile is highly skilled and automatically operates the automobile, he or she can do multiple things simultaneously. For example, the driver monitors the other cars to make sure they do not come too close, keeps an eye on the traffic signals, knows the geographic location, shifts gears, and applies the correct amount of fuel to keep the car moving at a safe speed. While all these complex tasks are being performed, the driver can also listen to what a passenger in the car is saying and engage in conversation.

This ability to engage in conversation while simultaneously performing the mechanical aspects of driving a car with expertise and without accidents is the hallmark of skilled driving. In this complex process, what is automatic are the mechanical components of driving the car. Engaging in conversation, which requires understanding what another person is saying and formulating an answer, never becomes automatic. Thus, when driving a car, lower-order mechanical skills can become automatic with practice, while thinking and understanding will always require considerable attention and will not become automatic, even with practice.

If you have watched beginning drivers, you know they cannot do all the things at the same time that a skilled driver can do. When beginning drivers are in traffic, they often find that the mechanical aspects of driving use up so much of their attention that they cannot engage in conversation.

How to Help Students Attain Automaticity

How does one become automatic at driving? The answer is through practice. There are only a few things that a good driving instructor can do to help a student learn how to drive a car. First, the teacher must motivate the students and provide experiences to develop the students' confidence that they will be able to drive. Some students may experience so much failure and anxiety during the early learning stages that they are inclined to quit before they have given themselves a chance to master the necessary skills. Confidence keeps the student from quitting. Second, the teacher must show the student how to perform the various skills so the student can perform them effectively. Third, the teacher must get the student to practice driving so that he or she can get to the point where the mechanical driving skills can be done automatically (requiring little attention and effort).

The learning and teaching processes involved in driving a car transfer well to reading and writing. When teaching the word recognition skills in reading, some teachers work towards the goal of word recognition accuracy, but they may ignore the need for automaticity. Automaticity is essential for fluent reading. Skilled readers who read fluently must be able to do two things at the same time. First, they must be able to decode the text easily, and second they must be able to comprehend it. The decoding and comprehension tasks require a balance of attention.

In the beginning reading stage, the word recognition decoding task requires a considerable amount of attention, especially if the beginning reader has only one strategy rather than several. The comprehension process also requires attention and effort. This is why beginning reading is tiring for students, and they need to use materials with pictures and language clues that facilitate word recognition and comprehension. If the students focus mostly on accurate decoding using strategies based only on phonics, so much attention is required for the word recognition task that they will have little energy left over for comprehension. If students focus on identifying words using only context and experience clues, they may not attend to the alphabetic principle system underlying our reading. From the teacher's perspective, the goal is to reduce the amount of attention required by students for word recognition, and this goal can be achieved through practice and learning a combination of strategies. If students learn effective strategies, as they practice reading the amount of attention required for word recognition lessens.

Effective readers recognize the words in the text and comprehend them at the same time. *Automaticity* simply means that through practice a complex skill can be performed with little attention. It also means that through practice two tasks, such as word recognition and comprehension, can be performed simultaneously, whereas during the beginning stage the word recognition and comprehension tasks have to be performed separately.

These stages in the learning process—where the student progresses from nonaccuracy to accuracy to automaticity—require confidence and a belief that one can learn the skills or ideas. Some students are self-motivated to read a lot and their skills increase; they are confident and believe they are readers. Other students, however, will need to experience success in beginning reading so that they can continue to feel they will be able to learn to read and thus have the self-motivation to continue to learn.

In order to illustrate how automaticity is developed, imagine an experimental setting where a beginning reader is sitting before a computer and performing a task. The task is to press a key as soon as possible whenever an animal word, such as *dog, mouse,* or *elephant,* appears on the screen. If a nonanimal word shows up, the student does not press the key. The computer measures accuracy of response and speed of response. The purpose of this hypothetical experiment is to study the stages in learning as a skill is practiced and becomes more automatic.

A Model of Learning Showing the Automatic Stage

A model of the learning stages that the student goes through in increasing proficiency and developing more automatic responses is shown in Figure 2-1. The three stages are shown along the base of the figure. Going from left to right, the first stage is the nonaccurate stage. During this stage the student expends a large amount of attention and effort trying to learn how to perform the task and learning what to attend to. The next stage is the accuracy stage, where the student becomes more accurate and less attention and energy are required in order to do well. The third stage is the automatic stage, where the task is performed accurately and with little effort and attention.

Let us now examine what happens to accuracy and speed of response as the hypothetical student practices. On the y axis, accuracy of response for the student is recorded and shown by a curved line that resembles, the letter s. Accuracy is indicated by percent correct. As one moves up the y axis, accuracy increases. Speed of response is indicated on the y axis on the right side of the figure. In the figure, speed of response is indicated by the large dots. Note that for speed of response data points that are in the upper regions are slow responses while those at the lower regions are the fast responses.

Going from left to right in the figure note that at first the responses have low accuracy and they are slower. This characterizes the nonaccuracy stage. Then as practice continues the student learns how to perform the task and accuracy of response increases rapidly. While accuracy increases, speed of response may also. Before long the student becomes 100 percent accurate. Even though the student is highly accurate, note that the speed of response is still increasing, so there is still room for improvement. As practice continues into the automaticity

FIGURE 2-1 • *Development of Automaticity*

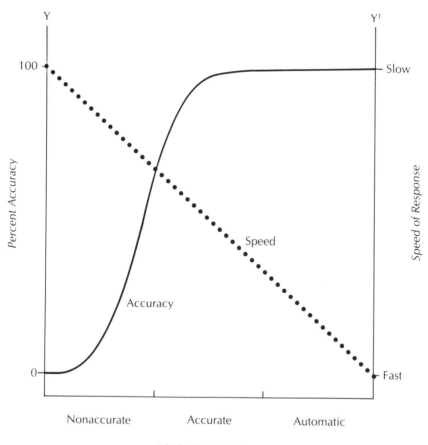

LEARNING STAGES

This figure illustrates the stages of learning that one goes through with practice (reading from left to right). With practice, responses become more accurate and speed increases. Practice continued after 100 percent accuracy is reached allows the student to become automatic. This model illustrates the role of practice in developing reading and writing skills.

stage, response speed continues to increase to a practical level depending on the student's capabilities. During the automaticity stage, response accuracy is still at 100 percent, and responses are performed with considerable speed. The hypothetical experiment of the student working with the computer parallels what happens as one practices reading or writing. With practice, reading and writing skills improve to the point of automaticity.

In reading, what becomes automatic are the lower-order decoding skills such as the recognition of letters, letter clusters, and whole words. It seems that what never becomes automatic are the higher-order thought processes connected to comprehension. We can apply the same psychological principles used in the development of automaticity in reading to explain the development of automaticity in writing. Many students have difficulty with penmanship or finding the correct typewriter or computer keys, or they may be concerned about poor spelling ability. When students expend considerable attention and effort on these lower-order writing skills, their lack of automaticity and knowledge may interfere with their abilities to express their ideas. If our goal is to help students express their thoughts in writing with some degree of ease, it is important that the lower-order skills, such as spelling and penmanship, become as automatic as possible. Again, automaticity in lower-order writing skills and knowledge can occur only through practice in writing.

How to Assess Automaticity

One way that a teacher can tell if a student is automatic at word recognition or spelling is that the skill is performed with speed and accuracy. For example, when reading aloud, the student's voice should sound the way it does in conversational speech. The reading rate may be a bit slower and there might not be quite as much expression, but there is an approximation. An excellent way that the teacher can tell if the student has gained automatic skills for reading is to ask the student to read aloud from a passage and then have the student retell what was read. To conduct this test of automaticity in reading, the teacher selects a brief passage ranging in length from one-half page to a full page. The passage should be at a recreational level of difficulty, that is it should be easy and one that has not been read previously. Instructions to the student are, "I want you to read this to me. As soon as you are done reading, I want you to tell me everything you remember."

In the retelling, if the student can preserve the main ideas and a few of the details, this means the student was able to decode and comprehend simultaneously the passage read aloud. Teachers can conclude that students who can read aloud with expression and recall the main idea of the passage are probably automatic at the decoding task. Students who are focussing most of their attention on decoding the passage will not have enough attention remaining for comprehension and will probably have difficulty recalling what was in the passage. Thus, the simple technique of oral reading and retelling is a good diagnostic device for determining if the student is automatic at decoding. Expression in oral reading is a good indicator of how automatic the student is at the decoding task. Usually, if the student is not automatic at decoding, the oral reading will be slow, the student may stumble over words, and there will be a lack of expression. When students fail to read out loud with expression it is because they are not automatic — not because they are uncooperative. As students practice reading and as they read and reread a passage using the repeated reading technique, they gain in automaticity. When they develop automaticity with oral reading they are able to read fluently, with expression. One of the advantages of using the method of repeated reading is that even poor readers learn rather quickly how to read with expression because they are using more than one strategy.

The method of repeated reading is a simple classroom technique. To use this technique the student reads a short passage of about 50–100 words repeatedly until the oral reading rate reaches 75 words a minute. As the student rereads the passage, he or she will find that accuracy, reading rate, and expression improve (Samuels, 1979). After the student reaches the 75 words a minute rate on the passage, the procedure is repeated on the next 50–100 word passage in the text.

Aiding Comprehension through Self-Assessment and Levels of Processing

Principle   *To facilitate reading comprehension, students should know how to ask self-assessment questions based on knowledge of text structure and levels of processing.*

Contrary to Durkin's Research, Questions Can Aid Comprehension

It has been more than a decade since Durkin (1978) published her landmark study of comprehension instruction. Her study found that, although many teachers thought they were teaching comprehension, they were not. What teachers were doing was asking questions that revealed if students understood what they read. Durkin's position was that asking questions that revealed if students understood a passage was not the same as teaching students how to understand the information contained in the text. In other words, she differentiated between testing and teaching.

Since Durkin's study was published, we have increased our knowledge of what factors influence comprehension. One of the things we have learned is that not all questions are alike. Some questions, which have no instructional purpose or are not based on educational theory, may indeed be a waste of time. Other questions, however, which are derived from a theory of how narrative texts are written, may promote active comprehension (Samuels, 1988; Singer, 1978).

Students Need to Learn How to Ask Self-Assessment Questions

While it is important for teachers to know how to facilitate comprehension, an even more important goal is for their students to acquire these skills in order to become independent learners. As Singer (1978) has suggested, to accomplish this we have to phase out the teacher and phase in the student. We have to transfer to the student the teacher's knowledge about how to promote comprehension so the student can become an autonomous and self-directing reader. Therefore, the teacher first needs to know what is important.

According to Singer (1978), active comprehension consists of forming questions and then reading to find answers to the questions. Singer found that when students were trained how to ask questions, the student-generated questions led to better comprehension than teacher-generated questions. Baker and Brown (1984) claim that the ability to ask relevant questions of oneself during reading is crucial to monitoring comprehension. Preschool children and children in primary grades can be instructed on how to ask questions and they can practice their question-asking skills when listening to stories and when reading. Instead of the teacher asking questions, the students can ask questions of each other.

Self-Assessment Questions of Narratives Can Be Based on a Story Grammar

In order to know how to ask relevant questions, the students must understand that all well-written texts have a structure, just as buildings do. For example, in one study (Samuels, Tennyson, Sax, Mulcahy, and Schermer, 1988), university students were taught about the text structure used in scientific research articles. They learned that these articles contained a problem for which an answer was sought, a literature review, a method section, a results section, and a discussion section. These university students were taught to ask self-assessment questions based upon the structure of a scientific text while reading. These questions took the form of: What problem is under investigation? What have other researchers found out about the problem? What methods were used in the present study to find answers to the question under investigation? What did the investigator find out about the problem? Other university students served as a control group and did not get this training. Then the experimental and control groups read the same scientific articles and they were tested for recall. Some of the articles they read had good text structure. Other articles were not well structured. The question was: Would the experimental group, which had been trained to ask self-assessment questions based on text structure, have better comprehension?

The experimental group had remarkably superior recall on both types of texts. In fact, the experimental group trained in question asking had higher scores on the poor text than the control group had on the good text. The finding that college readers who were trained to use text structure had better recall on poorly written texts than untrained readers had on well-written texts was impressive.

A similar study was done using school children (Taylor and Samuels, 1983). In this study no training on text structure or self-questioning took place. Taylor and Samuels simply found children who were aware of text structure and some who were not. Both groups read passages from a social studies text, and the passages were either well structured or poorly structured. As in the other study, recall was measured after reading.

In general, the results with school children were similar to those found with college students, but with some noteworthy differences. Although the children who were aware of text structure had superior comprehension, it was only on the well-written passage. On the poorly structured text passages, there was no difference between the students who were aware or unaware of text structure in the amount recalled. How can one account for the difference between adults and children on the poorly organized texts? One possibility is that the self-questioning training the adults had allowed them to locate important information in the poorly written texts, whereas the children who were not trained in this strategy were at a disadvantage. Thus, it seems, self-assessment questions based on a theory of text structure may be a powerful tool to enhance text comprehension.

Another interesting finding was that children who were unaware of text structure had equally poor comprehension scores on the well-written passages and the poorly written passages. For children who were not sensitive to the text structure of an expository structure, reading took place as a confused jumble of ideas.

What can be done to help students improve their reading comprehension? One helpful approach consists of teaching them about text structure and teaching them how to question themselves as they read. Although many students seem able to acquire awareness of text structure on their own, all students can be helped to learn these structures through instruction. Once they know about text structure, they can use this knowledge to improve their comprehension of what they read. Furthermore, knowledge of structure can help to improve students' writing. It appears, then, that awareness of text structure is highly important since it can lead to improved reading comprehension and better writing.

Many narrative stories that children read have the basic text elements found in the following short story.

"Fred, the Lucky Fish"

(*Setting*) Once upon a time there was a large red fish with a golden fan tail named Fred. He lived in a stream that ran through Farmer Brown's meadow.

(*Initiating Event*) One day as Fred was swimming, he saw a large fat minnow swim by.

(*Reaction*) Fred had not eaten that day. Looking at the minnow made Fred realize that he was hungry.

(*Goal*) Fred said, "I would like to eat that fat minnow."

(*Attempt*) He swam to the minnow and tried to swallow it, but the minnow escaped.

(*Outcome*) Although Fred was very disappointed, he did not give up.

(*Attempt*) Again he went for the minnow, only this time he was able to eat it.

(*Outcome*) "Delicious," he said. "This has been a good day."

To illustrate the structural relationships in a single episode narrative text, the model specified by Trabasso, van den Broek and Liu (1989) will be used. According to their model, a narrative story has six major components, consisting of a Setting, initiating Event, Reaction, Goal, Attempt, and Outcome. Thus a story can be represented as Narrative = S + E + R + G + A + O. These text elements are found in the story of "Fred, the Lucky Fish."

As seen in the Fred story, each component in the narrative serves a purpose.

The setting functions somewhat as a canvas does for a painter in that it provides the place and space for the action to unfold. The setting includes the actors, objects, time, and location for the events that will take place. An initiating event consists of an occurrence that causes an emotional reaction to take place in one or more actors. The emotional reaction is such that it causes the actor(s) to establish a goal. The goal in turn leads to actions or attempts to reach the goal. Each attempt has an outcome. At times the outcome is successful, and the goal is achieved. In this case the story is finished. In a multiple episode narrative, the outcome may be unsuccessful. The characters then attempt a new action to achieve the goal. This cycle of attempt and outcome can continue until the goal is reached.

For a story to become more complex, the author simply has to put in characters with conflicting goals. For example, in the Fred story the plot could have been made more complex by describing the minnow's goals. While Fred's goal was to eat the minnow, the minnow's goal was to escape. Thus, each goal and the characters associated with the goal can serve as a barrier to the goals and characters on the opposing side. Many of the most complex multiple episode plots are built out of the simple narrative structure just described.

Even in preschool teachers can begin to teach these narrative text structures through storytelling and teacher-directed questions. For example, theory-based questions on the Fred story might take the form: "Who was Fred? Where did he live? What happened one day when he saw the minnow? What did he want to do? What did he do to catch the minnow? Was he successful?" These questions all require literal comprehension. In order to answer a literal comprehension question, the student simply has to read the text because it contains all the necessary information. Any inferential comprehension question requires information from the text as well as information that is part of the student's background knowledge. The teacher may also want to ask inferential questions, such as: "How did Fred feel when he first saw the minnow? How did he feel when he ate the minnow?" Since the text does not provide answers to these questions, the information will have to come from the student's prior knowledge of different events and outcomes.

Teachers should work at having the students learn how to generate their own questions. Instead of teacher-led questioning, the students can take over the role of asking questions and deciding if the answers are satisfactory.

Craik and Lockhart (1972) introduced a powerful technique for helping young students understand what they read called *levels of processing theory*. They discovered that if a list of about 15 words, such as *table, chair, couch, sand, market,* and *hand,* were written on a chalkboard and the students were asked to remember the words, the ability to do so was related to the kinds of questions the teacher asked. For example, the teacher could say to the class, "Look at each word on the board and find the words that do not have letter *e* in them." In order to do this task, the students need only examine the words for superficial surface characteristics that have nothing to do with meaning. The teacher could also say to the class, "Find the words on the board that rhyme with the word *band.*" In order to do this task the students have to say each word, but again the task does not require the students to process the words for meaning. The best way to get the students to remember the words is to get them to examine them for meaning. Therefore, questions that force the students to examine each of the words for meaning, such as "Find the words on the board that are furniture," will lead to better recall than the other types of questions.

The levels of processing theory provides teachers with general guidelines about how to help students recall what they read. First, questions should focus the students' attention on deep meaning rather than on superficial aspects of a text. Second, have the students transform the text to be learned in a way that makes the material personally meaningful to them. For example, the teacher can say to students, "I am going to read you a story. When I am done reading it to you, draw a picture that shows what happened in the story." By drawing the picture, the students transform the events into their own interpretations, which are meaningful and personal.

Being Able to Draw a Cognitive Map Is a
Self-Assessment Technique that Helps Comprehension

Another way to help students understand what they read is to have them do a cognitive map of a story. A cognitive map has several essential elements. First, the key elements or ideas are extracted from the story. These key elements in a narrative are usually events having to do with setting, initiating events, goals, outcomes, and so on. Second, the map shows with the aid of arrows how the events interrelate with each other. Figure 2-2 shows a cognitive map of "Fred, the Lucky Fish." This map was done with teacher help towards the end of first grade by students who had been studying text structure. After the students gain experience doing cognitive maps with teacher help, they can work cooperatively in small groups to construct maps. Then, with additional practice, they are able to do the maps independently.

Cognitive maps can also be done on expository texts. What is different about maps done on expository texts is that categories such as setting, initiating event, and attempt are not present and the students must decide by themselves what ideas in the text are important and how the ideas interrelate. In order to illustrate a cognitive map for an expository text, a college student read this chapter and prepared a cognitive map of it. The map drawn by the student is the graphic organizer at the beginning of this chapter. Since the map is really the student's personal interpretation of the chapter, there is no one way for a map to be constructed that will hold true for all the students. The very act of preparing the map forces the student to process and to transform the text into a structure that represents meaning for the student, thereby aiding comprehension and memory for the text material.

Knowledge of narrative text structure can help the students write good stories. With the six components to a narrative as a guide, the class can dictate a group story while the teacher writes it down. With some experience writing group stories, the teacher can then have small teams of 2 or 3 students working

FIGURE 2-2 • *Cognitive Map of a Narrative Story*

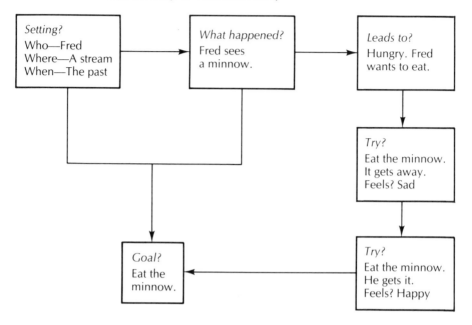

FRED, THE LUCKY FISH

Students in a grade 1 class did this map after listening to the story of "Fred, the Lucky Fish."

cooperatively to write a story. Through the experience and practice of writing stories in small teams, each student will develop the skills necessary for independent writing. Thus, we see that a theory explaining how narrative texts are structured combined with self-assessment questions can serve as a useful tool to help students become skilled readers and writers.

This chapter on principles of literacy instruction closes on a note of optimism. By building positive attitudes and feelings of confidence in our students, almost all of them can become skilled in reading and writing. Even the longest journeys start with a single step, and this chapter outlines the steps that should be taken to help students become literate citizens in their communities.

References

Baker, L., & Brown, A. (1984). Cognitive skills and reading. In P. D. Pearson (Ed.), *Handbook of reading research* (pp. 363–394). New York: Longman.

Bond, G., & Dykstra, R., (1967). The cooperative research program in first grade reading, *Reading Research Quarterly, 2,* 5–142.

Chall, J. (1967). *Learning to read: The great debate.* New York: McGraw Hill.

Craik, E., & Lockhart, R. (1972). Levels of processing: A framework for memory research. *Journal of Verbal Learning and Verbal Behavior, II,* 671–684.

Downing, J. (1973). *Comparative reading: Cross national studies of behavior and processes in reading and writing.* New York: Macmillan.

Durkin, D. (1978). What classroom observations reveal about comprehension instruction. *Reading Research Quarterly, 14,* 481–533.

Evans, M. A., & Carr, T. N. (1983). *Curricular emphasis and reading development: Focus on language or focus on script.* Symposium conducted at the biennial meeting of The Society for Research on Child Development. Detroit, MI.

Flesch, R. (1955). *Why Johnny can't read and what you can do about it.* NY: Harper and Bros.

Huey, E. (1968). *The psychology and pedagogy of reading.* Cambridge, MA: MIT Press. (Original work published 1908)

Mathews, M. (1966). *Teaching to read: Historically considered.* Chicago: University of Chicago Press.

Meltzer, N., & Herse, R. (1969). The boundaries of written words as seen by first graders. *Journal of Reading Behavior, 1,* 3–14.

Mulcahy, P., & Samuels, S. J. (1987). Three hundred years of illustrations in American textbooks. In D. Willows & H. Houghton (Eds.), *Illustrations, graphs, and diagrams: Psychological theory and educational practice.* New York: Springer-Verlag.

Samuels, S. J. (1979). The method of repeated reading. *The Reading Teacher, 32,* 403–408.

Samuels, S. J. (1985). Word recognition. In H. Singer & R. Ruddell (Eds.), *Theoretical models and processes in reading* (pp. 256–275). Newark, DE: International Reading Association.

Samuels, S. J. (1988). Decoding and automaticity: Helping poor readers become automatic at word recognition. *The Reading Teacher, 41,* 756–761.

Samuels, S. J., & Jeffrey, W. E. (1966). Initial discriminability of words and its effect on transfer in learning to read. *Journal of Educational Psychology, 57,* 337–340.

Samuels, S. J., Tennyson, R., Sax, L., Mulcahy, P., & Schermer, N. (1988). Adults use of text structure in the recall of a scientific article. *Journal of Educational Research, 81,* 171–174.

Singer, H. (1978). Active comprehension from answering to asking questions. *The Reading Teacher, 31,* 901–908.

Taylor, B., & Samuels, S. J. (1983). Children's use of text structure in the recall of expository material. *American Educational Research, 20,* 517–528.

Trabasso, T., van den Broek, P., & Liu, L. (1989). A model for generating questions that assess and promote comprehension. In A. Graesser (Ed.), *Questioning Exchange, 2,* 25–38.

Thorndike, E., & Lorge, I. (1944). *The teachers word book of 30,000 words.* New York: Teachers College Press.

Vellutino, F. (1979). *Dyslexia: Theory and research.* Cambridge, MA: MIT Press.

Weaver, P., & Shonkoff, F. (1978). *Research within reach: A research-guided response to concerns of reading educators.* Washington, DC: CEMREL.

CHAPTER THREE

Oral Language Competence and the Young Child

Advance Organizer

What does a caregiver or teacher who is working with young children need to know about language development in order to support, extend, and enrich that development? In this chapter, we discuss and describe the development and consolidation of the young child's language and listening skills during the preschool, kindergarten, and primary years. Patterns of growth during this period are charted. We outline how children refine and expand their control over increasingly complex syntactic constructions; broaden and deepen their vocabularies; begin to explore indirect, figurative, and idiomatic language; and use language for an expanding range of purposes in a widening arena of experience. Parent/child interactional patterns are contrasted with those typical of instructional settings. Aspects of instructional settings that have proven problematical for children are also discussed. Consideration of the factors found to support and enhance language development, as well as factors that inhibit it, lead to the description of practical strategies and suggestions to help teachers create a classroom environment designed to foster language growth. Finally, suggestions for the appropriate evaluation of listening and speaking competence are included.

Objectives

After studying this chapter, the reader should be able to —

- describe the general patterns of language development characteristics of children in the preschool, kindergarten and primary years;
- define the terms *grammar, semantics,* and *pragmatics* and describe the language growth of preschoolers and school beginners with reference to each of these aspects of language;

Graphic Organizer

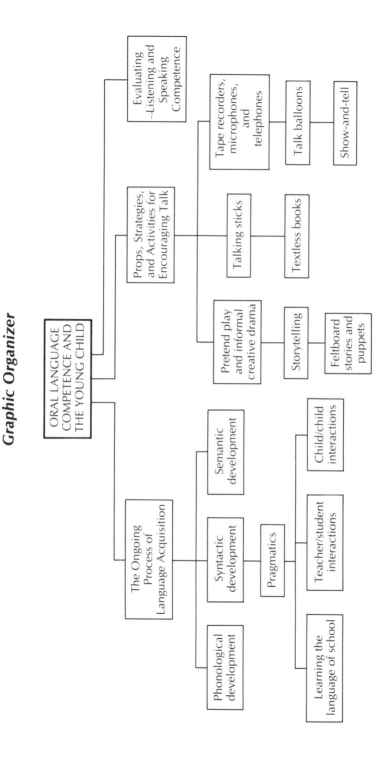

- compare and contrast the language learning environments typical of the home and the school;
- describe teacher/student interaction patterns traditionally associated with schooling and indicate which aspects of these can prove problematical for young children;
- describe ways of interacting with children that encourage their participation in extended and mutually satisfying conversational exchanges;
- indicate how peer interactions differ from adult/child interactions and why and how such interactions can contribute to language growth;
- describe and explain the value of a variety of practical classroom strategies and activities designed to foster, facilitate, and enrich oral language competence and listening skills in the classroom context;
- understand the need to evaluate communicative competence over time, in a variety of different contexts and situations with a variety of different tasks and interactional partners.

The Ongoing Process of Language Acquisition

Although most children have acquired an impressive amount of language by the time they are 3 or 4 years old, the language-learning process continues well into adolescence (Perera, 1984) and beyond. Despite the frequent claim that children have mastered the fundamentals of their mother tongue by the age of 5 (Cambourne, 1988; Slobin, 1979), much still remains to be explored, consolidated, and refined. Throughout their preschool and elementary years, children expend energy and effort developing, testing, and honing their repertoire of language resources. Vocabulary knowledge expands in breadth and depth; complex grammatical constructions are mastered and increasingly subtle relationships between ideas can be succinctly and accurately expressed. Children gradually become aware of, and more adept at handling, the rules and conventions governing the social exchange of talk as they learn how to engage appropriately in an ever-widening range of situations.

Because "language learning takes place through interaction" (Wells, 1985, p. 416) and through the learner's active attempts to use it, parents, peers, caregivers and teachers play key roles in facilitating and supporting language growth. If the adults responsible for helping children develop their language capabilities are aware of the conditions that foster language growth, and if they understand which aspects of language and communication are likely to pose problems for the young child, then they will be in a better position to offer timely and appropriate assistance.

It is worth reminding ourselves of the enormity of the task that learning to use language represents. Cambourne (1988) sums it up in the following way: "Each language is an amazingly complex, cultural artifact, comprising incredibly complex sets of sounds, words and rules for combining them, with equally numerous and complex systems for using them for different social, personal and cognitive purposes" (p. 30). Complex as it is, language is learned by almost all children. By the time they can walk with ease, most are able to use language to express an array of personal needs and to realize a variety of functions (Halliday, 1975; Tough, 1977). This accomplishment, seemingly managed incidentally, is deservedly recognized as "a stunning intellectual achievement" (Cambourne, 1988, p. 28). We should not forget, however, that the language-learning process is in many ways a life-long endeavor. In the following sections, some of the specific competencies, skills, and insights required of children as they mature will be outlined briefly. To help simplify the discussion, these competencies and skills will be categorized according to whether they primarily involve the phonological, syntactic, semantic, or pragmatic aspects of language. It is recognized, however, that such divisions are artificial and that any genuine language act involves the simultaneous interplay of all dimensions.

Phonological Development

By the age of 4 or 5 most children are able to articulate the majority of the vowel and consonant sounds and consonant clusters with a reasonable degree of intelligibility. Mastery of the phonetic inventory of the English language is usually complete by the age of 6 (Bryen, 1982). Phonological development continues well into adolescence, however, as children learn to employ and refine their use of stress, pitch, and intonational patterns to convey subtle distinctions of meaning. For example, the use of contrastive stress to differentiate between the meanings of *greenhouse* and *green house* or to signal the difference in meaning between the sentences "He *gave* it to her?" and "He gave it to *her?*" is learned over the course of the elementary school years. As with most other aspects of language, phonological development is best supported and enhanced by exposure to those who speak clearly and well and by the opportunity to participate as a speaker and listener in a wide variety of situations. Bryen (1982) and Crystal (1976) offer informative overviews of the process of phonological development.

Grappling with Grammar

In order to understand or use a language, a child must have a working knowledge of the grammar of that language. As used here, *grammar* refers to the rules and conventions that govern how words, phrases, and sentences may be connected, combined, and ordered so as to convey the meaning intended. Although most young children are not consciously aware of grammatical rules, their use of language reflects tacit familiarity with them. For example, children rarely produce nonsensical word orderings (e.g., "Dog with play will I the"). The knowledge that such an ordering is unacceptable is termed *grammatical* or *syntactic knowledge*. Similarly, children learn that some words need to be altered when they are used in connection with other words; e.g., "I have two sock" is not acceptable, but "I have one sock" is.

Common indicators of growing competency include the use of a greater number of words, the fluent production of longer sentences, the use of a greater variety of words and parts of speech, the increasing use of unusual words, the use of varied sentence types, greater complexity of structure, and superior coherence (Loban, 1976; Wilkinson, Barnsley, Hanna, & Swan, 1980).

Children gradually learn to express their ideas more succinctly and efficiently. This is accomplished by a variety of means, including precision in the choice of vocabulary, the use of modifiers, and the embedding and conjoining of phrases and clauses: e.g., a 3-year-old would likely say, "This my truck. My truck wood" whereas a 5-year-old would probably say "I have a wooden truck." Over time, children learn how to join simple sentences together in ways that accurately link their meanings. Not surprisingly, easily understood relationships are correctly expressed before more complex ones. For example, by the age of 3, children can combine "I have a friend. Her name is Anne" into "I have a friend *and* her name in Anne." However, the use of terms such as *if, so, because, yet,* and *although* to combine sentences is not fully mastered until well into the period of middle and late childhood (Menyuk, 1977). Complex relationships can be expressed by means of embedding: e.g., rather than saying "That boy ate the chips. He ate all of them. He was greedy. He lives across the street," a child becomes able to state, "That greedy boy, who lives across the street, ate all of the chips."

A considerable number of grammatical constructions are more likely to occur after the age of 5 than before it (Perera, 1984). Common errors throughout early and middle childhood include the following:

- the lack of agreement between subjects and verbs: ("She swim to the boat");
- the use of the wrong determiner ("a ordinary car, them kids");
- vague or inappropriate pronoun references so that the listener is not clear as to whom or to what the child is referring (". . . and he put it on that thing and it broke them");
- omission of the auxiliary *be (*"Her name Tracy");
- failure to maintain the correct tense ("We went to the store and then we go home and after we went to my Grandma's");
- the use of incorrect or overgeneralized forms of irregular nouns and verbs (*mouses, bringed*);
- errors in tag questions ("He liked that, don't he?").

There are many grammatical constructions that are not fully understood by the time the child starts school (Perera, 1984). For example, children confuse direct and indirect objects and consequently many 4–7-year-olds find it difficult to interpret who is doing what to whom when presented with an apparently simple sentence such as "Mummy gave Leah the pencil." Young children seem to assume that events take place in the same order they are mentioned. Therefore, while they will be able to manage easily the instructions to "Cut out the triangle shapes, get the glue from the shelf, and stick the shapes around the edge of the circle," many will have difficulty with "Before you glue on the shapes, fold the paper in half" because what is said first has to occur last.

Embedded sentences also offer challenges to comprehension, particularly if lengthy or if alternative interpretations are plausible. For example, children presented with sentences such as "The horse that kicked the man chased the boy" have been found to understand it as meaning "The man chased the boy" (de Villiers and de Villiers, 1979). Negatives can prove problematic well into the middle childhood years. Although, as any parent will attest, "children understand and use the fundamental aspects of negation almost from the start" (p. 59), the use of the negative with indefinites, such as *some, none,* and *any,* is not easily acquired: e.g., "He didn't see nothing," "Nobody can have some." Similarly, negative sentences, such as "Nicola's lunch was neither healthy nor hot," are frequently misinterpreted by 7-year-olds to mean that the lunch *was* healthy and hot. Excellent descriptions of the maturing child's growing ability to manipulate the grammatical options of the language are provided by Menyuk (1977) and Perera (1984).

If the young child still has much to learn about grammar, does that imply that grammar should be directly and systematically taught? The answer is no. For the young child, explicit instruction that focuses on the rules and terminology of grammar has been found to be unnecessary, highly abstract, and confusing. Erasmus, writing in 1515, expressed this position in the following way: "It is not by learning rules that we acquire the power of speaking a language, but by daily intercourse with those accustomed to express themselves with exactness and refinement and by the copious reading of the best authors." Parents, teachers, and caregivers can contribute a great deal to the ease with which children become familiar with, and gain control of, the grammatical options by providing models of language richly and appropriately used and by arranging opportunities for children to explore and participate in the course of everyday interactions. It is through such exposure and experience, rather than by means of isolated language lessons, that the intricacies of the grammatical system are most efficiently and effectively learned.

Semantic Development: Learning How to Mean

Semantics refers to the capacity of language "to refer and to mean" (Bruner, 1983, p. 17). Fundamentally, it involves learning the meanings of words and how those meanings are changed and shaded depending on the linguistic, social, and situational contexts in which they are used.

Vocabulary growth   Children's vocabularies expand at a remarkable rate after the first words are uttered. Estimates vary, but many 18-month-old toddlers can use about 50 words appropriately. Average growth is approximately as follows: "2 years, 150 words; 2½ years, 400 words; 3-4 years, 1,000 words; 5-6 years, 2,000–3,000 words" (Allen, Brown, and Yatvin, 1986, p. 42). The rate of acquisition has been estimated at between 15-20 words per day (p. 120) — a rate unmatched by any formal program designed to teach vocabulary.

Vocabulary development is both a process of learning concepts and the words that represent them and of elaborating and restricting the meanings attached to words already known. One trend in the order in which children learn word meanings is a progression from generalization to specificity. For example, young children will commonly use a single word to refer to a number of different objects, such as initially calling all drinkable liquids *juice.* As they gain experience, they differentiate and label the members of the semantic class: e.g., *milk, pop, cocoa, tea,* etc. Meaning is progressively refined. Simultaneously, the child also is learning to comprehend and use abstract and superordinate terms – a progression from the specific to the general. At first this may involve relatively straightforward classifications, such as including a cow, a horse, a pig, and a chicken under the label *animals.* As they mature, however, children are increasingly able to use terms that "represent wider and wider groupings of words on the basis of more and more abstract features" (Menyuk, 1977, p. 104). For example, where a young child would have difficulty identifying and/ or classifying terms such as *anger, hatred, affection,* and *sorrow* as *emotions,* an older child likely would not. Not surprisingly, those properties most easily observed by the child are the first to be linguistically encoded. For this reason, children will use adjectives such as *fat* or *big* to describe a person before using more abstract ones, such as *greedy* or *selfish.*

Adults need to keep in mind that the meanings children attach to various words (e.g., *friend, sorry*), may differ markedly from what adults mean by the same words. Holzman (1983, p. 129) provides a delightful illustration of this point. Her 4-year-old daughter started to say "Last year before I was born . . ." Holzman interrupted, "Last year you were already born; you were 3-years-old," to which the child indignantly replied, "I meant *very* last year." Holzman comments that "even though my daughter had the same words in her vocabulary as adults have, the words did not reflect the same verbal understanding as the adults'."

The issue for teachers is whether vocabulary should be directly and formally taught to young children. Genishi (1988) concludes:

> *. . . the answer is no, not any more than we "teach" experiences. We might introduce a word like* chalky *to describe the way something feels, but the child's experience of touching the object is as valuable as the introduction of the word. Children do ask questions about words, usually as a result of some event or experience. The concepts behind those words need to be experienced; words are learned, not taught, in contexts and activities that teachers have arranged and sustained, often through talk. (p. 22-23)*

Nonliteral language, metaphor, and idiom   Use of figurative, metaphoric, idiomatic, and ironic language poses challenges for young children because the words are deliberately *not* intended to carry literal meanings: e.g., "It's raining cats and dogs," "You are the sunshine of my life." By relying heavily on tone and context, even quite young children seem able to understand the general gist of many such expressions. However, the ability to fully interpret metaphors or to appreciate irony continues to develop throughout the elementary and high-school years (Billow, 1981; Winner, McCarthy, and Gardner, 1980).

Clearly, learning "how to mean" involves far more than the mere acquisition of a larger vocabulary. It includes learning the shades and subtle connotations of words and understanding the constraints of number, tense, and gender: e.g., *several* doesn't mean "lots"; it is semantically incorrect to say "we did go tomorrow"; a bachelor cannot be referred to as *she*. It involves perceiving and appreciating ambiguity and nuance and understanding when and why the words uttered are not intended to mean what they say. When children play with puns, nonsense verses, riddles, and jokes that turn on double meanings they are exploring the semantic subtleties, constraints, and possibilities of language. Exposure to language richly used, through books, play, or the ongoing exchanges of everyday life is the best resource to stimulate the child's understanding of how language can be made to mean. The provision of opportunities for young children to practice such language for themselves should be one of the primary goals of every early childhood teacher.

Pragmatics: Learning How, When, and with Whom

Knowledge of the socially expected and accepted ways of using language to communicate in specific contexts of situations is referred to as *pragmatics*. Language is functional; we *do* things with words (Halliday, 1988). For the young child, this means knowing the sorts of things that are listed in Box 3-1.

The list could go on and on. The point is that language permeates almost everything we do, while rules, conventions, and expectations govern every situ-

---

BOX 3-1 • *Learning the Pragmatics of Language Use*

Young children need to learn—

- how to initiate a conversation;
- how to observe turn-taking rules;
- how to sustain a conversation;
- how to gain and hold the floor;
- how to initiate a play encounter;
- how to gain access to an ongoing play activity;
- how to address adults;
- how to talk to and with peers;
- how to ask for help or information;
- how to explain;
- how to verbally express feelings;
- how to greet and take leave;
- how to argue;
- how to speak on the telephone;
- how to anticipate the needs of the listener so as to be able to adjust the communication accordingly;
- who is allowed to speak, to whom, when, and how.

ation in which language occurs. Children have to learn these rules. However, the rules and expectations for using language in the home frequently differ from those of the daycare center, preschool, or primary classroom (Tizard and Hughes, 1984; Ward, 1989). The adults who work with children need to be aware of unstated expectations that shape and surround various language events so that they can make these expectations explicit. Learning the "language of school" engages the attention and energies of children throughout their early school years (Ward, 1989).

Learning the Language of School

Upon entering school, the young child encounters a language environment that differs dramatically from that of the home. The size of the social group increases significantly, as does the adult/child ratio. Whereas at home most children enjoy a close relationship with their parent(s) and a background of shared experience, at school opportunities for one-on-one exchanges with adults are reduced. Opportunities for contact with a variety of peers, however, are increased. New rules for engaging in and responding to talk need to be learned, but not all of these rules will be explicitly stated. Most must be inferred, and many will become obvious only as a consequence of inadvertent transgressions. After spending a year observing in a kindergarten, Ward (1989) identified a series of general rules that governed classroom talk. For example, during group instruction the children had to learn that they must raise their hands if they wished to answer; that they were to talk to the teacher and not to each other; that they were *not* to answer questions directed at someone else (and that if they did, their answer would be ignored); and that they *were* expected to answer questions addressed to no one in particular, and so on. Some of the children she observed failed to participate simply because they were unsure of what they were supposed to do. Although active and effective communicators outside of school, many found the unfamiliar expectations of school inhibiting and their confidence as speakers undermined rather than enhanced. Unaware of why they were having difficulties, their teacher was unable to help them.

Typical classroom speech is quite unlike ordinary conversation. Many of the interactional routines regarded as normal and perfectly acceptable features of the school experience (e.g., the asking of known-answer questions, the public evaluation of answers) would be considered inappropriate and even rude outside of school (Delamont, 1983). Teachers need to be aware that children entering school have to learn to use language in ways that may differ markedly from what they are used to (Heath, 1983).

Teacher/Student Interaction Patterns

Although children at home are usually more or less free to talk whenever they choose, there are definite constraints at school. Numerous studies have confirmed Goodlad's (1984) finding that teachers at all grade levels outtalk their "entire class of students by a ratio of about 3:1" (p. 229), and this appears to hold true for informal as well as traditional classrooms (Delamont, 1983). Teacher-posed questions predominate. Most are not genuine questions in the sense that the asker is seeking knowledge he or she does not have (e.g., "Which of these stories did you like best?"), but are in fact questions to which the answer is already known (e.g., "Who did Little Red Riding Hood meet in the forest?"). Children who are not familiar with knowledge-display questions (from playing naming games with parents) are initially confused by them (Heath, 1983). Furthermore, children ask very few questions in school.

Well-chosen questions can spark curiosity and result in probing discussions. Research suggests, however, that the majority of teacher-posed questions require little more than literal recall or the provision of factual information. During his study of 1,000 American classrooms, Goodlad (1984, p. 229) found that less than 1 percent of instructional time was devoted to questions that "required some kind of open response involving reasoning or perhaps an opinion from students." All too often the child's task is to come up with the one "right" answer. Peter Ustinov parodied this expectation when recalling his schooldays (Edwards and Westgate, 1987):

Teacher: Name me one Russian composer.
Pupil: Tchaikovsky.
Teacher: Wrong. Rimsky-Korsakov. (p. 98)

Unfortunately, these questioning patterns have been found to be well entrenched in classrooms at every level (Delamont, 1983; Rogers, Perrin, and Waller, 1987).

In their study of the home and preschool experiences of 4-year-old girls, Tizard and Hughes (1984, p. 187) note some striking contrasts. Compared with the home, children at school engaged in much less one-on-one adult/child talk. School conversations tended to be dominated by adults, very brief, concerned with the here and now, and focused upon a much narrower range of topics than conversations at home. Even in the supposedly informal and child-centered setting of the preschool, "the characteristic shape of a school conversation was a question-and-answer session, with the children's role confined mainly to answering questions." Sadly, for many children the functional range of talk experienced outside of school is richer and wider than that experienced in it (Edwards and Westgate, 1987; Halliday, 1988; Preece, 1985; Wells, 1985).

Teachers are in a position to provide children with rich and stimulating opportunities for language growth. In order to do so, however, they need to be consciously aware of how talk is handled in their classrooms.

Rogers, Perrin, and Waller (1987) offer as a model of positive teacher/child interaction a description of the way one particularly skilled teacher engaged preschoolers in extended, mutually satisfying conversations. These conversations were spontaneous and unpredictable, with both teacher and child contributing equally. Most of the exchanges were initiated by the child and followed the child's rather than the teacher's agenda. When questions were asked they were genuine inquiries that invited the child to elaborate or explain what he or she was doing so that the teacher could better understand. Fewer than 5 percent of this teacher's questions were factual, assessment, or known-answer questions. The child's responses were listened to attentively and accepted rather than evaluated. Mechanical replies, such as "Great" or "That's neat" were not used; rather, the teacher's replies built on the child's comments and encouraged the extension and sharing of ideas. This teacher offers a model worth emulating.

Child/Child Interaction Patterns

Because peer relationships are more balanced in terms of status, power, and experience than are adult/child relationships, peer interactions provide children with very different language-learning challenges and experiences. Language contributes powerfully to social competence. Children who are popular and accepted by their classmates display a constellation of interactive characteristics not demonstrated by unpopular or socially isolated children (Hazen, Black, and Fleming-Johnson, 1984). Socially adept children are able to use language to initiate and maintain play encounters, to engage other children in dia-

Children need many opportunities to talk productively with their peers.

logue, to join ongoing play or activity sessions, and to handle disputes. They display flexibility and persistence in their communication attempts, and they *create* opportunities for interaction with their peers. When initiating or attempting to enter a play or activity session, they clearly direct their request to a specific child either by using the child's name, making eye contact, or touching them. When attempting to play or work with a group of children, the socially aware child distributes attention equally to all members of the group. In addition to simply stating that they wish to participate, the socially aware child has available a wide range of social initiation strategies. These can include such things as suggesting a possible role for themselves ("I'll be the Dad, OK?"); offering something that will contribute to what the others are doing ("You can use my felt pens if you want"); slipping into an appropriate pretend role and using it to enter the ongoing play ("I'm the policeman and I've come to give you a ticket"). In contrast, less socially successful children are inclined to make indirect or uninterpretable bids to join in; to hang around on the fringes hoping for an invitation; to nag, whine, disrupt the ongoing activity, or demand to be included. When teachers are aware of the strategies that socially capable children use, they can assist those less capable to acquire some of these strategies. By providing children with many opportunities to work, play, and talk with each other, and by modeling and pointing out successful interaction strategies, teachers can play critical roles in helping their students learn the pragmatics of peer interactions.

Props, Strategies, and Activities for Encouraging Talk

Teachers play vital roles in creating language learning environments rich in possibilities and support. Fundamental to such an environment is a teacher who believes children have worthwhile and interesting things to say, who listens attentively to what they say, who finds ways to help them say what they want to say, who provides models of language used with power and skill, and who creates opportunities for them to *use* language for meaningful and varied purposes of their own.

The props, activities, and strategies described in the following pages are offered as examples of some of the ways teachers can encourage and stimulate talk in their early childhood centers and classrooms. All are open-ended, and all invite and help children to explore and exploit their language abilities to the fullest on their own terms.

Pretend Play and Informal, Creative Drama

Some of the most sophisticated language produced by young children is generated in the course of pretend or sociodramatic play (Garvey, 1977). When children pretend to be someone or something else, they try to assume the language and speech behaviors of the characters adopted. Pretending grants the child license to experiment with the language used by others in ways not otherwise possible. In addition to assuming roles, children who are attempting to engage in pretend play with other children must also use language to negotiate who can play, who will be whom, who will do what, and how (Garvey and Berndt, 1977). They must be able to move in and out of roles and signal that they have done so. For these reasons, pretending taxes and stretches children's linguistic resources in ways that make it one of the most fertile areas for language development.

Throughout the preschool, kindergarten, and elementary years, play props and settings should be provided and rotated in order to spark and reflect children's interests. The traditional housekeeping corner easily can be transformed into a vegetable stand, an ice-cream parlor, an optometrist's office, or a bakery. Each setting offers the children different opportunities to explore different interactional roles and registers and to encounter specialized vocabulary.

Children also should be encouraged to informally dramatize the experiences and problems found in the stories they have heard, read, or invented (Paley, 1988). They should be invited to approach them from different perspectives, portraying the events that occurred before or after those presented in the stories or elaborating the themes or issues raised. For example, children might be asked to imagine they are trolls, just like those in the *Three Billy Goats Gruff,* and to act out their feelings and frustrations with the goats that repeatedly trespass on their bridge (Kelly-Smith, 1988). These dramatizations should aim for maximum participation and allow each child the freedom to explore and interpret the story, situation, or problem in his or her own way. They should not be performances, and they should not be scripted. Too often, older children are denied these role-playing or fantasy experiences in school. It needs to be stressed that children of all ages have much to gain and learn from them. Guidance and helpful suggestions for teachers are available in Barton (1986), Barton and Booth (1990), and Wagner (1976).

Talking Sticks

Many cultures use talking sticks of various sorts to concretely signify whose turn it is to speak. The person in possession of the talking stick is the only one entitled to talk. Because talking sticks tangibly mark the speaker and concretely signal turn-taking transitions, they have proven invaluable props with young children.

A fairly impressive stick (e.g., a fancy or carved walking stick) is needed. The teacher produces the stick, explains what it is for, and then takes the first turn in modeling how it is used. For example, during any group activity that involves talking turns, the teacher explains to the children that the person holding the stick is permitted to talk. When that person is finished, the stick is handed over to someone else, who then has a turn. Those not holding the stick are expected to be attentive listeners.

There are a number of different ways that the stick can be passed. It can be handed from one child to another in sequence around the group, or the teacher might decide the order of turns. Alternatively, the passing of the stick can be child-determined, with the speaker deciding who will hold the stick next. This has the advantage of giving children opportunities for making decisions. One drawback, however, is that it can (and frequently does) result in girls handing the stick only to girls, boys passing it only to boys, or friends passing it amongst themselves. A simple rule that a boy must pass the stick to a girl, and vice versa, usually takes care of this problem. On occasion, a child chosen as the next speaker may not wish the role; when this occurs the speaker simply selects another child.

Talking sticks are ideal in collaborative sessions in which children contribute to the telling of stories. Stories can be original, extemporaneous creations or retellings of familiar favorites. It is wise to begin with retellings of well-known and clearly structured stories, such as *Little Red Riding Hood*. Once children become comfortable with the process, they can be encouraged to make up tales of their own. Given support and an interested audience, even 4- and 5-year-olds can collaborate to tell imaginative, coherent, and entertaining stories (Preece, 1985, 1987).

Talking sticks also can be used to facilitate the retelling or verbal reconstruction of actual events: e.g., children might take turns recounting the steps they followed in a cooking project, the incidents that occurred during a fieldtrip, or the various steps in a science experiment. The turn-taking procedure lends itself to sequenced accounts; each child can talk about one step or part and then pass the stick along. Similarly, talking sticks are well suited to surveys and opinion polls.

A talking stick helps make the process of learning how to take turns in a group more explicit and concrete. Although almost any old stick will do, the shape and size can have an impact. Once, in a first-grade class, I happened to have two sticks. One was a large, gnarled stick that stood as high as my 6-year-olds, and the second was a small Irish shillelagh. During sharing time one of the children asked if she could use "that little stick" instead of the big one for her turn because "I just have a *little news* to share." For the rest of that sharing session the children chose either the large or the small stick in accordance with their perception of whether they were presenting "big" or "little" news.

Telephones

Telephone conversations are one of "the most highly structured of informal engagements" (Garvey, 1984, p. 35). After initial hellos are exchanged, further greetings ("So, how are you?") and social enquiries ("And, how have things been going?") are offered before the real or main topic of the call can be raised ("Are you free next Friday to help with that project I mentioned?"). After the main topic has been dealt with, openings generally are provided for either speaker to raise additional topics ("That takes care of it then?"). If neither has anything more to say (usually indicated by a phrase such as "Well, OK," or "All right, then"), the conversation is closed with an exchange of goodbyes. If any of these steps are omitted, most adults will recognize that something was not quite right about the call or will feel that it was somewhat abrupt and abbreviated.

As Garvey (1984) points out, observations of young children attempting to use the telephone in both real-life and pretend settings have revealed that they first master the opening and closing markers. To begin with, a pretend telephone conversation might consist of nothing more than "Hello. Goodbye." During the next stage:

> the child supplies the greetings: "Hello. How are you? Fine. Goodbye." The next stage may elaborate these moves and add a hint of a substantive topic: "Hello. How are you? I'm fine. I'm ironing. Goodbye." At this level of sophistication the child begins to leave pauses for the replies of the pretend interlocutor and to use a vacant stare into space, the "telephone gaze." By 4 years of age a pretend conversation with an imaginary or actual partner is likely to have more topic talk and occasionally a preclosing move: "Well, I have to go now. I have to do some work for the baby," before the final round of goodbyes." (p. 36)

It seems that children first grasp the boundary markers of the speech event, then the social courtesies, then the content, and finally recognize the reciprocal role of the listener or conversational partner. This pattern of development appears to apply to many other situations that involve the exchange of talk.

Telephones are designed for talk. Consequently, they are ideal instruments for encouraging language production with young children throughout the preschool and primary years. It is a good idea to provide a number of telephones for play purposes. Real phones are preferable to toy ones. Telephone companies often will donate discarded phones or loan a battery-operated set. Try to obtain a variety of types, ranging from the old-fashioned crank models to the modern, multifunction marvels. The props can make a considerable difference. For example, in one first-grade class, three regular black dial telephones, two black touch-tone telephones, and a pastel pink princess phone were scattered about the room. The children used these phones for different types of play interaction: everyday matters were handled on the black dial phones, important business calls on the touch-tone phones, and personal calls to friends or pretend husbands and wives on the pink one. Body language, stance, volume, and tone of voice all differed depending on the nature of the call and the telephone chosen. The different telephones provided genuine practice opportunities for adjusting register.

When telephones are placed in pretend settings (e.g., a bank, shoe store, or flower shop) they should be accompanied with the usual things that one would expect to find beside a telephone in such a setting (e.g., a *Yellow Pages Directory,* a book for important numbers, message pads, calendars, and order forms). All such items add to the reality factor, increase the likelihood that the props will be used, and indirectly provide information about the functions of written language.

Telephones are ideal props for encouraging language production.

In addition to free play with telephones, it is worthwhile occasionally to organize more structured situations around them. The obvious case is that of teaching young children how to use the telephone in an emergency situation; practice in providing essential information can prevent tragedies. Similarly, it is wise to ensure that young children know how to answer the telephone safely so that they do not provide information that might put them in jeopardy, such as telling a caller that no adult is home. The proliferation of telephone-answering machines requires that people learn how to record and leave call-back messages. A great deal of language practice (and a considerable amount of fun) can result from the creation of such messages, even when they are "just pretend" and recorded on an ordinary tape recorder.

Practice in dealing with a range of situations can be provided by outlining a hypothetical problem or situation to children and suggesting that they discuss it over the phone, with each assuming the role of one of the characters involved. The nature and complexity of the problem easily can be adjusted to make the activity appropriate for children of various ages, and the task can be varied by pairing an older child with a younger one. Children are very adept at generating their own scenarios and clearly enjoy doing so. Two girls (aged 7 and 8) pretended to be the manager of a toy store and a parent trying to buy a Cabbage Patch doll. In quick succession, the girls assumed the roles of a jazz dance instructor and a mother trying to arrange lessons, a teacher calling a mother to complain about her son's ghetto blaster, a teacher informing a mother that her son had been injured, and two children plotting to disobey their parents. Box 3-2 presents the call about the accident. Shannon's use of "Oh, gracious" is clear evidence of her awareness of adult language in situations warranting restraint and courtesy. It is doubtful she would use such an expression were she being herself. Her immediate inquiry as to whether anything was wrong also reveals her awareness of the pragmatic implications of a call from the teacher. On many levels, pretend telephone calls offer low-risk opportunities for children to experiment with language, to stretch their linguistic resources, and to learn how to conduct conversations in socially acceptable ways.

Tape Recorders and Microphones

Real or play microphones are irresistible props that children of all ages will happily use to pretend to be rock stars, roving reporters, talk-show hosts, air traffic controllers, etc. Play microphones can be used to add variety to class news, sharing sessions, or interviews. Using a microphone and a tape recorder if appropriate, children can interview each other, teachers, or visitors. There are many good reasons for having children undertake such interviews in pairs. In order to prepare for the interview, they need to discuss with each other the sorts of questions they might ask and how to phrase their questions. During the interview they can support each other and take turns asking the questions.

BOX 3-2 • *Excerpt from a Pretend Telephone Call*

Bronwyn: Brriiiingg!!

Shannon: Hello?

Bronwyn: Oh, hello. This is Mrs. Lundall.

Shannon: Oh, he-llo. How do you do?

Bronwyn: Oh, just fine.

Shannon: Is something wrong?

Bronwyn: Are you the mother of . . . Gregory?

Shannon: Yes, I am.

Bronwyn: Oh, I thought so. Um, well, it's a little emergency.

Shannon: What happened?

Bronwyn: Well, he was hit by a swing in the playground and he's in *quite* bad condition—like he's bleeding very bad in the leg.

Shannon: Oh gracious! Oh, gracious! I'll be right down. Thank you. Goodbye.

Bronwyn: Goodbye.

The excerpt in Box 3-3 is taken from an interview conducted and tape-recorded by two 6-year-olds. Their subject was a teacher who taught in their school. Although Dianne and Ricky obviously have a great deal to learn about how to relate one question to another so as to conduct a coherent interview, the interview provided them with a genuine opportunity to extend their language skills. In contrast to the usual school interaction pattern, they were placed in the position of asking the questions while the adult answered them. With their permission, the tape was placed in the listening center so that those who wished could hear their interview, and the teacher later transcribed it and included a portion in the class newsletter. By doing this, the children were provided with a real audience, and the activity was given point and purpose.

Most preschool, kindergarten, and primary grade classrooms feature a listening center (see Chapter 7). Usually, commercially produced tapes and teacher-produced tapes of stories are provided. Careful selection and rotation of tapes can offer children deeply satisfying listening experiences. One easy and inexpensive way to ensure a continuous supply of fresh recordings is for teachers to tape-record themselves when reading to the children during daily read-aloud sessions. Although comments made by the teacher and the children during the reading also will be captured on tape, these have proven to enhance, rather than detract from, their appeal. The children should be informed that the tape will be available for a week or so and then erased and used again. This serves to encourage regular visits to the listening center and guarantees rotation of the materials in it.

Many different types of language should be available on the tapes in addi-

---

BOX 3-3 • *Interviewing the Teacher*

Dianne: Did you have a nice day today?

Ms. Nichol: Yes I did, thank you. I had a very nice day.

Dianne: Did anybody in your class get dirty?

Ms. Nichol: I suppose somebody got dirty, not *really* dirty, just a little bit.

Ricky: Are you married?

Ms. Nichol: No.

Dianne: What did you have for breakfast?

Ms. Nichol: An egg and some toast.

Dianne: Hey! The same thing I had. Did you catch any kids that were bad today?

Ms. Nichol: (*in a low whisper*) I caught my whole class today, and I chased them around the gym.

Dianne: Did you get lots of nice things for Christmas?

Ms. Nichol: (*points to Mickey Mouse watch on her wrist*) Yes, I got a new watch.

Dianne: Hey, that's a boys' and girls' one.

Ms. Nichol: Well, I'm a girl.

Dianne: No, you're a teacher, not a girl!

tion to stories. (See Box 3-4.) Tapes based on nonfiction books are easily created; in addition to the text, a commentary on the illustrations and any charts or graphs in the book also should be included. Nonfiction tapes of this sort offer children needed exposure to the nature and structure of expository language. Just as they learn narrative structure from listening to countless stories, listening to nonfiction helps students throughout the elementary grades internalize the very different language and organization of exposition. Older students benefit considerably from the opportunity to listen to recordings of key and difficult passages from their textbooks. Nonfiction books with excellent illustrations and clear, brief passages of text should be selected for recordings intended for young children. A recorded commentary to accompany photographs taken of a class activity (e.g., hatching chicks) or a fieldtrip is ideal material for the listening center, particularly if the children contribute the commentary.

Children should be encouraged to suggest selections for recording and to participate during the recording sessions. Young children can choose favorite short poems or finger plays; older students can be asked to make tapes for younger children in other classes. This can prove especially beneficial for students who are not confident readers, as it provides a legitimate and face-saving opportunity for the practice and rehearsal of easy material. Students can record their reactions to stories they have heard or read, retellings of favorite stories, and retellings of personal experiences. Class survey tapes prove particularly popular. A question is posed and each child gives his or her opinion: e.g., "How do you think our playground could be made more interesting?"

BOX 3-4 • *Tapes Should Offer a Rich Variety of Language*

Listening-center tapes could feature:
- skipping rhymes
- favorite poems
- tongue twisters
- instructions
- announcements
- recipes
- classroom news
- playground chants
- jingles
- riddles and jokes
- interviews
- advertisements
- plays
- opinion polls

Children should be encouraged to make recordings for use in the listening center.

Storytelling

There are a number of significant differences between listening to someone *tell* a story versus listening to someone *read* a story. With no book between them, the storyteller is free to make direct eye contact with the listener throughout the telling; this facilitates the establishment of rapport and lends the experience an immediacy and intimacy that can make it compelling. The absence of illustrations allows each listener to imagine the story in his or her own way, using the cues of tone, rhythm, pacing, and expressiveness provided by the narrator. The storyteller can use gestures and props to bring the story to life. Stories, read *and* told, should be a regular feature of classroom life. Box 3-5 offers some guidelines for selecting and preparing stories for telling to children. Children also need to be encouraged to create and tell their own stories and to retell

---

BOX 3-5 • *Guidelines for Storytelling*

1. Choose a story that appeals to you and that you feel will have appeal for your listeners. It should be a story worthy of the time invested in its preparation and telling (Rosen, 1988).

2. Stories best suited for telling are those that have a small number of well-defined characters; a well-developed yet simple plot with a clear underlying theme, an easily detected structure or sequence of events, repetition of events or key phrases, colorful or evocative language and memorable dialogue (adapted from Morrow, 1979).

3. Thoroughly familiarize yourself with the story by reading or going over it as many times as is required. It is neither necessary nor desirable to memorize it. Make sure you can remember all of the relevant details and the significant events in the order in which they occur. The story should be so well known to you that you can recast and reshape it in response to your listener's needs and reactions (Rosen, 1988).

4. Decide whether you will use props (puppets, feltboard figures, objects, pictures presented or sketched as you talk) and plan how and where these will be introduced.

5. Prepare a short introduction, which will relate the story to the listeners' experiences and indicate its relevance to them (Rosen, 1988).

6. Practice and rehearse the story until you feel confident in your ability to do it justice.

---

and recast stories they have heard and enjoyed. Strategies designed to provide such opportunities are described in the following sections.

Textless Books

Textless or wordless books are picture books in which the pictures alone communicate the story. Well-known examples include books by John Goodall, Mercer Mayer, Brian Wildsmith, Peter Spier, Brinton Turkle, and Peter Collington. Operating as a scaffold, the illustrations provide children with the structure and content of the story but leave them to provide the language themselves. The open-endedness of the task means that young children can bring to it whatever language resources they have, create their *own* versions, and be guaranteed some success.

Textless books can be used in many different ways. They can simply be made available for private browsing. They can be shared with a small group, with the teacher telling the story and offering a model of how such a story might be told. He or she can then invite the children to collaboratively contribute to a second account of the same story. Individually, or in pairs, children can create a story and then record it for use in the listening center. If selected with care, textless books offer children incentive and support for storytelling and language production; for refining descriptive language; for inferring cause and effect; and for building familiarity with the way stories are organized, structured, and sequenced.

Examples of the language generated by a 7-year-old girl when telling the story portrayed in *Deep in the Forest* by Brinton Turkle (1976) will serve to illustrate some of these points. This evocatively illustrated book plays on the story of *Goldilocks and the Three Bears*. However, instead of a little girl visiting the home of three absent bears, a baby bear visits the home of a little girl and her parents. With minor variations, the plot unfolds just as in the traditional tale. In this instance, both the illustrations *and* knowledge of the fairy tale serve to undergird the child's efforts to tell the story. In the following excerpt, the child establishes the setting and begins the tale:

> *It was very dark in the forest. These . . . this family lived deep down in the forest. Trees surrounded their house . . . and bears lived near them. That morning . . . that morning Little Baby Bear went wandering into the forest. He saw this house . . . and it didn't look like anybody was inside. The door was shut tight. The owls were howling. So he walked in. There were three bowls of cereal on the table . . . one for Papa, one for Mama, and one for Little Girl . . . and a jug of big milk. The curtains were open on the windowsill. Everything was neat and tidy.*

The child begins by sketching the setting in a way that conveys mood ("It was *very* dark in the forest") and strikes a note of foreboding ("The owls were howling"). All of the characters are quickly introduced, and the situation is defined ("... and it didn't look like anybody was inside. . . . So he walked in"). The selection of words reveals relatively mature vocabulary control for a 7-year-old (e.g., *surrounded, wandering, windowsill*), although there were some difficulties with the word order of modifiers ("and a jug of big milk"). The account is logically sequenced and the sequence clearly marked ("That morning . . ."; "So . . ."). As this example demonstrates, the generation of stories from textless books provides meaningful language practice and opportunities for children to exploit their language resources to the fullest.

Talk Balloons

Talk balloons, which are typically used in cartooning, are encircled spaces where the words purportedly uttered by the characters are written. The drawing of an empty talk balloon on a picture explicitly signals the expectation that language appropriate to the situation and the character is to be added.

Introduce the concept to young children with a set of unrelated pictures that portray immediately recognizable situations or familiar characters. Books, magazines, humorous calendars, and children's drawings and paintings are excellent sources. A talk balloon can be drawn in the appropriate place on each picture or a precut paper or cardboard talk balloon can simply be placed on top of the picture. To start with, each picture should have only one talk balloon. The pictures may then be presented to the children with a question to elicit words that might plausibly be spoken by the character and to encourage them to justify or explain their choice of comment. Just as with the generation of stories based on textless books, this technique provides support and structure but is sufficiently open-ended to permit children to interpret the task in their own ways.

The task can be made more challenging by offering a single picture that features many characters and has many talk balloons. After that, a series of sequenced, related pictures can be presented. Cartoons can be used or adapted, or a series of pictures can be taken from damaged or discarded books and placed in sequence. The sequenced pictures require the children to make comments that logically relate to each other and convey the progression portrayed.

Talk balloons also can be used with many textless books; talk balloons made from laminated tagboard can simply be placed appropriately on each page as the child proceeds through the book. At first, it is best simply to ask for suggested comments from volunteers. Later, individual children can be assigned the roles of specific characters and given the task of generating the language appropriate for that character throughout the entire story. This requires that the child sustain the ongoing monologue or dialogue, which is a far more complex task than coming up with a comment to fit an isolated illustration. It is also a substantially different task than the straightforward telling of a story. With talk balloons the story must be communicated entirely via the dialogue.

Feltboard Figures and Puppets

Feltboards with sets of characters and props offer children a concrete and easily managed vehicle for creating, telling, and retelling stories. Felt figures can be purchased, traced, and cut out of felt, or drawn by the children and backed with felt. As the story is told or read, the relevant figures are simply placed or moved around the feltboard. Initially, the process should be modeled by the teacher, and then volunteers can be invited to manipulate the figures as the teacher reads the story. Children should then be encouraged to create their own versions. Some children delight in mixing the characters and prop pieces from different stories to create new and imaginative plots or to add unexpected twists. I recently watched a felt story told by two 6-year-olds who gleefully introduced Cinderella and her ugly stepsisters into the story of *Jack and the Beanstalk,* modifying the traditional plot to incorporate the new characters.

For many, telling a story *with* the felt figures is easier than without them. Because attention is directed to the placement and movement of the figures, it is deflected from the narrator. Consequently, many children seem more relaxed and less self-conscious when telling stories with the support of the figures. This results in longer, more elaborate stories delivered with greater spontaneity and dramatic effect.

Because puppets also serve to deflect attention from the speaker and because they can be made to represent almost anything and to do whatever the imagination dreams up, they too are ideal tools for fostering language development. Puppets offer children a mouthpiece, a voice that is, and is not, their own. For shy or self-conscious children, puppets offer the security and protection of an intermediary. After all, it is the puppet who is speaking.

A variety of puppets of different types should be attractively displayed and

Spontaneously created stories are delivered unselfconsciously and with dramatic effect using felt figures.

readily accessible; many simple puppets can easily be made by the children themselves. (See Chapter 8.) The development and performance of puppet plays provide meaningful opportunities for the creative and dramatic use of language. They also encourage the sharing and coordinating of ideas and talents. Young children should create their own unscripted puppet plays. Simple adaptations of familiar stories and rhymes are ideal. It is unnecessary and inappropriate to have children memorize lines for their puppets, other than ones they have made up themselves. Performances should be kept simple and unpressured, and the audiences should be small and familiar.

Second Thoughts about "Show-and-tell"

When organized thoughtfully, show-and-tell sessions can be stimulating and enriching experiences for presenters and listeners alike and can serve as a gentle introduction to public speaking. Without careful and sensitive planning, however, they can become a tedious, stressful chore.

Puppets deflect attention from the speaker.

There are *many* ways that show-and-tell sessions can be made interesting and involving. To avoid having the sessions degenerate into bring-and-brag events, many teachers encourage children to talk about something they have made or done or found interesting rather than presenting a personal possession. For example, Oken-Wright (1988, p. 52) notes that show-and-tell times provide excellent opportunities for children to recall, evaluate, and share objects, anecdotes and insights that result from their ongoing work and play. She suggests that children be invited to present such things as "sculptures they've made in the junk center, books they've written or read, or special pictures they've drawn or painted." She also suggests that they talk about problems, solutions, plans, and feelings they have experienced. Different sessions might focus on questions such as: "Who did something this morning that made them feel proud?" or "Who discovered something today that they didn't know before?". In this way, the emphasis can be shifted from what the children have to what they are doing and discovering.

If effectively set up, show-and-tell sessions offer a gentle introduction to public speaking.

Another way to vary show-and-tell is to have children select an object from home that is unique or special in some way and place it in a bag. The child may then offer the audience several clues as to what the object is and encourage them to guess. The children should take the responsibility for asking questions of the presenters. The teacher can facilitate this by informally providing models of the sorts of questions that are appropriate to ask. Simple rules will help the sessions run smoothly: e.g., a limit of 3 questions from the group for each presenter. The speaker may choose which questions are heard, or another child could be given that role. Although the teacher will want to offer support to the speaker as necessary, whenever possible, requests for elaboration and clarification should come from the audience. When the children are given active roles as questioners they listen more attentively and become involved. If the group is a large one, 2 or 3 smaller groups could be formed. In this way, more children will have a chance to share their news in a less intimidating setting, and more

Children should be invited to talk about the things they've made and discovered.

audience members will be able to ask questions. However it is managed, it is desirable to have the students run the sessions.

Evaluating Listening and Speaking Competence

The reader is referred to Chapter 9 for a full discussion of the assessment and evaluation of communicative competence. There are several points, however, that should be stressed here, though, as they are significant enough to bear repeating.

First, teachers should evaluate the language learning environments provided by their classrooms *before* they attempt to evaluate the capabilities of their students. To an extraordinary degree, language is sensitive to context. If the curriculum is narrow and the opportunities for children to express themselves limited, then shortcomings in children's language performance may reflect shortcomings in the program rather than inadequacies in the children.

Second, children's language should be assessed over time in a full range of authentic contexts. A variety of situations (formal and informal, spontaneous and planned) should be monitored. The child's confidence and effectiveness when communicating with a partner, a small group, a large group, adults, and peers should be considered. Similarly, the functional range of a child's competence should be evaluated, and the focus should be placed on the things a child is able to *do* with language. As always, intent and content should be monitored as well as the ability to enact the appropriate conventions. Both the cognitive and the social dimensions of talk need to be considered: children need to learn how to use language to explore and relate ideas and to relate to people. Both aspects need to receive equal weight and attention in an evaluation plan.

Fundamentally, teachers need to know whether the children with whom they work are able to use language as richly and powerfully as they are capable, whether they can use language to do what is required of them, and whether they can use language to help them do the things they want to do. They need to evaluate what they can *do* with language, with whom, and how well. The guiding questions should be:

1. Are the children expanding their repertoires of language resources and their awareness of the linguistic options available to them?

2. Are they able to use that repertoire appropriately in an ever-widening range of situations, with varied audiences, for increasingly sophisticated purposes?

References

Allen, R. R., Brown, K. L., & Yatvin, J. (1986). *Language learning through communication*. Belmont, CA: Wadsworth Publishing.

Barton, B. (1986). *Tell me another*. Portsmouth, NH: Heinemann.

Barton, B., & Booth, D. (1990). *Stories in the classroom: Storytelling, reading aloud and roleplaying with children*. Markham, Ontario, Canada: Pembroke.

Billow, R. M. (1981). Observing spontaneous metaphor in children. *Journal of Experimental Child Psychology, 31,* 430–445.

Bruner, J. (1983). *Child's talk: Learning to use language*. New York: Norton.

Bryen, D. N. (1982). *Inquiries into child language*. Boston: Allyn & Bacon.

Cambourne, B. (1988). *The whole story: Natural learning and the acquisition of literacy in the classroom*. Auckland, New Zealand: Ashton Scholastic.

Crystal, D. (1976). *Child language, learning and linguistics*. London: Edward Arnold.

Delamont, S. (1983). *Interaction in the classroom* (2nd ed.). London: Methuen.

de Villiers, P. A., & de Villiers, J. G. (1979). *Early language*. Cambridge, MA: Harvard University Press.

Edwards, A. D., & Westgate, D. P. G. (1987). *Investigating classroom talk*. Philadelphia, PA: The Falmer Press.

Garvey, C. (1977). *Play*. Cambridge, MA: Harvard University Press.

Garvey, C. (1984). *Children's talk*. Cambridge, MA: Harvard University Press.

Garvey, C., & Berndt, R. (1977). The organization of pretend play. Abstracted in the JSAS *Catalog of Selected Documents in Psychology, 7,* (107).

Genishi, C. (1988). Children's language: Learning words from experience. *Young Children, 44*(1), 16–23.

Goodlad, J. I. (1984). *A place called school: Prospects for the future*. New York: McGraw-Hill.

Halliday, M. A. K. (1975). *Learning how to mean: Explorations in the development of language,* London: Edward Arnold.

Halliday, M. A. K. (1988). Relevant models of language. In M. B. Franklin & S. S. Barten (Eds.), *Child language: A reader.* Oxford: Oxford University Press.

Hazen, N., Black, B., & Fleming-Johnson, F. (1984). Social acceptance: Strategies children use and how teachers can help children learn them. *Young Children, 39*(6).

Heath, S. B. (1983). *Ways with words: Language, life, and work in communities and classrooms.* Cambridge, England: Cambridge University Press.

Holzman, M. (1983). *The language of children: Development in home and school.* Englewood Cliffs, NJ: Prentice Hall.

Kelly-Smith, L. (1988). Role drama as a process for promoting self-esteem. *Journal of the Association of B. C. Drama Educators, 9*(2), 3–5.

Loban, W. (1976). *Language development: Kindergarten through grade twelve.* Urbana, IL: National Council of Teachers of English.

Menyuk, P. (1977). *Language and maturation.* Cambridge, MA.: MIT Press.

Morrow, L. M. (1979). Exciting children about literature through creative storytelling techniques. *Language Arts, 56,* 236–243.

Oken-Wright, P. (1988). Show-and-tell grows up. *Young Children, 43*(2), 52–58.

Paley, V. G. (1988). *Bad guys don't have birthdays: Fantasy play at four.* Chicago: University of Chicago Press.

Perera, K. (1984). *Children's writing and reading: Analyzing classroom language.* London: Basil Blackwell.

Preece, A. (1985). *The development of young children's productive narrative competence in conversational contexts: A longitudinal investigation.* Unpublished doctoral dissertation, University of Victoria, Victoria, British Columbia, Canada.

Preece, A. (1987). The range of narrative forms conversationally produced by young children. *Journal of Child Language, 14,* 353–373.

Rogers, D. L., Perrin, M. S., & Waller, C. B. (1987). Enhancing the development of language and thought through conversations with young children. *Journal of Research in Childhood Education, 2*(1), 17–29.

Rosen, B. (1988). *And none of it was nonsense: The power of storytelling in school.* New York: Scholastic.

Slobin, D. I. (1979). *Psycholinguistics (*2nd ed.). Glenview, IL: Scott, Foresman & Co.

Tizard, B., & Hughes, M. (1984). *Young children learning: Talking and thinking at home and at school.* London: Fontana Press.

Tough, J. (1977). *The development of meaning.* London: Allen & Unwin.

Turkle, B. (1976). *Deep in the forest.* New York: E. P. Dutton.

Wagner, B. J. (1976). *Dorothy Heathcote: Drama as a learning medium.* Washington, DC: National Education Association.

Ward, A. (1989). *Communicative inequality: The participation of native Indian and non-native children in instructional dialogue in a cross-cultural kindergarten class.* Unpublished doctoral dissertation, University of Victoria, Victoria, British Columbia, Canada.

Wells, Gordon. (1985). *Language development in the preschool years.* Cambridge, England: Cambridge University Press.

Wilkinson, A., Barnsley, G., Hanna, P., & Swan, M. (1980). *Assessing language development.* Oxford: Oxford University Press.

Winner, E., McCarthy, M., & Gardner, H. (1980). The ontogenesis of metaphor. In R. P. Honeck and R. R. Hoffman (Eds.), *Cognition and figurative language.* Hillsdale, NJ: Lawrence Erlbaum.

CHAPTER FOUR

Emerging Reading

Advance Organizer

The process by which children learn to read begins in the home and advances by imperceptible degrees. Schools must recognize the crucial role played by the home and develop programs that help to enhance the natural learning proclivities of young children. School programs must recognize that children learn by active exploration of their environment. The teacher's role, while exercising leadership, is subsidiary to the child's initiative. The teacher acts as a coach who demonstrates expert performance, invites the novice to try, rewards success, and withdraws support as the learner grows in competence and confidence. Learning to read involves the making of meaning and the identification of words. Children who are perceived to be functioning below expectation are best viewed as delayed rather than deficient. For these children, the only modification in instruction required is a reduction in the size of the instructional group.

Objectives

After studying this chapter, the reader should be able to—

- recognize that much fundamental learning about the nature and function of written language begins at home;
- realize that for those children whose homes have not provided such fundamental learning it must be provided by the school before any sense can be made of instruction in the technical details of written language;
- appreciate that children need to make the connection between experience, talk, writing, and reading;
- understand that learning to read is best accomplished through observation and emulation of expert behavior;
- recognize that the skills dealing with technicalities of written language,

Graphic Organizer

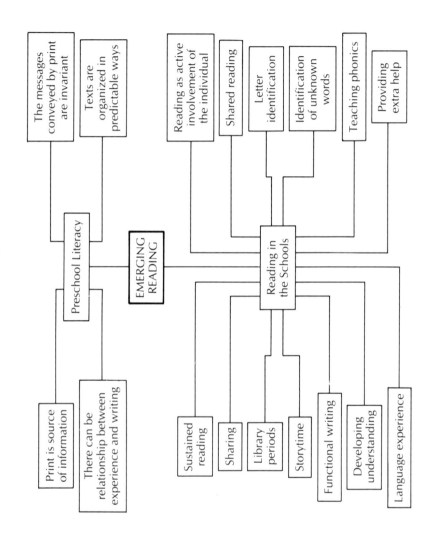

such as sight vocabulary, phonics, and word structure, are best learned while trying to understand a meaningful text;

- appreciate that children need copious opportunities to practice newly acquired accomplishments in literacy by reading meaningful texts;
- understand that progress in learning to read moves from the global to the specific;
- understand that children who need extra help need extended experiences with meaningful texts in a smaller group with instruction at a slower pace and with a higher rate of active involvement.

Preschool Literacy

At the present time, elementary school programs seem to be relatively successful with children who come to school having already learned the following generalities:

- Print (or writing) is a source of information.
- Messages conveyed by print are invariant.
- There can be a relationship between experience and writing.
- Texts are organized in predictable ways.

We do not suggest that preschool children can actually express these generalities, but that the children can function comfortably in social situations where these things are assumed to be true.

Print Is a Source of Information

Information may be interpreted to mean such things as news of a distant relative via a letter, TV advertisements, signs indicating where parking is available, stories that tell of things that never happened, texts that tell you about aspects of the world you have never seen, and texts that tell you how to live a moral life. All children are likely to have preschool experience with functional texts such as signs, shopping lists, and advertisements. But such texts are rarely used in elementary school for teaching reading. Schools specialize in three kinds of texts: narrative, poetry, and exposition.

Narrative: texts organized by time. Most narratives used in school are fictional, although biographies and histories are also used to some extent.

Poetry: texts using compressed, symbolic, metaphorical, rhythmical, or rhyming language.

Exposition: texts that explain or describe some aspect of the real world. Informational books that tell about such things as earthquakes, turtles, pollution, or Nigeria are usually in expository form.

Each of these kinds of texts is written for a particular purpose and is organized in a characteristic manner. Learning to read involves two phases. Children must understand what use print serves. They must also learn the details of the code: that is, the relationships between speaking and writing. But children who come from homes where such texts are not read aloud to them will be very confused if the teacher incorrectly assumes that they already understand in general the way in which written language works. Becoming involved with fine details, such as the identification of words and learning the relationship between specific letters and sounds, makes sense only when children understand the larger purpose that is served by such effort. They need to understand that being able to read will give them independent access to people, places, and processes in real and imaginary worlds and a greater degree of independence in the way they deal with environmental print. Being able to read gives them access to unicorns, the solar system, and the right bathroom.

The Messages Conveyed by Print Are Invariant

Invariance is a characteristic that is fairly peculiar to the printed word. Much in the young child's life changes: friends and relatives change their clothing, activities, and facial expressions. The weather, life on the street, the garden, and the TV screen are subject to constant change. Only very ritualized oral language is not subject to change: e.g., prayers, songs, traditional stories, greetings, and farewells tend to have fixed forms. But most oral language is subject to change. Even a repeated statement may be rephrased or receive a changed emphasis. In contrast, the sign in the park that says, "Please don't pick the flowers" always says just that. Red Riding Hood always meets the wolf. An expository text on pandas always says that pandas have a sixth thumb. It is clear from the behavior of preschool "readers" that they do not approach the printed word with this assumption. Observation of early attempts at reading indicate that the child talks in the presence of print. The topic of the talk is associated with the content of the text, but the parallel is very approximate (Holdaway, 1976). No two readings are identical. For example, a child whose preschool experiences have taught her that the words and meaning are somehow held by the print may benefit from a program that includes a concern with word identification. But a child who does not yet fully appreciate that print conveys meaning will be very confused by such instruction.

There Can Be a Relationship between Experience and Writing

Full appreciation of this generalization is likely to come about through writing rather than reading. Printed texts do not reflect the process by which speech and writing were produced. Young children are likely to regard a printed text the same way they regard a toy, a TV set, or a shoe. They are very familiar with the products but unaware of the means by which they were produced. Young children need to participate in the creation of many written documents such as letters, greeting cards, signs, and shopping lists. They need to witness adults and older children creating such texts and to participate in the process. To appreciate the sound/symbol relationship between speech and print the child should be part of a situation in which a need to communicate by writing arises. The adult involved articulates the need and composes aloud:

> *We won't be here when Daddy gets home. We must leave him a note. We have to tell him where we have gone.* Dear Alan (*speaks and writes*) *That's what I call Daddy.* We have gone to (*speaks and writes*) *Where are we going? (Child: Grandma's). Grandma's, right. Grandma begins with a G.* Grandma's (*speaks and writes*).

When the note is complete the child may be asked to add his name, add kisses, or draw an appropriate picture. Similar modeling may occur during the writing of letters, the sending of greeting cards, or the compilation of a shopping list.

Children who have participated in hundreds of such events will develop a functional notion of print. They will realize first and foremost that writing serves a function. The externalization of the adult's thought processes in the form of dictation will help them appreciate the speech-writing connection. Such 6-year-old children who encounter a teacher who is concerned with conventional spelling will appreciate that this is the mere filling in of details of an already well-established process. On the other hand, children who do not yet appreciate that the function of print is to encode meaning will be very confused by a concern with conventional spelling.

Texts Are Organized in Predictable Ways

Narrative is the kind of text that has been subject to the greatest amount of research. Applebee (1987) has shown how children develop a sense of story. The degree to which an appreciation of story structure contributes to the understanding of a narrative has been shown by the research into story grammar (Mandler and Johnson, 1977). Meyer (1985) has shown that an awareness of discourse structure is important in understanding expository text. Meyer worked with high school students, however. It is not clear how important an awareness of expository discourse structure is for younger readers, although logic would suggest that it is of prime importance. What is clear is the massive overinvestment in narrative in the elementary school. The majority of texts that children read and write in the elementary school are fictional narratives (Martin, 1984). The imbalance is maintained despite the fact that elementary school children are going to move into higher levels of education (secondary, college, university) and a work force that makes maximum use of expository texts and very little use of fictional narratives (Diehl and Mikulecky, 1988).

Thus we are presented with a dilemma. For parents to prepare children for elementary schools, as they are presently constituted, they would be well advised to familiarize their children with fictional narratives, although a longer view would suggest that extensive experience with expository texts would be of greater value. The resolution of the dilemma is to help elementary schools adjust their offerings to be more in line with future expectations.

Summary

Activities pursued by children in school will help to promote a broad view of literacy. Elementary school reading programs seem to work best with children who come to school with the perceptions of literacy discussed above. Reading programs seem to be less successful with children who have not yet developed such perceptions. Teachers need to do a better job of harnessing the undoubted power of the home, providing those parents who need direction in preparing their children for literacy with appropriate counseling so that a higher proportion of children come to school better able to benefit from what the school has to offer. The reader is urged to take note of the advice offered regarding the role of parents in Chapter 10.

Children who come to school without an awareness that print is a source of information, that messages conveyed by print are invariant, that experience and writing are related, and that texts are organized in predictable ways will not have their needs met in programs that assume they know these things. Such children need to be read to. With the teacher they need to discover that texts can help you learn about rockets, dinosaurs, volcanoes, and insects. They need to know that texts tell stories full of hope, effort, failure, success, love, and loss. They need to learn that written language can help you bake a cake, cross the road safely, or order the kind of lunch you would like. Induction into reading in the classroom should convey the message that the printed word is a source of pleasure and power. This message is conveyed by programs that put print to use; not by exclusive attention to syllables, letter formation, or digraphs. Hall (1987) notes that, "Most language that children experience is embedded in the pursuit of other ends. . . . Language is not the focus of these interactions; it is a medium for fulfilling objectives." Hall's remarks apply with equal force to both spoken and written language.

Reading in School

Sustained Reading

A significant portion of the reading program for young children should be the regular opportunity to read using whatever ability the child has. For some beginning readers this may be no more than turning the pages and looking at the pictures.

Shared, silent reading   Reading opportunities should take two forms: quiet, sustained reading times and library periods. Many teachers refer to quiet, sustained reading times as SSR (Sustained Silent Reading) or DEAR. (Drop Everything and Read). Such periods, however brief, should begin in the pre-school, be well established by the child's first school year, and maintained throughout the rest of the child's school career.

Children should be free to choose their own books and be allowed to select as many as might be necessary to hold their attention. The teacher may wish to share his or her own book and make a general invitation for others to share theirs. However, no individual should be pressured to share. The sessions should be attuned to the children's attention span. The period should be terminated as soon as signs of a general restiveness are observed.

Some teachers are very strict regarding what is permitted in sustained reading periods. Each individual must give exclusive and sustained attention to the text. Forester and Reinhard (1989) are much more relaxed in their attitude. If children wish to share a book together and such sharing involves discussion of their reactions, then such behavior is allowed. Such tolerance is acceptable as long as the reading of texts remains the central focus for the majority of the class for most of the time. However, if the bounds of behavior are loosened to include tidying out one's desk, finishing off an art project, or social chat, then the original intent of the experience will have been lost.

A reading period when children read self-selected books is the major feature of an approach advocated by Hansen (1989) and Forester and Reinhard (1989). Sharing responses is no more than talking about what one has just been reading in a small-group and in a whole-class meeting. During both sessions the teacher models how to share one's reading and how to react to someone else's sharing. Children are commended and counseled to adopt the practices and attitudes modeled by the teacher.

Sharing

Readers may share their reading in the following ways:

* retell all or a portion of the story;
* express opinions regarding the story;
* compare the story to previous reading;
* tell one thing you liked, one thing you disliked and one thing that puzzled you;
* compare the story with another by the same author;
* compare an expository text with another on the same topic;
* read aloud a favorite portion of the text;
* read aloud a section to support a judgment.

Reacting to the sharing of others   When listening and responding to the sharing of others, the children should be encouraged and required to:

* express genuine interest in what the person has said;
* ask questions to which you don't know the answer and would truly like to know;
* treat the speaker with courtesy and dignity.

In small-group sessions children are expected to adopt the exemplary behavior modeled by the teacher and children in the large-group meetings.

Absent from the books by Hansen (1989) and Forester and Reinhard (1989) is any suggestion for the use of worksheets or comprehension questions. Nevertheless, Hansen offers compelling research evidence to support the effectiveness of such a regime. It is noteworthy that Hansen and Forester and Reinhard run complementary writing programs that are fully integrated with the reading program. The suggestions proposed in this chapter are intended to be used in concert with those ideas presented in Chapter 5.

Library Periods

The library period is a second type of reading opportunity in school. Book selection from the classroom library can be very informal — whenever the routines of the classroom permit it. Visits to the school library may have to be scheduled. We recommend that teachers of early primary classes stay with the children and not regard library time as spare time. The browsing that occurs during library time is an excellent opportunity for teachers to learn the interests of the children and to offer individual guidance.

We recommend that the librarian prepare book talks based on authors, illustrators, or topics of current interest and mention several books rather than just one. This procedure will capitalize on the interest stimulated by the book talk because a larger number of children will have access to the books while their initial enthusiasm is still high. We do *not* recommend that librarians read entire texts to children. To be of benefit, reading aloud to children must occur much more frequently than librarians can provide. Nor does storyreading capitalize on the professional expertise librarians have. Librarians know collections of books. They should use that knowledge to help the novice find his or her way around. However, we do not recommend that young children be taught library science in a lecture format. The mechanical use of the card catalogue and the classification system is best learned one-on-one in a tutorial system as children seek information on topics of genuine interest.

We have a particular reason for advocating that librarians give book talks. Unlike shops and museums, libraries do not display their wares in order to catch the attention of the consumers. Libraries are more like warehouses where things are organized for convenience of access. Even in those sections of the library devoted to picture books, the books are displayed with their narrow spines showing rather than their illustrated covers. The textual information on the spine (title and author) is not much use to the emergent reader. The pictorial information, which might aid them in making a selection, is not readily visible.

While many teachers and librarians are assiduous in arranging book displays, the proportion of books shown broadside at any one time is minimal. As a consequence of all these perfectly reasonable arrangements, it is difficult for the emergent reader to take full advantage of what the library has to offer. The book talks, which offer mini-guided tours of library territory, are invaluable to the young child.

After the book talk the children should be free to browse or read. Teachers should permit children the freedom that they allow themselves. Browsing may involve the search for a particular author or topic. It may involve an unfocused examination of the books on display. It may involve a chat with a friend over the possibilities of a particular book. Teachers and librarians should model and talk about the process of selecting a book: scanning the shelves, pulling a book out, scanning the pictures, sampling the text, and repeating this procedure with 2–3 books before making a choice. Such modeling should be done informally with individuals or very small groups of 2–3 children. Children should be invited to talk about how they go about selecting a book.

Storytime

Children should be read aloud to on a frequent and regular basis. Quality literature and a high level of involvement on the part of the children should be requirements.

Frequency

Language in printed texts is organized quite differently from oral language (Halliday, 1985). Ideas are organized in different ways, sentences are constructed differently, and the vocabulary in texts is often different from that used in daily conversation. In order to become literate, children must become very familiar with printed language. The only way in which the nonreader can acquire such familiarity is if someone reads printed language aloud. Parents and family members provide the main body of experience, but teachers must also assist.

Regularity

Reading aloud to children is pleasant and easy. It does not require extensive preparation. Because of our work ethic, reading aloud is sometimes regarded as too easy to be of any benefit (no pain, no gain). Consequently reading aloud to children is often seen as an optional, recreational activity—it is often used as a bribe and its withdrawal is used as a threat. The importance of reading aloud to children is well established in the research literature (Wells, 1986).

Quality

Children's literature is a literal treasure trove that has been ignored for too long. Some of the world's finest literature has been written for young children. Max, Curious George, Samantha, Charlotte, Sylvester, Francis, Little Tim, Viola Swamp, Paddington, Madeline, Drummer Hoff, and Toad are among the most memorable characters in the world of literature. Authors and publishers are beginning to learn how to present factual information to children. There are stunning books on tadpoles, the solar system, ecology, architecture, Vikings, transportation, electricity, the human body, sailing ships, war, food, dogs, camels, and teeth. See Box 4-1 for a list of professional references to assist teachers in selecting books for children.

The books made available to children should represent a balance among narrative, exposition, poetry, and functional texts.

Narrative   Good narratives provide the reader a chance to discover what it might be like to be someone else. Such reading encourages readers to reflect on their own experience, to think about who they are and what they might become. The very best narratives are not entirely explicit. Some things are left for the reader to provide; some questions are left unresolved for the reader to ponder. By means of a well-developed theme, they comment on a significant aspect of life. Events are selected and structured to form an organic plot. Main characters are well developed and exhibit change and growth. Pace, style, setting, and point of view are deployed to present theme, plot, and characterization in a unified work of art.

Exposition   Expository texts explain how some aspect of the real world works. Expository texts for children must take into account the relatively restricted range of world knowledge that the young reader brings to the text. Texts, illustrations, charts, tables, graphs, maps, and diagrams should work together to present a coherent view of some aspect of reality. Distortions of reality, such as anthropomorphism and teleology, should be avoided.

BOX 4-1   •   *Bibliographies of Children's Literature*

The books below provide extensive lists of selected books. In many cases critical annotations are provided. It is recommended that books such as these should be included in school libraries.

Butler, D. (1980). *Babies need books.* New York: Atheneum.

Dunkle, M. (Ed.). (1987). *The story makers: A collection of interviews with Australian and New Zealand authors and illustrators for young people.* Melbourne, Australia: Oxford University Press.

Glazer, T. (1986). *Literature for young children* (2nd ed.). Columbus, OH: Charles E. Merrill.

Kobrin, B. (1988). *Eyeopeners: How to choose and use children's books about real people, places, and things.* New York: Penguin.

Lansberg, M. (1985). *Michele Lansberg's guide to children's books.* New York: Penguin.

Rudman, M. K. (1984). *Children's literature: An issues approach* (2nd ed.). New York: Longman.

Trelease, J. (1989). *The read-aloud handbook* (2nd ed.). New York: Penguin.

Anthropomorphism is the endowment of animals with human feelings and aspirations. One book on bees showed the queen bee in a bridal gown. *Teleology* invests natural phenomena with human intent: e.g., a book on atomic structure showed atoms with hands, eyes, and smiling mouths. Phrases such as "hot air tries to rise" "the moon hides behind the earth" imply motives.

One structural problem common in nonfiction is the presentation of factual material in narrative form. Narrative deals with the particular (*"Once* upon a time . . .") and is usually told in the past tense ("there *was* a little girl"). Exposition deals with the general ("polar bears live in the arctic") and is normally in the present tense. The presentation of nonfiction in narrative form can be very confusing: for example, "herbivores, such as rabbits, are *threatened* by predators but never caught." By using the narrative form, the rabbit becomes the "hero" of the story. It does not do to have one's hero torn to shreds by an owl on page 4 and fed to a family of baby owls on page 5. In books about owls or foxes, rabbits are dispatched without a qualm. With the exception of biography and historical events, nonfiction is best presented in expository form.

Poetry   Good poetry is honest. Good poetry for children offers them enjoyable sensory experiences through rhyme, rhythm, and repetition or offers reflective comments about those aspects of the world to which they can relate. Good poetry reminds the reader of feelings they too have had. Great poetry helps the reader realize that they have felt that way but have never been able to express it. Great poetry makes the commonplace an object of wonder as it helps the reader look at a familiar world with wiser eyes.

Much of the poetry offered to young children is sweet, sugary, and sentimental. While optimism is a universal characteristic of youth, the young also experience rejection, self-doubt, confusion, rage, frustration, and contempt. Poetry that deals with negative feelings is an excellent means for allowing children to express such feelings and to realize that they are not alone in experiencing them. Poetry should reflect the entire spectrum of human feelings. Poetry is appreciated best when it is performed and the performance is shared with an interested audience.

Involvement

One of the problems in reading to large groups (25 or more) of children is holding everyone's attention. Some children seem to need very close personal attention and the opportunity to participate almost continuously. Reading at home almost takes on the form of a three-way conversation: text, adult, and child. All participants have equal access. Some of this experience can be reproduced in the classroom, although the student/teacher/text ratio means that each child's degree of active participation will be severely restricted. We suggest that as the text is read the teacher invite the children to ask questions of the text: for example, having read the title, first sentence, first paragraph, or first page, what do you now wish to know? Some teachers refer to this procedure as "interrogating the text." Questions raised by the children are answered or remain unanswered as the ensuing text is read aloud. Unanswered questions may lead to speculative discussion or to further reading in search of the answers. We advocate extreme caution in asking children questions about the text. Questions should not quiz. We would advocate only two types of teacher questions—genuine and surprising.

Genuine questions are those that one adult might ask another if both have shared the same book, TV show, or movie. They are questions to which the questioner does not know the answer: e.g., questions soliciting opinion ("What did you think of it?") or questions seeking assistance ("I didn't understand why she didn't phone home. What did you think?").

Questions that surprise are those that get you to think about the text in a new way: "How do you think Mr. MacGregor felt about rabbits? Do you think he was surprised to see a rabbit wearing a blue jacket and shoes?"

When we studied readers interrogating texts, it was interesting to note how questions raised in the early parts of the text evolve into predictions as the storyline or argument develops.

Functional Writing

Cambourne (1987) and many other writers have advocated that children should be immersed in written language. Some teachers have interpreted this excellent advice by covering the classroom walls with written texts. Too much print is visually confusing, however. Children wisely ignore things they find confusing. Moreover, much of the print is not functional. A poem, a brainstormed list of "happy" words, or a 2-month-old language experience story are not functional. If left unconsulted, and thus unread, they are simply visual clutter.

Truly functional print includes the signs that show children where to hang their coats, which seats have been assigned to them, labels on boxes of equipment, or signs announcing special events.

Another legitimate way of introducing functional print into the classroom is through play activities. When the playhouse becomes a travel agent's office, grocery store, post office, or doctor's office, the areas should be provided with real examples of the kinds of texts that are actually used in such environments. They should also be equipped with writing materials. Hall (1987) has documented the remarkable effect the provision of such materials can have on the emergent literacy behavior of young children.

Developing Understanding

Many of the texts that are simple enough for young children to read present little conceptual difficulty. This is particularly true of the predictable texts that many teachers now use to teach reading in school (see the section on Shared Reading in this chapter). The features that make the text predictable—structure and frequent repetition—also render them conceptually unchallenging. The reader rarely stops to reflect why the yellow bird is looking at the brown bear in *Brown Bear, Brown, Bear, What Do You See?* Teachers of heavily structured texts rarely invite children to speculate about the motives of the characters or the wisdom of their actions. Dickinson (1989) found that the quality of language actually decreased in a kindergarten class when the teacher switched from reading stories to the children to reading shared texts.

Reading texts to children rather than having them read to themselves promotes understanding in young children. Teachers should read stories to children that have intricacies of plot, obvious and hidden motives, and events that parallel or comment on the lives of the children. All these issues should be freely discussed. It is through such discussions that children come to appreciate the deep satisfaction that may be derived from books. The rollicking rhythms of predictable texts used to teach children to read should accompany rather than displace texts that use more complex language to address more complex ideas.

As these texts are shared, they should be predicted, commented upon, questioned, challenged, accepted, and rejected. Children should be invited to say how the texts relate to their personal experiences, what they believe, and how they feel. Comprehension is not the process of answering someone else's questions but integrating the information available in the text with one's prior knowledge. The process of integration may involve the raising of questions, but these questions should be raised by the reader and addressed to the text, not by the teacher and addressed to the children.

As the children become able to read more complex texts by themselves, the behaviors learned under the guidance of the teacher are applied covertly by the reader to the independent reading of self-selected texts.

Language Experience

There are three reasons why language experience is an excellent way of introducing literacy:

- It shows the relationship between experience, speech, writing, and reading.
- It shows one process by which a text is created.
- It is based on the language and experience of the child.

Language experience involves the interconnection of four aspects: an experience, talk about the experience, dictation resulting in the creation of a text based on the experience and the language, and reading back of the resulting text.

A typical group language-experience episode might involve watching workers repair the roof of the school and interviewing them. Back in the classroom the experience is discussed. What was seen? heard? smelled? What did the workers say they were doing? A text based on oral suggestions from the children may be written in draft form on the chalkboard and then in final form on a chart:

Workers are fixing the roof.
They have hot, black tar.
It smells like old engine oil.
They are trying to stop a leak in the roof.

The chart may be surrounded by children's illustrations of the event. Personal dictation may be added to each picture. The text is read and reread for as long as the children's interest is maintained.

The intent behind the language-experience approach is not that children will learn specific vocabulary items, such as *worker, roof,* or *tar,* nor that they will learn any particular phonic relationship, although both of these may occur for some children. The intent is to show the children the process by which a text may be created and how rereading that text invokes some of the words and memories of the original experience. The fact that the episode is based on a recent experience and the oral language produced by the children increases the likelihood that the text will have meaning and relevance for them.

There are numerous variations on the procedure, which fall into two categories — group and individual. Group experiences are manageable but diluted. Individual experiences are concentrated but stressful.

Group approaches produce texts based on a common experience. The class has a single focus, thus the process is relatively easy to manage. But it is diluted because the actual oral language contributed in the creation of the text by each individual child is minimal or nonexistent. The 5 sentences in the example above might easily be based on oral contributions by no more than 6 or 7 children. The text is based on scraps of language from each. The remaining 15–16 children may have contributed nothing. Much of the composition, selection, sequence, grammar, and spelling is controlled by the teacher.

Individual experiences involve a single child dictating to the teacher. The dictation may be a comment on or caption to a picture, an explanatory comment about a model that has been constructed, or a label for something brought from home or a natural object found outside. Written texts record the oral comments made by the children:

This is my dad going fishing. (Adolphus)
This is an XMJ-1400 Rocket Blaster. (Jason)
A wasp's nest. I found it in our garden. (Anna)

Such episodes are more concentrated because the child is more fully responsible for creating the entire text. The language produced is personal to each child. The picture or artifact (and thus the text) has some particular significance for the individual. However, the procedure places great stress on the teacher since it involves sustained one-on-one interactions, which are very difficult to maintain in the classroom. The stress may be reduced by using volunteers such as parents or aides.

With the increased awareness of and interest in early writing development, many teachers are encouraging, or even insisting, that each child attempt to make some mark on the paper to represent their ideas as writing (see Chapter 5). The practice of dictation should not be prolonged. The child should take over the responsibility of creating the written text as soon as possible.

There are as many variations on the language-experience approach as there are practitioners. The suggestions below are merely examples.

Group Experiences

The class goes on an excursion (pond, park, store, crosswalk). The children observe, discuss, create a text, and read.

A new version of a familiar song, poem, or rhyme is created.

A record of what was learned from a visitor is composed. A thank-you letter is also sent.

Rules for classroom routines are drawn up: e.g., behavior at learning centers, behavior during storytime, procedures for care of the class pet, responsibilities of classroom helpers, safety in crossing the road.

Record of the weather, daily attendance, bus schedule is made.

Individual Experiences

Each child draws a picture based on an experience and dictates a caption.

Each child brings one toy stuffed animal. A comment is dictated.

Each child draws a picture of his or her family. Dictates comment.

Each child is provided with a sentence frame: I like my _____. The frame is completed and an appropriate picture is drawn.

Reading as Active Involvement of the Individual

Young children learn best through active exploration of their environment. Learning to read is no exception. Sustained periods of private reading, library time, and related discussions should not be seen as marginal in importance nor used as fillers for unassigned classroom time. They should be regarded as central to the process of learning to read and command the majority of the time allocated to reading instruction. There is a need for direction and intervention by the teacher (discussed in the next section), but such sessions should be brisk and brief (15–20 minutes) once or twice a day.

Shared Reading

Reading instruction has undergone a radical transformation in recent years. We have come to realize that the beginning of instruction in elementary school is far from being the child's first encounter with written language. We have rejected the didactic model, in which the teacher tells the novice ·what to do, and have adopted an apprenticeship model in which the expert (the teacher) models the reading process for the novice (the child). Rather than teaching children the names of a limited number of words and then having them labor through artificial texts made up of those words, the teacher presents the children with a natural text and shows them how he or she reads it. A natural text is one that is written to inform or entertain rather than written for the purpose of reading instruction or assessment.

The most widely used term for introducing reading through the apprenticeship model is *shared reading*. The procedure is developed from the bedtime story, wherein the adult reads aloud from a text that the child can see. Through repeated readings of the same text the child begins to appreciate the complex relationship between the words on the page and the meaningful sounds emanating from the reader's mouth.

In a shared reading session, the teacher gathers a group of children around an enlarged text. The text is enlarged so that all the children in the group can see the visual information that the teacher is indicating. The text may take the form of a big book, a pocket chart, or a wall chart. The texts are usually short, rhythmical, robust, and repetitious. For example:

Star bright, star light,
First star I see tonight.
I wish I may,
I wish I might
Have the wish I wish tonight.

Rhymes, poems, songs, and cumulative stories are widely used. See Box 4-2 for materials suitable for shared reading.

Box 4-2 • *Children's Books with Natural Repetition*

Allen, P. (1983). *Who sank the boat?* New York: Coward-McCann.
Allen, P. (1984). *Bertie and the bear.* Melbourne, Australia: Thomas Nelson.
Barrett, J. (1970). *Animals should definitely not wear clothing.* New York: Atheneum.
Barton, B. (1973). *Buzz, buzz, buzz.* London: H. Hamilton.
Baskin, L. (1972). *Hosie's alphabet.* New York: The Viking Press.
Battaglia, A. (1972). *Old Mother Hubbard.* Racine, WI: Golden Press.
Berenstain, S., & Berenstain, J. (1971). *B Book.* New York: Random House.
Blegvad, E. (illus.). (1980). *The three little pigs.* New York: Atheneum.
Bonne, R. (1961). *I know an old lady who swallowed a fly.* New York: Scholastic Press.
Brooke, L. (1903). *Johnny Crow's garden.* New York: Frederick Warne.
Brown, M. W. (1949). *The important book.* New York: Harper and Row.
Brown, M. W. (1954). *The friendly book.* Racine, WI: Golden Press.
Burningham, J. (1970). *Mr. Gumpy's outing.* London: J. Cape.
Burningham, J. (1980). *The shopping basket.* London: J. Cape.
Cameron, P. (1961). *I can't said the ant.* New York: Coward, McCann & Geoghegan.
Carle, E. (1969). *The very hungry caterpillar.* New York: Putnam.
Charlip, R. (1964). *What good luck, what bad luck.* New York: Scholastic Press.

Considine, K., & Schuler, R. (1965). *One, two, three, four.* New York: Holt, Rinehart, and Winston.

Einsel, W. (1962). *Did you ever see?* New York: Scholastic Press.

Emberley, B. (1967). *Drummer Hoff.* Englewood Cliffs, NJ: Prentice-Hall.

Gag, W. (1928). *Millions of cats.* New York: Coward-McCann.

Galdone, P. (1970). *Henny Penny.* Englewood Cliffs, NJ: Scholastic Press.

Galdone, P. (1974). *The little red hen.* New York: Scholastic Press.

Guilfoile, E. (1957). *Nobody listens to Andrew.* New York: Scholastic Press.

Handy, L. (1984). *Boss for the week.* Auckland, New Zealand: Ashton Scholastic.

Hewitt, A., & Broomfield, R. (1970). *Mrs. Mopple's washing line.* Harmondsworth, England: Puffin Books.

Hutchins, P. (1969). *The surprise party.* New York: Macmillan.

Hutchins, P. (1971). *Titch.* New York: Macmillan.

Hutchins, P. (1972). *Goodnight, owl.* New York: Macmillan.

Hutchins, P. (1976). *Don't forget the bacon!* New York: Greenwillow Books.

Joslin, S. (1970). *What do you say, dear?* New York: Young Scott Books.

Joyce, I. (1967). *Never talk to strangers.* Racine, WI: Golden Press.

Krauss, R. (1948). *Bears.* New York: Scholastic Press.

Krauss, R. (1952). *A hole is to dig.* New York: Harper.

Kraus, R. (1972). *Good night little ABC.* London: J. Cape.

Latham, R., & Sloan, P. (1985). *Planet Earth.* Melbourne, Australia: Methuen.

Martin, B. (1967). *Brown bear, brown bear, what do you see?* New York: Holt, Rinehart, and Winston.

Martin, B. (1970). *A ghost story.* New York: Holt, Rinehart, and Winston.

Sloan, P., & Latham, R. (1985). *Australian animals (*Set 2). Melbourne, Australia: Methuen.

Snowball, D., & Bolton, F. (1984). *Super springers.* Melbourne, Australia: Methuen.

Sutton, E. (1973). *My cat likes to hide in boxes.* London: H. Hamilton.

Tolstoy, A. (1968). *The great enormous turnip.* New York: F. Watts.

Watson, C. (1971). *Father's Fox's pennyrhymes.* New York: Crowell.

Wildsmith, B. (1962). *Brian Wildsmith's ABC.* London: Oxford University Press.

Withers, C. (1948). *A rocket in my pocket: The rhymes and chants of young Americans.* New York: Holt.

Wright, H. R. (1965). *A maker of boxes.* New York: Holt, Rinehart, and Winston.

Big book. An enlarged version of a standard-sized text. Most major publishing companies now produce them. An enlarged version may measure 24" x 18". The letters may be 1/2"–3/4" high.

Pocket chart. A nylon sheet with transparent plastic strips sewn across it to form pockets. Sentence strips and word cards are displayed in the pockets.

Wall chart. The text is usually hand-printed by the teacher or an aide on a piece of paper, which may measure 30" x 24".

The teacher reads the text aloud, using a pointer or her hand to underscore which portion of the text is being read. The teacher reads slowly but maintains sufficient speed to allow for natural expression in the oral reading. As the teacher reads, the children are expected to track the tip of the pointer so that they begin to associate what they see with what they hear.

It is important that the teacher read with natural expression. Sentences have intonational contours that are important in conveying meaning. The appropriate intonational contour is not marked in the text. The words on the page do not tell the reader how the voice must rise and fall to render the sentence meaningful. The teacher supplies the appropriate sentence melody from her store of linguistic knowledge. The children must learn that they too must provide the melody. Reading is not the sequential naming of words. Oral reading is the mellifluous blending of speech sounds into the contours of spoken language. Consequently, it is important to model natural expression and to require it from the children. Some of the children may pass through a stage that Clay (1972) calls "voice pointing." At some point children perceive the one-on-one relationship between oral and written words. At this stage, the reading may become jerky as children bite off one word at a time. Teachers should understand this is a stage, continue to model desired behavior, and gently press for more mature performance from the children.

As the children become familiar with the text, they are invited to join in. If the text selected is already known aurally/orally by the children they may join in on the first "reading."

We suggest that teachers avoid becoming mired in a pointless debate over a definition of what the children are doing at this stage. Some people have objected to shared reading on the grounds that during the initial stages the children are not really "reading." They are merely reciting the words from memory in the presence of the text. While this observation is true, the objection is not. The problem lies in what one accepts as really reading. If one demands that the child be able to correctly identify each individual word, then it is true that many of the children are not really reading. But, as we discussed above, the sequential naming of the words is not really reading either. Marie Clay has relieved us of the burden of this circular debate by introducing the magnificent phrase, *emergent reading* (Holdaway, 1976). The child is engaging in readinglike behavior. The performance has some of the characteristics of mature reading but not all of them. As in so much of their learning, children first adopt the gross aspects of the behavior, and with increased experience they refine their performance in the direction of maturity.

The process of learning to read is no exception. The children proceed from gross to fine, from general to particular, from global to local. They first identify the text. They then learn the identity of sentences or lines, then words and/or phrases, and finally letter/sound correspondences. It must be stressed that these are very general trends. To say that words are learned before letter/sound correspondences is not to suggest, for example, that a child who cannot identify the words *dog, door,* or *drop* could not recognize that each begins with the letter *d* as does his name, David. The teacher can gradually shift the responsibility of reading the text to the children by means of the following activities.

Oral cloze   As the children become more confident, the teacher engages in oral cloze. Beginning at predictable points, the teacher's voice fades out, leaving the children to provide the unsupported word for themselves:

Old King Cole was a merry old _____.

Visual cloze The use of oral cloze can lead into visual cloze. Using some form of masking, the teacher covers highly predictable content words and asks the children to identify them:

He called for his pipe and he called for his _____.
And he called for his fiddlers _____.

The function of initial letters and letter groups can be brought to the attention of children by leaving the initial part of the masked word in view:

Old King C_____
And a m_____ old soul was he
fiddlers thr_____
He called for his p_____
And he called for his b_____

Refining attention to the text The teacher capitalizes on the natural learning proclivities of the children by introducing a series of text identification strategies in a very rough developmental sequence.

Framing Using cupped hands the teacher frames a line of text and asks the children to identify it:

(Old King Cole was a merry old soul.)

The teacher moves around the text until most of the children can identify most of the lines most of the time.

Then the teacher frames phrases and/or words and asks the children to identify them:

(Old King Cole)	(King Cole)
(Merry old soul)	(soul)
(his pipe)	(pipe)
(his bowl)	(bowl)

Then the situation is reversed by citing a portion of the text and inviting volunteers to frame it.

Who can frame, "He called for his bowl"?
                 "He called for his fiddlers three"?
                 "And a merry old soul was he"?
Who can frame, "Old King Cole"?   "fiddlers three"?
                 "King Cole"?   "bowl"?
                 "merry old soul"?   "pipe?"

Tracing The procedure for tracing is identical to framing except that the teacher draws his or her hand or pointer below the portion of text to be identified. Framing carefully delineates the portion of text under examination. The introduction of tracing removes some of that support and requires the child to focus selectively on a portion of the text somewhat more independently.

Letter Identification

The teacher presents a portion of the text:

He called for his pipe

and says, "One of the words in this sentence begins with the same sound as *Cole* in *Old King Cole*. Who can frame that letter?" Correct identification is commended. "Yes, that's the letter *c* (see). It reminds us to say *cuh*. Does anyone's name begin like *Cole* or *called?*". Deal with complexities of *k* and soft *c* *when they are noted by the children.*

Many publishers of big books provide multiple copies of standard-sized versions of the enlarged text. These texts can be read chorally by small groups and made available as part of the classroom library. Individuals should be allowed to reread a favorite text as often as they wish to do so. Rereading familiar texts helps to build self-confidence. Some children will spend a month rereading the same text (Forester and Reinhard, 1989). Such behavior parallels the behavior children exhibit with regard to bedtime stories. Such massive *self*-imposed repetitions appears to be an important language learning strategy for young children.

Freedom for individual rereading should not of course be limited to books presented in shared reading sessions. Children should have daily access to the classroom library. The child should be permitted to stay with any book for as long as it holds their attention. By the same token, children should not be coerced into reading a text that does not appeal to them.

Identification of Unknown Words

A useful word identification strategy is the combination of context and letter/sound information. The teacher should model word identification procedures repeatedly during shared reading sessions.

Text	*Teacher*
Jack and Jill went up the hill To fetch a pail of water	Jack and Jill went up the hill to _____ hmm, something a pail of water. The picture shows they were going to *get* water but *get* begins with a *g* and this word begins with an *f,* fuh. Oh, I know. It's *fetch*. To fetch a pail or water. I know it's *fetch* because it ends with a *ch* (points to *ch*).

As the children develop more experience, they can be invited to assist with the identification of unknown words.

Text	*Teacher*	*Children*
Mary had a little lamb Its fleece was white as snow	(Points to fleece) This is a new word. Let's find out what it says. Read	

the line but say *Some-thing* instead.	Its something was white as snow.
It belongs to the sheep. What color is it?	White
What does the sheep have that's white?	Its coat
Let's try *coat*.	Its coat was white as snow.
Does that make sense?	Yes
Let's look at the word. Do the letters at the beginning remind you to say *cuh?*	No
What does it tell you to say?	fuh fluh
We need a word that means the coat of a sheep that begins with *fluh.* Any ideas?	fleece
Great. Let's try it.	Its fleece was white as snow.

It is quite possible that no one would know the word *fleece*. In this case the teacher would provide it. The primary goal is not to have the children accurately identify the word but to model the combining of context, letter information, and world knowledge.

The teacher's demonstrations should be based on the following principles:

* Read to the end of the sentence or line.
* Guess what would make sense.
* Check your guesses against the spelling of the unknown word.
* Reread the word in context to check that it makes sense.

If the word is still unknown and you can understand the meaning of the text without the word, then carry on reading. If understanding the word is crucial, then ask for help. Always ask for confirmation or disconfirmation of a hypothesis:

Ask: Does this word say *fetch?*
Not: What is this word?

Another strategy we would advocate is identification of spelling/sound patterns based on familiar words.

Text	*Teacher*
Jack and Jill went up the hill To fetch a pail of water	Jack and Jill went up the hill To fetch a some-thing of water. It looks like *tail* except for the *t*. This word begins with a *p* (puh). Take off the *t* (tuh) tuh-ail, puh-ail. It must be *pail*. That's another word for a *bucket*. To fetch a pail of water.

It will help if the teacher's think-aloud commentary is accompanied by writing the appropriate words, spelling patterns, and letters on the chalkboard. Letter names and letter/sound approximations should be used almost synonymously. For example:

t   That's a *t* (tee). It reminds us to say *tuh.*

ch   We have to write *chuh.* We need a *c* (see) and an *h* (aitch). *c* and *h* often work together.

Children should also become aware of the morphemic structure of words. A simple structure that is readily learned by young children is compounding. *When I was Young in the Mountains* (Rylant, 1982) contains the following compound words: *Sometimes, cowbells, grandfather, grandmother, pocketknife, bobwhite, anywhere.* As the children share the text of this delightful story the teacher may pause to point out the compound nature of some of the words.

Compound word	*Commentary*
sometimes	". . . and we sometimes saw snakes, . . ." This words says *sometimes: some* (traces underneath) and *times* (traces underneath). It's two words put together, *some* and *times* ". . . we sometimes saw snakes, but we jumped in anyway."
grandmother	". . . Grandmother spread the table with hot corn bread. . . ." This word is *grandmother. Grand* (traces underneath) and *mother* (traces underneath). *Grand* and *mother* have been put together to make one big word, *grandmother.* ". . . Grandmother spread the table with hot corn bread, pinto beans, and fried ocra."

After two or three examples the children may be invited to look for a few examples of compound words as they occur in the text. Children do not need to learn a specified body of compound words; what is important is that they learn that compounding occurs and that some long and unfamiliar words are sometimes made up of familiar shorter parts. Decontextualized exercises on compound words have little value. Children may be invited to contribute to a compound word collection. On some occasions the children may be challenged to find compound words in a given story, exposition, or poem.

A similar approach may be taken towards the use of prefixes and suffixes added to root words. Word structure is best approached in context. The opening lines of *When I was Young in the Mountains* provide several opportunities for examining suffixes:

When I was young in the mountains, Grandfather came home in the evening covered with the black dust of the coal mine. Only his lips were clean, and he used them to kiss the top of my head.

The opening lines of *The Incredible Painting of Felix Clousseau* (Agee, 1988) contain an example of a prefix:

In Paris, the Royal Palace was holding its Grand Contest of Art. From all over the city, painters came to show their pictures. One of them was the unknown painter named Felix Clousseau.

Curiously enough, a focus on the meaning of word parts is not very rewarding. The following words and phrases occur in *When I was Young in the Mountains:*

in the evening
swimming hole
looked alike
afterward.

Evening is a word and concept likely to be familiar to young children. Little is gained by trying to explain the contextual meaning of the root word, *eve,* and how this meaning is modified by adding *ing.* The addition of the *n* is to facilitate pronunciation rather than meaning. Discussion of word parts may stay at the perceptual level.

Text	*Teacher*
Grandfather came home in the evening.	The word is *evening.* This part (gestures) says *eve(n).* This part (gestures) says *ing.* It's the spelling pattern we see in *ring* and *thing.* Does anyone else know of a word with *ing* in it? They put the *n* in so that it is easier to say.

The same argument can be offered against trying to explain the meaning of the parts in *swimming, alike,* and *afterward.* Each word is readily understood as a unit.

One advantage of addressing examples as they occur naturally in texts is that the appropriate balance is maintained. It soon becomes very clear from examining actual texts that while the practice of adding suffixes is very common, the use of prefixes is much less so.

The goal of such instruction in word identification is *not* to teach children specific sound/symbol associations or spelling "rules." The intent is to:

- show children that there is a somewhat systematic relationship between how we speak and how we write *but* that this relationship is so unstable that one should hold a series of disposable working hypotheses drawn inductively from experience (rather than Authoritative Immutable Rules passed down by Infallible Authorities). For example: "When two vowels go walking the first vowel has its 'long' sound";
- provide children with a few flexible strategies wherein one orchestrates the information available (prior knowledge, context, word structure, and spelling information) to form a reasonable hypothesis;
- show that the identification of unknown words is the responsibility of the reader;
- show that reading is an active process that requires the extension of effort by the reader (meaning does not spring unbidden from the page into the eye or brain).

Some children will need numerous demonstrations of word identification before they internalize the procedures for themselves. Instruction should involve repeated modeling, invitations to join in the process, the gradual fading of support by the teacher, and lavish praise and support for any signs of progress. As the children have experience with reading the texts of others and composing their own texts, they move gradually towards conventional usage.

It is important to note that learning is under the control of the learner not the teacher. What the teacher can provide are opportunities for learning. Thus the goals of instruction should remain at the strategic level listed above. The acquisition of specific sound/symbol associations — the finer details — occur in the recesses of each individual brain, not in the teacher's lesson plan nor according to a schedule printed in a teacher's guide.

We do not recommend the teaching of verbal rules such as what happens when two vowels go "walking," or when a magic *e* follows a vowel and a consonant. Such rules are too abstract, have low utility, and are often misleading. The greatest argument against them is their level of abstraction. Such generalities are drawn from familiarity with an enormous number of examples by someone who is an experienced reader. Teachers who have taught such rules will admit they did not note them for themselves but read them in a teacher's guide. Young children do not learn by being handed abstract generalizations, which they are expected to apply on all future occasions. Young children learn inductively from experience. What they need help with is drawing up working hypotheses based on *their* (limited) experiences. Thus, any generalities about speech and spelling should be devised privately by each child.

Nor do we recommend the teaching of syllabication. There are several grounds for our prohibition:

- Syllables are an abstract and meaningless aspect of language, and thus not readily learned by children.
- There are no agreed-upon rules for breaking words into syllables.
- The notion that words are broken into discrete syllables is mistaken. Discreet breaks between one syllable and the next do not occur. Words have vocalic centers that are "hinged" at the syllabic boundaries. For example, in pronouncing the word *pattern,* the speaker moves from *pa* to *ern* by pivoting on the *t.* The action is fluid and continuous. At no point does one syllable start and the second begin.

As should be evident from our examples, word identification should occur only when readers are trying to make sense out of naturally occurring texts. Decontextualized exercises on subword units of language are difficult for children to learn, and it is almost impossible for them to relate the isolated exercise to the demands of reading real texts. Strategies for word identification should be modeled by the teacher during shared reading. The assistance of the children should be increasingly urged as the teacher's support is withdrawn. A similar philosophy, more finely attuned to the current competence of the individual, should guide the teacher's behavior during reading conferences. Teachers should insist that children *never* ask for the identity of a word. Rather they should seek confirmation or rejection of a hypothesis.

Summary

We have deliberately chosen our examples from good literature. However, it would be a dreadful mistake to perceive *When I was Young in the Mountains* as a vehicle for word analysis and miss the lilt of the language and the charm of the story. Discussion of word identification and word structure should be light, brief, purposeful, and infrequent. The major portion of the instruction should be concentrated on the meaning and aesthetics of the story. Activities that would address these aspects would include—

- discussing situations in the book that parallel one's own experience (Have you ever overeaten and had a tummy ache? Would you pick up a snake and drape it across your neck?);
- reading the story in chorus so as to bring out the rhythm and repetition of the language;
- creating a parallel version based on experiences of children in the class;
- reexamining the text and pictures to determine when and where the story might have taken place.

Teaching Phonics

The teaching of phonics is embedded in many of the activities already described. Whenever the children's attention is addressed to how a particular word might be spelled or what letter or letters aid the identification of an unknown word, the children have the opportunity to learn the sound/symbol associations involved.

Two techniques for teaching phonics within the context of natural and meaningful language are (1) morning news and (2) morning messages.

Children can be helped to appreciate how spoken and written English relate to one another by using these techniques. Morning news can be used right from the start. Morning messages works better with children who have some phonic skills.

Morning news   As one of the opening exercises of the day, the teacher invites some of the children to talk about something of note that occurred the previous evening or over the weekend. With whatever help the children can provide, the teacher records the news on the chalkboard. As she does so, she models her composing processes and points out any regularities. For example, Cathleen might report that her cat had kittens.

Teacher says	*Children say*	*Teachers writes*
We need to say, "Cathleen's cat had kittens."		
What letters do we need to write *Cathleen?*	C	C

If Cathleen can spell her name, she is invited to do so.

Now we need cat? What letters do we need?	C	C
Cat begins like *Cathleen*. What other letters do we need?	t tuh	
Yes, we need a *t*. It goes here. Anything else?		c t

If the children offer the letter *a* it is inserted. If not, it is provided. Children may suggest letters in order of perceived importance.

Most important:	beginning letter(s)
Next most important:	final letter(s)
Least important:	middle letter(s)

As words become familiar, the children will adopt the sequential identification of letters.

When the teacher gets to *kittens* she might proceed as follows:

Teacher says	*Children say*	*Teacher writes*
Now we need *kittens*. It begins with the same sound as *Cathleen* and *cat* but you write with a different letter. I need a *k*.		k

If children suggest unconventional spellings the results may be recorded and compared.

Teacher says	*Children say*	*Teacher has written*
We have two ways of spelling *cat*. Which way is it spelled in a printed book?		kat cat

If the children have any visual memory of the conventional spelling they will identify it. If no one is sure, then the teacher provides the identification.

Morning messages   The teacher writes a brief message on the chalkboard ready for the children to read when they come into the classroom. The message might deal with some of the activities planned for that day:

Good morning *T*oys and *B*irls,
Today we will work on our sp*i*ce project.
We will read *Where the Wild Strings* are again.

Each error is clearly marked by using a piece of chalk of contrasting color or underlining it. The substitutions can be adjusted to the sophistication level of the children and selected to ensure that children pay close attention to such things as initial consonants, vowels, phonograms, blends, and digraphs:

Substitution convention

initial consonants	toys/boys	shown in the example above
vowels	spice/space	
blends	strings/things	
phonograms	singed/singing	
digraphs	lurch/church	

Children enjoy the silly nonsense and helping the teacher correct it.

Providing Extra Help

There is no research evidence that children who seem to be developing more slowly than their peers have brains that function in significantly different ways from those of more advanced learners. Consequently there are no a priori grounds for assuming that children whose abilities are emerging more slowly must be taught in some manner that differs in a significantly qualitative way from more able children. There is certainly no reason to think that while competent learners learn to read by making sense out of the context, children who develop more slowly must concentrate exclusively on sound/symbol relations.

A very small percentage of children who experience very severe difficulties may require the attention of a specialist. However, the majority of children can be helped by using the same methods employed with the more able children. The only difference is that the instruction should be done in small groups (3–5 children). The small size of the group allows the teacher to adjust the level and pace of the instruction more precisely to the needs of the children. It also means that while the pace of instruction is slower, the level of active participation of each child can be higher. It is much easier for the teacher to monitor the responses of each child and thus modify the flow of instruction to individual needs. In most cases, it is safe to assume that development is delayed rather than presuming some component skill is missing. Thus diagnosis becomes a search for the appropriate developmental level rather than a search for some discreet skill that must be remediated. Instruction is essentially the same as that used for the majority of the class but at an earlier stage. Thus, if the achieving children are ready for the identification of words and letters, these other emerging readers may need extended practice reading chorally with vigorous and continuing support from the teacher's voice.

It is a good idea to get these emerging readers ahead of the rest of the class rather than have them trailing ever further behind. Thus, if the teacher is planning to introduce a new text to the children, for example, "Old Mother Hubbard," the teacher might present this to these emerging readers first. This prior experience may enable some of them to shine before their more able peers when the text is introduced to the whole class. The positive effects on these emerging readers' self-esteem can be considerable.

The small-group instruction of these emerging readers, where possible, should be conducted by the regular classroom teacher. If aides or parent helpers are available, they should provide general supervision of the majority of the class in some independent activities while the regular teacher provides those who need extra time in a small-group setting.

Where aides or parents are not available, the teacher needs to develop a classroom environment and regime wherein children have the means and self-discipline to conduct independent work for 5–15 minutes, thus allowing the teacher time for interruption-free instruction of small groups.

Providing such periods means developing learning centers, self-corrective games, and reading, writing, craft materials to which the children have independent access (see Chapter 7). It also means training the children in the procedures for obtaining, using, and returning materials independently. It means counseling the children in cooperation and dispute resolution. Appeals to the teacher should be seen as a court of last resort. It means having a series of ongoing projects in science, social studies, or art that can be pursued without direction from the teacher. If every lesson involves the teacher taking a central role as traffic controller, materials manager, and thought director, the children will remain dependent. Teachers will find it very difficult to find time to spend with individuals or small groups. If children are taught independence, then small-group instruction and individual conferences become much more viable options.

With all learners, but most particularly with these emerging readers, it is crucial that the learners, not the teacher nor the program, set the pace of instruction. In practical terms, this means letting the children choose the text to be read and the number of times it will be reread. Some children will reread the same text an astounding number of times before they are willing to move on. Teachers should exercise tolerance and patience. While rereading *The Old Woman and Her Pig* for the fortieth time may be repetitious for the teacher, the experience may be the occasion when some feature of the text, for the first time, comes to the notice of the learner.

Conclusion

Literacy learning is not confined to the elementary school or the language arts lesson. One of the most powerful forces in the child's life is the home. As teachers we must know what is, what is not, and what can be learned in the home. We must recognize that the influence of the school is limited and that we must learn to harness the power and influence of the home for language learning.

Reading in school has two major facets: individual, independent exploration of the world of literacy; and intervention by the teacher. In the first aspect, the teacher's role is to provide a receptive environment in which literacy can flourish. The teacher acts as role model and counselor. Storytime invites children to engage with conceptually challenging written language. Language-experience helps to connect experience, talk, writing, and reading. The second major aspect of reading in school is the active intervention of the teacher in the form of shared reading. The role adopted by the teacher is one of a coach, an expert who demonstrates the procedure for the novices and then invites them to join in. The attention of the children is drawn initially to the global and meaningful aspects of the text. As the children become more familiar with a given text, and with texts in general, the teacher helps the children refine their attention to the finer details of text.

Emergent readers may need a higher degree of individual attention, a slower pace, and a higher rate of active participation. They are best regarded as developmentally delayed rather than as deficient.

References

Agee, J. (1988). *The incredible painting of Felix Clouseau.* New York: Farrar, Straus and Giroux.

Applebee, A. M. (1987). *The child's concept of story: Ages two to seventeen.* Chicago: University of Chicago Press.

Cambourne, B. L. (1987). *Natural learning and literacy education.* Sydney: Ashton Scholastic.

Clay, M. (1972). *Reading: The patterning of complex behavior.* Portsmouth, NH: Heinemann.

Dickinson, D. K. (1967). Effects of a shared reading program on one head-start language and literacy environment. In J. Allen & J. M. Mason (Eds.), *Risk makers, risk takers, risk breakers: Reducing the risks for young literacy learners* (pp. 125–153). Portsmouth, NH: Heinemann.

Diehl, W. A., & Mikulecky, L. (1988). The nature of reading at work. In E. R. Kintgen, B. M. Kroll, & M. Rose (Eds.), *Perspectives on literacy* (pp. 378–390). Carbondale, IL: Southern Illinois University Press.

Forester, A., & Rienhard, M. (1989). *The learner's way.* Winnipeg, Canada: Peguis.

Hall, N. (1987). *The emergence of literacy.* Portsmouth, NH: Heinemann.

Halliday, M. A. K. (1985). *Spoken and written language.* Victoria, Australia: Deakin University Press.

Hansen, J. (1989). *When writers read.* Portsmouth, NH: Heinemann.

Holdaway, D. (1976). *Foundations of literacy.* Toronto, Canada: Scholastic.

Mandler, J. M., & Johnson, N. S. (1977). Remembrance of things parsed: Story structure and recall. *Cognitive Psychology, 9,* 111–151.

Martin, J. R. (1984). Types of writing in infants and primary school. In L. Unsworth (Ed.), *Reading, writing and spelling: Proceedings of the fifth MacArthur reading language symposium.* Sydney, Australia: MacArthur Institute of Higher Learning.

Meyer, B. J. F. (1985). The structure of text. In P. D. Pearson (Ed.), *Handbook of reading research.* New York: Longman.

Rylant, C. (1982). *When I was young in the mountains.* New York: E. P. Dutton.

Tizard, B., & Hughes, M. (1984). *Young children learning: Talking and thinking at home and at school.* London: Fontana.

Wells, G. (1986). *The meaning makers: Children learning language and using language to learn.* Portsmouth, NH: Heinemann.

CHAPTER FIVE

Emerging Writing

Advance Organizer

In this chapter we discuss young emerging writers and how they can be encouraged and guided in their writing growth. The first section provides characteristics of beginning writing, which often show up prior to school. Next we focus on young writers in school and the very important role of the teacher in helping them develop enjoyment, pride, and skill at this craft. Children and teachers can choose from a wide range of writing experiences, and several of these are explored. The writing process as an effective method of instruction is described. Then strategies for evaluating growth in writing and record keeping are examined. Many schools now have computers, and these have been used effectively with young children's writing. The use of the word processors as a tool for writing is described next. The chapter closes with ways to teach handwriting and spelling—also important tools of the young writer.

Objectives

After studying this chapter, the reader should be able to—

- identify some of the characteristics of emerging writers;
- explain how a teacher can organize the classroom environment to promote children's writing;
- describe five practices of teachers to help children write;
- explain what the ideal of "providing a wide range of writing experiences for young writers" entails;
- list the steps in the writing process and describe each step briefly;
- identify several effective strategies for helping children in the prewriting stage;
- name three different types of writing conferences and describe the characteristic of each;

Graphic Organizer

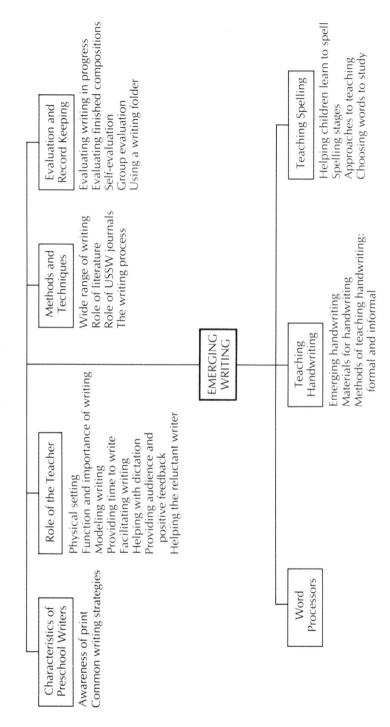

Characteristics of Preschool Writers

Awareness of print
Common writing strategies

Role of the Teacher

Physical setting
Function and importance of writing
Modeling writing
Providing time to write
Facilitating writing
Helping with dictation
Providing audience and
  positive feedback
Helping the reluctant writer

Methods and Techniques

Wide range of writing
Role of literature
Role of USSW journals
The writing process

Evaluation and Record Keeping

Evaluating writing in progress
Evaluating finished compositions
Self-evaluation
Group evaluation
Using a writing folder

EMERGING WRITING

Word Processors

Teaching Handwriting

Emerging handwriting
Materials for handwriting
Methods of teaching handwriting:
  formal and informal

Teaching Spelling

Helping children learn to spell
Spelling stages
Approaches to teaching
Choosing words to study

- describe ways to evaluate young children's writing;
- define *writing folder* and discuss its use in the classroom;
- discuss the advantages of using word processors to help children write;
- identify some initial handwriting activities to be used in the classroom;
- discuss important considerations in teaching spelling in the classroom.

Characteristics of Preschool Writers

Awareness of Print

Most young children in North America encounter print on a daily basis. There is print on doors at supermarkets, print on cereal boxes, jackets, T-shirts, alphabet blocks, and road signs. Books, newspapers, posters, and magazines add to the long list of common print items. An awareness of the communication function of print comes at different times for different children. Parents point out words to their children. An older sibling may print "Don't touch" on a sign and then attach it to a Lego design that the child made so that nobody will touch it. The child sees how useful print can be. Some children, because of interests, opportunities, and personality, choose to look at logos, letters, words, and drawings more carefully than other children.

Once children are aware of print, they naturally move towards reproducing it. Early writing is often seemingly without any purpose and begins with drawings, scribbles, random lines, and circles. Children play with the different patterns of numbers, letters, and words that they see in their environment. However, just as children differ in personalities, they also differ in the early developmental writing patterns (Vygotsky, 1978). There is no one specific sequence of steps or group of strategies that all children follow in becoming writers. Children's emerging writing is not always a linear pattern; children may use more immature forms of writing at the same time as conventional writing forms. Preschool children may also become engrossed in writing for periods of time, only to lose interest for awhile, and then become engrossed again.

Some Common Writing Strategies

Although all children will not exhibit exactly the same behaviors, there are some common strategies that many children do try as they learn about writing. In many cases, they use a combination of different forms of writing in one message. Ferreio and Teberosky (1982) found the initial marking and scribbling of the youngest children represented objects, not letters. Other researchers (Clay,

1975; Harste, Woodward, & Burke, 1984; Read, 1970) have found that children often exhibit the following attempts at early writing.

Drawing Many children will use drawings to communicate their ideas.

Scribbling Some children's initial attempts at writing start as early as 1 or 2 years of age, while others are still scribbling in kindergarten. Some of the scribbles may be wavy at the start, then take on circular or boxlike shapes, add simple angles, and gradually become more letterlike. Both drawing and scribbling give the child practice in control and lead to the writing of letterlike forms.

Progressing from letterlike units to letters Researchers (Ferreiro and Teberosky, 1982; Freeman and Whitesell, 1985) reported that many young children had developed concepts about words by themselves. They believed that a certain number of letters (usually 2–4) was required to make a word readable. Also, children thought that there should be some variation of letters in order to be words. Many children use a combination of strings of shapes that look like letters, actual letters, scribbling, and drawing as they form concepts about writing. As they progress, they will often show a preference for drawing on one part of the paper or a separate page and putting their "letters" and "sentences" in another part of the page or on a separate page.

Copying print Many children spend time doing this activity before branching off into composing their own writings.

Invented spelling Many children begin to explore the phoneme/grapheme relationship, usually starting with words in isolation. Often, one letter (the first one) may stand for a word or the first and last letters may be used. Later, many children will begin to include vowels in the middle of the word. Finally, the whole word is written out the way it sounds to the child. See Figure 5-1 for an evaluation scale on the different forms of writing.

Some other insights about how young children emerge as writers and how the school influences their progress in this development come from Davies's (1989) study of how children learn to print their own names in playschool (see Figure 5-2). She found:

1. Name writing does appear to be a constructing process that is predictable and observable, but the process is influenced both in terms of scope and sequence by the others in the environment. Children are informed by others. They do not discover graphic combinations accidentally.

2. From the children's perspectives, the functions of children's written names were ownership, labeling, invitations, and expressions of gratitude. These functions were embedded in and limited by the routines and interactions among and between participants in the playschool.

3. The findings of the study indicated that the developmental pattern is largely im-

FIGURE 5-1 • **Class Forms of Writing Evaluation Scale**

GROUP SESSION

SULZBY PELP
School Code:
Teacher Code:
Classroom:
Researcher:
Date:

FORMS OF WRITING

Child's Name	Drawing	Scribble-Wavy	Scribble-Letterlike	Letterlike Units	Letters-Random	Letters-Patterned	Letters-Name Elements	Copying (Inv. Print)	Invented Sp.-Syllabic	Inv. Sp.-Intermediate	Inv. Sp.-Full	Conventional	Other	Not Observed	Refusal	"I didn't write"
	1	2	3	4	5	6	7	8	9	10	11	12	13	1	2	3
1																
2																
3																
4																
5																

Source: Sulzby Forms of Writing, Copyright reserved, Elizabeth Sulzby.

FIGURE 5-2 • *Changes in Children's Written Names*

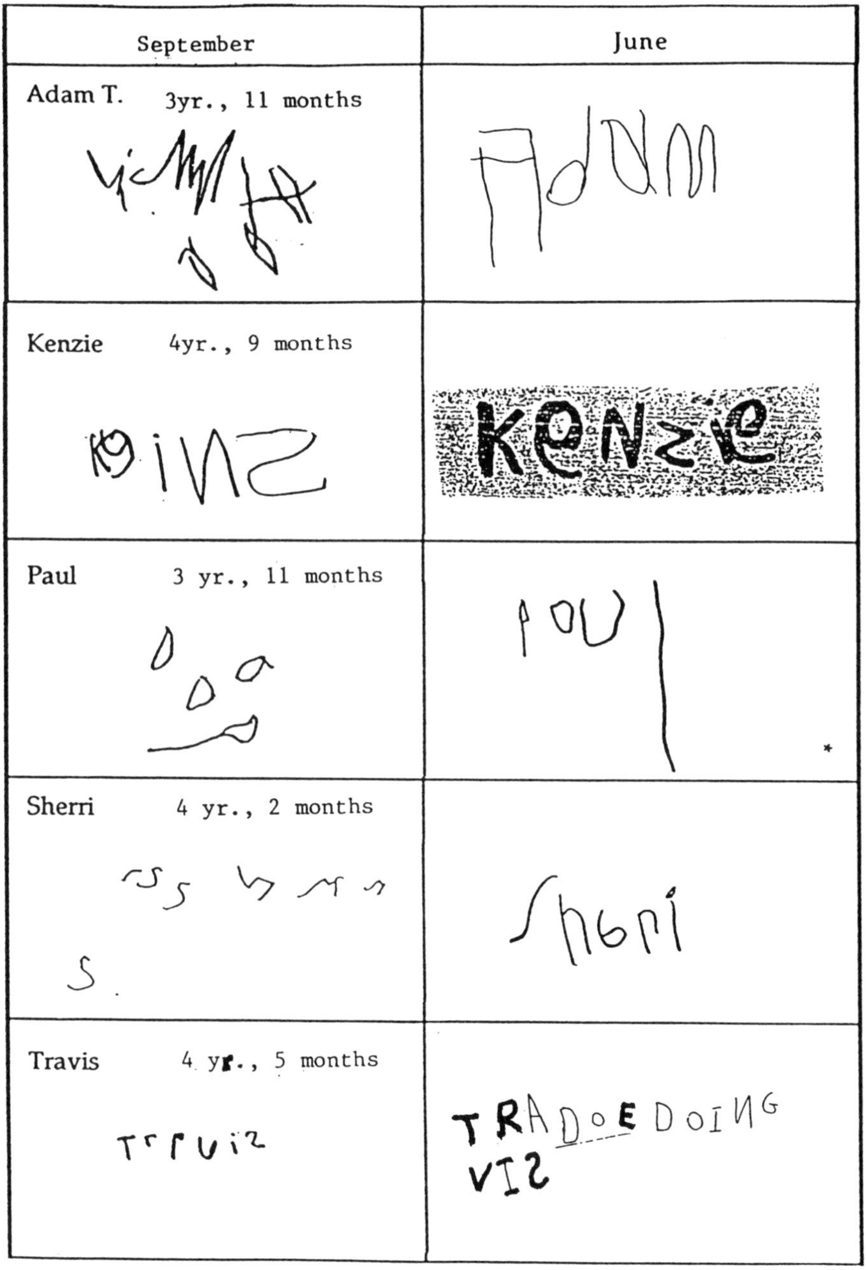

September	June
Adam T. 3yr., 11 months	
Kenzie 4yr., 9 months	
Paul 3 yr., 11 months	*
Sherri 4 yr., 2 months	
Travis 4 yr., 5 months	

Source: Ann Davies, 1988, Ph.D. Dissertation. Used by permission.

posed or directed by adults. The children learned to attend to words in ways demonstrated and taught by teachers as they wrote their own names.

The Role of the Teacher in Helping Children Write

The teacher of preschool, kindergarten, and primary children has a crucial role in setting up a nurturing and facilitating environment where children will value writing and will grow and flourish as writers. Each child brings his or her own knowledge of writing, which is unique and different from others in the class. The teacher's challenging role is to find out what each child knows about writing and act as a facilitator to extend this knowledge and to help each child discover both a personal usefulness for writing and feel successful as a writer. How a teacher does this will be discussed next.

Developing a Physical Setting for a Writing Classroom

The first observation a visitor would make about a writing classroom is the abundance of print throughout the room. Names of children are taped above hooks so each child knows where to hang his or her coat. Invitational signs, such as "Use these paints to make a picture," encourage children to participate in a variety of activities. Bulletin boards showcase children's drawings and writing. The writing table displays key words that children have requested and have had written down for them. Chalkboards record daily class news or individual news, such as "Megan's cat had four babies last night."

The teacher enhances the desirability of writing by providing easy access to a wide variety of practical and desirable materials for writing, such as paper, pencils, erasers, felt-tip pens, crayons, and rulers. Art supplies are available to decorate the writing. Differently shaped, prepared booklets, large chart paper, individual chalkboards, computers, and typewriters can be made available (see also Chapter 7 for a detailed description of a writing center). Many children also enjoy writing together at tables or desks pushed together. This close proximity promotes cooperative learning in which the sharing of ideas helps with the writing.

Helping Children Understand the Function and Importance of Writing in their Lives

Children need to understand the purpose of writing, that writing can do jobs that speech cannot. The various purposes of writing can be easily demonstrated daily by the teacher while going about classroom business. Written reminders of things for the children to do the next day can be done at the end of the day. The class can write letters to prepare for a fieldtrip, thank-you letters to sick children, and so on. These are all meaningful examples of the functions of writing. Children, in turn, are asked to communicate their thoughts in a variety of meaningful writing experiences. Not only do they dictate or write stories for the teacher and others to read, they also write functional messages to their parents about bake sale days and school concerts. Letters of complaint or suggestions, riddle writing, tips for good classroom parties, "me" books, autographs, captions for pictures. Children need to be able to choose their own topics and purposes for writing. However, the teacher needs to have on hand a number of possible topics to help those children who have difficulty deciding about what to write.

Modeling Writing

By modeling writing teachers show purposes, principles, and techniques for accomplishing this task. For instance, the teacher points out to the children that she is writing a note to remember to get some more red paint for the class. During the year, the teacher can write impromptu stories for the class, modeling the steps of the *writing process* (to be described later in this chapter) as he or she composes the story. Journal writing or Uninterrupted Sustained Silent Writing (USSW) is when everyone, including the teacher, writes. The teacher can share problems with writing as well as triumphs to give the children a realistic picture of what every writer experiences.

Providing Time to Write

To be a writer one has to have time to write. It is the teacher's responsibility to provide ample time for children to compose in the classroom. Some teachers insure that writing takes place daily by setting aside a 15–20 minute period for personal journal writing or USSW. In other classrooms, there are writing centers where children may go if they wish to write. Some primary teachers plan formal writing sessions using such structures as the *writing process* to extend children's writing. Other teachers rely on more informal and free-time periods. Others use a mix of formally planned writing periods as well as informal free time for writing, but the important point is to give children adequate time to write.

One of the difficulties for teachers in planning writing activities is the variability in time it takes different children to write a composition. Some children write quickly producing many pages. Others work laboriously over a few lines. For some children, a few words or a caption is all they can accomplish. Some days a child feels like writing, other days inspiration won't come. A teacher needs to be sensitive to these writing behaviors and provide adequate time for children to complete unfinished work.

Facilitating the Writing and Extending the Skill

As was mentioned earlier, children come to school with their own abilities, attitudes, and understandings about writing. The teacher, through observation and discussion, evaluates where children are and then begins to help them advance in their writing from that point. To find out where children are, one of the simplest techniques is to have them write. The teacher circulates around the room watching how they approach the task. Do the children use conventional print? Which children are using invented spelling effectively? Are the sentences making sense? Is there evidence of story elements, variety of sentence patterns, and good vocabulary present in the writing? Teachers can create a climate where children can take risks, initiate their own purpose for writing, discuss and share their writing with others, and receive positive feedback and constructive criticism.

To develop as good writers, children need to read and be read many different types of writing. From this reading, children develop a sense of story and lan-

Parent volunteer helping with dictation for a child's drawing.

guage that spins off into their writing. The effective writing teacher will not overemphasize accurate punctuation and spelling, as this tends to inhibit writing and gives children the message that form is more important than content. Instruction in the mechanics of writing can be given at other times with young children. With older primary children, punctuation and spelling can be incorporated into lessons while editing some of their initial drafts.

Helping with Dictation

Teachers of young children will spend some of their time acting as scribes. The teacher writes what the child says. Then teacher and child will read it together while the teacher points out the words being read. If the child "reads" a completely different thought than what he or she originally dictated or makes obvious gross errors, the teacher may read the writing again. As one can see, the child is learning about writing and reading at the same time.

Many teachers employ the aid of parent helpers, older students, or teacher aides to help with dictation. A Writing Center (see description in Chapter 7), where children can go to dictate their thoughts, works well. In upper primary classes, students in the same class can help each other with their writing, and some teachers use a buddy system where younger and older children meet on a regular basis as buddies involved in a variety of learning activities together (see Chapter 8). Besides acting as scribes for individual children, the teacher can work with the whole class or small groups of children recording common experiences by grouping different individuals' thoughts into one composition.

Providing an Audience and Positive Feedback for the Writer

An attentive audience, who provide positive feedback and constructive criticism when appropriate, gives the young writer a sense of purpose for writing and provides a good motivation to continue writing. When the children's writing is displayed prominently, when they read what they have written to others, when they share their writing with other individuals, small groups, or the whole class, they are receiving the message that what they have to say is of value. The teacher needs to promote a positive, accepting climate where children feel able, take the risk, and bask in the warm rewards of exposing their written thoughts in front of peers, teacher, principal, or others.

A writing classroom can often be noisy as children are encouraged to share ideas and their writing in progress with each other. Often children get further ideas for their writing and useful comments in this cooperative learning situation. Understanding that this exchange among children is providing feedback and a genuine audience, teachers should tolerate a higher than usual noise level and be able to differentiate it from unproductive noise, which interferes with learning.

Children should be allowed to choose whether or not they want to share their writing with the class. Some children may be reluctant at first, or they may produce what they consider a poor composition or something very personal that they do not wish to share with others. As children see others sharing and the positive feedback others get from reading their writings, these reluctant children will invariably begin to share their writings. Children, especially older children with longer compositions, should be asked to practice reading their writings several times before sharing with the audience. The value of good expression, a loud clear voice, and fluency can be discussed and demonstrated at these times also. With younger children, sometimes the teacher can read the writing with the child standing next to her. This is often helpful with shy or timid children or children whose writing has not developed the sentence variety, sparkle, or imagination of the more developed writers in the classroom. The teacher can make this undeveloped writing more interesting by her expression and interjected comments so the child gets positive feedback and the rest of the audience gets some enjoyment.

Following the sharing by the child, the teacher could conclude with a positive comment, have other individuals from the audience provide some appropriate positive feedback, initiate applause, or use some other reinforcing closure. Audiences must be taught how to give positive feedback. Roleplaying and modeling positive feedback are effective ways of helping young children understand their role as a responsive audience. However, the teacher should be sensitive and quick to observe signs of inattentiveness and restlessness in the audience. Scheduling a few students everyday to read their current favorite piece of writing is better than having a whole class do it.

Helping the Reluctant Writer

Even in the best of all classrooms, there will be some children who love to write and others who, in varying degrees and for varying reasons, do not. Some children do not like to write because they lack certain writing skills. For instance, some young children do not like to write because they spend great amounts of time printing individual letters. Some suggestions for these children is to circumvent printing by having a scribe help record their stories; to teach them how to use a word processor; and to suggest writing shorter pieces, such as captions and messages, rather than longer stories. Some children are reluctant to write because they have great difficulty grasping the phoneme/ grapheme relationship, are not satisfied with their invented spelling, or have difficulty building up memories of common words. Some ways to help children who have problems putting down words are providing easy access to word banks and personal and class word lists; letting children know by the teacher's actions that content is more important than form; and keeping an eye on an easily frustrated child and being quick to help with this aspect of writing.

Other children are reluctant writers because they have a difficult time deciding what to write. All writers, including young writers, will sometimes get "writer's block" or have a time when they just can't write. However, some reluctant writers consistently experience great difficulty choosing a topic, developing ideas, or deciding what comes next. Many of these children are helped by writing activities that are initially very structured. Patterned sentences, such as "I like my _____ because _____," lead reluctant writers into idea possibilities. The children might paraphrase predictable books, such as changing *Brown Bear, Brown Bear* (Martin, 1970) to a Halloween theme of "Little ghost, Little ghost, what do you see, I see a _____ looking at me." Gradually, the structure can be lessened for these children.

Another type of activity that helps children write is having them first draw a picture; then talk about it with a classmate, buddy, parent volunteer, or the teacher; and finally begin to write. With older primary students, extra time spent in prewriting activities, such as brainstorming ideas or developing a semantic map or timeline of events, may be helpful. Talking about the writing with the teacher or other children often helps children think through their ideas and compositions.

Some children need more help in writing because they have a difficult time staying focused on such a sedentary activity as writing. These children have short attention spans, enjoy active play, and generally would not choose literacy activities in a classroom. Attentive supervision, encouragement, and modifications in writing activities to suit their needs as active learners and to match their developmental level is necessary. Teachers working with these children must maintain a firm but kind atmosphere, where children know that some writing is expected and know that they should attempt the task. Allowing the student to choose a topic to write about is a good strategy. Motivational feedback, both intrinsic (e.g., recognition for a job well done) and extrinsic (e.g., stickers, a note to parents) are also helpful with this kind of reluctant writer.

Methods and Techniques of Writing Instruction

A Wide Range of Writing Experiences

When people think of children's writing, they most often think in terms of creative story writing. There is a wide range of writing experiences, however, to which children need to be exposed and involved in so they can grow as writers. Four dimensions of writing that need to be considered for teaching writing are function, mode, purpose, and form (Britton, 1970).

Function   Teachers should provide opportunities to foster children's experiences with the three major functions of writing:

1. Practical or functional writing focuses on the information to be communicated to the reader: e.g., writing notes, making lists, filling in forms.
2. Expressive or personal writing focuses on the writer's experiences. It is more free

flowing and loosely structured: e.g., story writing, journal writing, descriptive writing.

3. Poetic or artistic writing focuses on the language and its structure.

Mode   English books commonly refer to a variety of modes (evaluative, narrative, expository, descriptive, argumentative, persuasive, discourse, and analysis) and genres (poetry, familiar essay, fiction, exposition, argument, and personal narrative). Ideally, children should have selections from each mode and genre read to them and available for independent reading. Although the teacher will not have the time to cover each mode in depth, examples of these writings should be available, and the children should be encouraged to experiment with different modes and genres as appropriate.

Purpose and form   There is a wide variety of purposes and forms of writing from which children can choose. For instance, the children's purpose may be that they want to inform or advise their parents about some school event. To achieve this purpose there are a number of writing forms, such as an invitation, a reminder note, or a poster. Box 5-1 presents a variety of choices for different forms of writing that young children could use successfully.

Young children's best writing often grows out of their personal experiences. They can write best about what they know. With this in mind, the teacher would probably suggest topics that children can draw from their own experiences. Even though "Adventures in the Jungle" could be an exciting topic, most young children would not have sufficient background information and ideas to write well on the jungle.

The Role of Literature

Literature is one of the core components of a writing program. Not only are books read for the enjoyment of good writing, but also as models of effective writing. Through listening to and reading books, children become aware of language use, form, style, and mood. They develop a sense of character, setting, and plot—the elements of a story. They also experience the rhythm, rhyme, and descriptive words of good literature.

As a story is read, techniques used by the author can be discussed. Books and poems written in various styles are selected to help children understand how language can be used to suit the purpose of the author. Discussion of the literature at the end of storytime helps children become more aware of the writer's craft.

The Role of USSW Journals

Children need to write frequently to become good writers. Uninterrupted Sustained Silent Writing (USSW), patterned after Uninterrupted Sustained Si-

Box 5-1 • *Writing Forms Young Children May Enjoy Using*

ads (for newspapers, magazines, etc.)	fables	pattern writing
advice columns	fairy tales	persuasive letters
autobiographies	fantasies	plays
awards	fortunes	poems
billboards	good news/bad news	postcards
biographies	greeting cards	posters
books	headlines	puppet shows
book jackets	instructions	questionnaires
book reviews	interviews	questions
bulletins	invitations	recipes
bumper stickers	jokes	riddles
cartoons	journals	sequences
captions	jump-rope rhymes	signs
certificates	labels	silly sayings
complaints	legends	songs
descriptions	letters	story problem
diaries	lists	thank-you notes
directions	movie reviews	titles
dramas	mysteries	want ads
endings	newspapers	wishes
exaggerations	nursery rhymes	weather reports
explanations	party tips	

lent Reading (USSR), is a daily, independent, short writing time. Guidelines for this process include:

1. The USSW writing period lasts no longer than 10–15 minutes. The emphasis is on the child's enjoyment of writing.
2. Everyone writes, including the teacher.
3. Writing is continuous, with interruptions being kept to a minimum.
4. The writing is recorded in one of the child's own exercise books especially designated for journal writing. The writing is private and can be shown or withheld from teacher and classmates as the child chooses.
5. No corrections or changes are made by the teacher.
6. If the child cannot spell a word correctly, invented spelling is encouraged. The free flow of ideas is an important aim of USSW.
7. The children can write anything they like, including copying something they would like to have or rewriting a former entry.
8. Some teachers include a sharing time at the end of USSW when children who wish to share their writings with others in the class may do so.

The Writing Process

Frequency and exposure to a variety of writings alone will not necessarily produce writing growth. What children also need are purposeful and guided

A child working on her journal during USSW time

lessons in which the writing task is divided into manageable steps. A number of educational writers (including Anderson and Lapp, 1988; Graves, 1983; Proett and Gill, 1986) have described the *writing process* as a method of teaching writing that can be effective with both young writers in the primary grades as well as with older students.

Although this process can be broken down into several stages, the primary teacher may wish to concentrate on the steps of prewriting, writing, rereading, sharing, editing, proofreading, and publishing. Teachers of beginning writers will concentrate their efforts less on editing and proofreading and more on prewriting, writing, rereading, sharing, and publishing. Young children need to be free to express their thoughts and ideas. They are still struggling with invented spelling and handwriting and do not need to be concerned about conventional punctuation and spelling at this stage. Correct form will come later with more knowledge and skills and when more effort can be placed on editing and proofreading. Even with older primary children, fluency will precede form, with perhaps every fourth or fifth piece of writing going through all the steps in the writing process, including editing and proofreading. We will now discuss the stages in the writing process.

Stage 1: Prewriting   This first stage is very important because it is a preparation time that allows children to think about ideas and get ready to write, establish a purpose for writing, and focus on a topic. The quality of the prewriting experience often is the major factor in the quality of the writing produced by young children, so 10–15 minutes of a 40-minute writing period should be spent on preparing to write.

Good motivators can be natural situations or experiences that generate thoughts, emotions, opinions and questions; books; videos; and interesting school, classroom, or personal experiences. The teacher sets up the environment but must remember to allow children to pursue their own ideas. Some specific examples used effectively by primary teachers include:

1. Stage an event in the classroom. Create a mystery: e.g., during the Easter season have the children come in one morning to find spilled paint, rabbit tracks leading from it, a piece of carrot here, jelly beans there, an open window, etc.
2. Use titles or first lines — "No valentines," "1,000,000,000 Worms," "I got sick on my birthday," "Charlie Brown got in trouble with the principal."
3. Stimulate children's imaginations with pictures. Use their own drawings, class photos of an event, pictures from magazines, and so forth.
4. Provide framework models. Use predictable books, such as *Fortunately, Unfortunately* (Charlip, 1964); patterned poems, such as "I Like Bugs"; or songs and chants.
5. Use high interest, familiar topics frequently: e.g., holidays, home and school, friends, fears, wishes, likes, and dislikes.
6. Develop a story based on a book idea: e.g., use *Alexander and the Terrible, No Good, Very Bad Day* (Viorst, 1975) to develop a story about the child's own very good or very bad day; or use *There's a Nightmare in my Closet* (Mayer, 1968) to develop a story about the child's own experience with good or bad dreams.

The next step in prewriting is to broaden the idea, to think out possibilities for writing, and to build vocabulary lists that can assist the young writer. There are several techniques that may be used.

1. Brainstorming and categorizing — The teacher records what the children know about a topic on the chalkboard or sentence strips, which are then displayed. All children's contributions are accepted. After the subject has been sufficiently discussed and many ideas generated, the teacher and children categorize the recorded comments. This helps children generate a number of ideas, provides a readily available word bank, and consolidates their ideas.
2. Clustering — The topic is recorded and then encircled in the middle of the chalkboard or paper. Then children contribute ideas, which are clustered around the central topic.
3. Word lists — The teacher records what words the children think would help them write about this subject on the chalkboard or chart paper.
4. Discussion with partners or small groups — After picking a topic, children are paired or grouped to talk about the topic before they write. This talking often clarifies the topic for the children as well as gives them new ideas.

Stage 2: Writing   After motivating the children and facilitating a broad base of ideas through discussions, brainstorming, and other prewriting activities, this next writing stage should be fairly easy for the children. As children write their rough drafts, the room has a busy sound to it with children writing, stopping to think, rereading what they have wrote, sharing parts with others, and asking for help. This productive talking and sharing of writing are to be en-

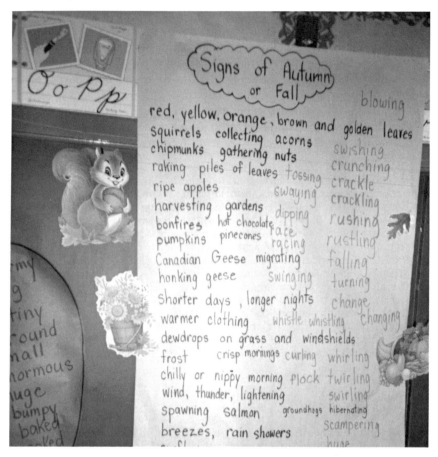

A word list developed by a grade 3 class to help them as they write stories about fall

couraged. Also, the teacher will circulate around the room giving suggestions and providing help and encouragement. She may ask a few children to read what they have written and point out special features in a child's work. This should typically take about 15–20 minutes with young children, although some will need more time than others.

Stage 3: Rereading   After the children have written their compositions, they should be encouraged to reread them to see if their writing makes sense, if something was left out, if additional thoughts should be added, if the writer would like to share it with the group, and so forth. (This rereading by young children is their introduction to revising and editing.) This rereading is sometimes called the *author's mumble,* a phrase children enjoy and have fun living up to.

Stage 4: Sharing   If they wish the children may share what they wrote with an audience. This should be a positive, happy experience that results in children wanting to write more. With younger children, the teacher may stop at this step in the writing process, only occasionally going beyond to editing, proofreading, and publishing. Special events, such as an "author's tea" (i.e., a school open house where the children's writing is displayed prominently, refreshments are served, and various authors read their works), and special projects, such as producing some of the children's writing in a booklet, are reasons to complete all the steps in the writing process.

Some students should get a chance to share their writing every day. The teacher has to figure out some equitable way so that all who wish to share get a chance. Experience shows that almost everyone in the class wants to share. Sharing writing can occur with a teacher, a partner, in a small group, or with the whole class. With younger children, sharing with the teacher and the whole class are usually done more frequently than the other suggestions above. Older primary students, who have been coached in ways of giving constructive criticism and positive encouragement, can work effectively as partners or in small groups listening and commenting on each others' writing.

Stage 5: Editing and proofreading   While much of the primary writing experience is designed to stimulate the flow of words, there should be some practice, especially in the upper primary grades, in editing, proofreading, and publishing. For editing, the writing has previously been reread by the author, been commented on by others in the sharing time, and is now ready to be changed, if necessary. There may be only a few changes to the first writing or draft, such as substituting a word or changing a sentence structure. On the other hand, the changes could be major, to the point of reworking the whole piece. Proofreading is checking the mechanics of writing (i.e., spelling, grammatical structures, and punctuation).

In his observations of young children writing Graves (1983) reports a dominance in the order of changes that children make to their work. The change that children see as most important is spelling; next come handwriting, punctuation, and capitalization conventions, topics, and information; and finally major revisions (i.e., reorganization and addition or exclusion of ideas or information).

Graves (1983) expands on the general order of children's problems in writing development with the following points:

1. For some learners, spelling and handwriting issues last a lifetime. For others this is conquered by age 7. If teachers never go beyond spelling, aesthetics, or conventions, then the children will not learn to take ownership of their writing.

2. Attention to topic and information depends on the teacher. If children are continually asked questions about their information through conferencing with teachers and peers, they begin to address and judge the imbalances in their writing.

3. The next stage includes adding and deleting information. Children find the addition of information one of the easiest ways to revise, while excluding information comes later in the child's writing development. It takes considerable time before a writer spon-

taneously wants to delete information. (Many adult writers exhibit these same tendencies.)

4. Finally, young authors become interested in better organization for better language use. Children in this stage struggle with drafts and refinements and compose over many days or weeks. (pp. 236–237)

Experienced teachers have developed a number of strategies to help children develop proofreading and editing skills. Several of these are:

1. Have children concentrate on one or two areas at a time. For instance, the teacher may suggest that the children will check their writing for spelling errors and capitalization. On another day, the children reread to see if they should combine any sentences.

2. Provide children with their own checklist of things to look for in editing and proofreading. For instance, for proofreading the teacher could make up a checklist, such as "I have checked my—"

   a. spelling _____
   b. capitals _____
   c. indentation _____
   d. punctuation (. , ! ?) _____

Teachers can acknowledge the children's ability in using these conventions independently by giving each a "can do" list, which they can keep in a writing folder. The content of these lists may vary from child to child based on each child's abilities and experience. For editing, the teacher could make up a self-evaluation question or reminder list, such as:

   a. Does my writing make sense?
   b. Did I say what I wanted to say?
   c. Did I leave out any good ideas?
   d. What do I like about my writing?
   e. What can I do to make my writing better?

As the teacher emphasizes different aspects of editing, this list could change to include questions about sentence structure, logical sequence, word choice, audience appropriateness, good beginnings, and good conclusions.

3. Model editing and proofreading. Using an overhead projector with a piece of unrevised writing on it, the teacher discusses the different steps to revise and improve the writing.

4. Use peer editors to help children improve their writing. Hogan (1984) gives specific guidelines for helping children become effective peer editors:

- Prior to beginning peer editing, model positive responses and have children practice giving positive reactions in role-playing situations.
- Establish parameters that include rules such as only authors can write on their own papers and authors have the final say about editing and changes.
- Give written guidelines for editing and teach children to concentrate on a few specific aspects of editing at a time.

5. Conference with the writer. The strategy of a teacher's conferencing with one or a small group of 4–6 writers after the first rough draft has been completed can be an effective way of helping children edit and proofread their work.

Teaching conferences arise from the observed needs of the children. For example, the teacher sees that several children are having difficulty using *is* and *are* correctly and therefore brings them together for a short lesson in usage. The teacher uses the children's writings as the basis for the lesson. The teaching is meaningful because the skill is taught in the context of the children's own work. The children can directly see the use of the skill and see how it can be applied in writing.

Specific writing skill areas that might be used as the basis for teaching conferences include —

1. choosing a topic and/or title;
2. thinking through a topic before writing about it (a review of prewriting activities);
3. reteaching of specific skill areas (punctuation, grammar, capitals, paragraphs, spelling, strategies, etc.);
4. reviewing editing and proofreading procedures;
5. discussing what makes a good sentence or paragraph, choice of wording, adding ideas or taking out parts of the writing; and
6. developing an awareness of audience and how to communicate effectively.

In another type of conference, the teacher guides the children in a discussion of the content, expression, focus, and direction of their completed drafts. The teacher leads the discussion but is careful not to dominate it. The teacher asks questions to help the children express and clarify their views and leads them to see how they might improve their writing. Graves (1983) discusses three main classifications of questions for conferences. These include (1) opening questions, such as "How is it going?" and "What is your piece about?"; (2) following questions, asked to keep children talking and provide more information; and (3) process questions, such as "What do you need help with?", "What do you think you'll do next?", "Can you think of another way to say this?", and "How do you feel about your story?".

Stage 6: Publishing   One of the most rewarding aspects of writing for young children is the recognition they get from having their writing read. Publishing or displaying written work provides a reason for editing and proofreading, aspects of the writing process that young children often would rather not do because they are difficult. Publishing also heightens the children's sense of audience.

Teachers help motivate children to write by structuring a writing-sharing time every day for children. Teachers also motivate children to write by "publishing" their work in a variety of forms. A picture of the child can be attached to the writing for added recognition. Ideas for publications include:

1. Printing, illustrating, and binding a book (the how-tos of simple bookmaking techniques can be found in Appendix B or in the crafts section of the library) — This homemade book could either include a child's own story or progression of stories, or it could be a collection of patterned writing or stories done by the whole class. The book could be placed in the class or school library or circulated to other classrooms. Children also enjoy borrowing these books to take home to share with their families. There are many other types of writings besides stories that could be published, such as recipe books, alphabet and number books, how-to books, riddle and joke books, poetry books, book-of-lists books, informational books, and "me" books.

2. Displaying work on bulletin boards — For instance an "Author of the Week" bulletin board is devoted to one child's writings and illustrations may include a prominently placed picture of the child.

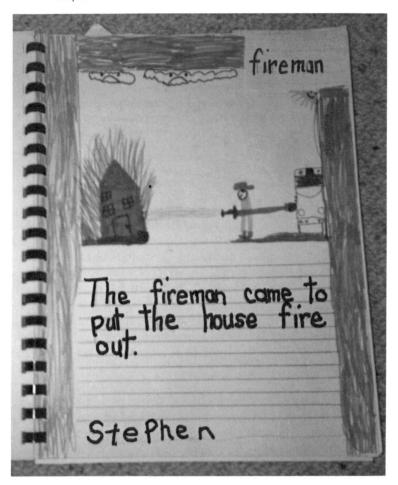

An example of a homemade book with each child in the grade 1 class
contributing a page

3. Writing letters or notes — Letters can be written to favorite authors, parents, sick children in the class, grandparents, pen pals in another school, and others.

4. Displaying work outside the classroom and the school — Work can be submitted for publication in a local newspaper. The local library may appreciate a display of children's storywriting. Sometimes, following a fieldtrip, thank-you notes can be written and pasted on a large section of colored paper or the children can make a mural of the fieldtrip that incorporates their descriptive writing.

Evaluation and Record Keeping

Evaluation of Writing in Progress

Writing is evaluated to provide the teacher and children with information to help improve the children's writing. There are several points to remember when

---

BOX 5-2 • *Evaluation of Writing*

A Sample Writing Evaluation

Does the child do the following:

___C___ Is doing   ___X___ Having difficulty   ___O___ Does not apply

Prewriting:

_____1. Thinks about and discusses the topic with others

_____2. Organizes his or her thought through brainstorming, clustering outlines, word lists, etc. so he or she has a clear focus or purpose before writing

_____3. Has a sense of audience for the writing

_____4. Has some ideas of what format he or she will use to publish the writing

Writing:

_____1. Keeps to the topic

_____2. Has a unified sequential plot, if needed

_____3. Has developed a good story structure (beginning, middle, and end)

_____4. Has developed a setting to the story

_____5. Develops characters, _____ uses imagery _____ conversation, and _____ other writing devices

_____6. Uses correct and varied sentence structures

_____7. Reads and rereads as writing progresses to see if the writing "makes sense"

_____8. Uses a variety of vocabulary words (richly and appropriately)

_____9. Has a knowledge of the different uses of punctuation and capitalization

_____10. Has developed some spelling strategies

Revising and editing:

_____1. Rereads and rethinks writing to see if writing can be made better through change, addition, deletion of parts

_____2. Edits and proofreads for grammar and usage as well as spelling and punctuation

_____3. Uses other students, teachers, dictionaries, etc. to help in the revision

---

giving children feedback. The teacher reacts first to the content and later to the form. Although evaluation is often thought of as a judgment of how good a finished piece of writing is, some of the best evaluation takes place at the initial stages of writing. The teacher provides immediate verbal response to the writing and can help children clarify and elaborate areas that need further work. Until children are able to read and interpret the teacher's written comments, evaluation will necessarily be oral.

The teacher's first verbal response to the writing should be encouraging and positive. This is more effective than criticism in helping children write (Hillocks, 1986). After setting an accepting tone, the teacher can proceed with questions that will help the child. Box 5-2 gives an example of a writing evaluation checklist that could be used to help the teacher develop comments about a child's writing.

Evaluating Finished Compositions

When the teacher analyzes and evaluates the finished piece of writing, this evaluation is also usually an oral conference about the product. As the child's reading develops, comments may be written on the finished work. Appropriate evaluation questions include:

- What do you think is your best piece of writing?
- Why do you think it is better than some of your other work?
- Are there any lines or parts that you really like? Why do you think they are so good?
- Can you think of any ways to make this writing better?
- What does a writer do to make a good composition?
- Who is your favorite author? What do you like about his or her writing?

The teacher may provide suggestions for improvement, but will limit them to one or two specific areas so the child is not overwhelmed by the enormity of the task.

Self-Evaluation

Some children may be able to use a self-evaluation checklist, which provides a focus as they think about the quality of their own writing. The teacher may develop one with the class and gradually add to it as the children understand more about their own writing growth and take more responsibility for it. Questions on a self-evaluation checklist may include:

- Does my writing make sense?
- Have I stuck to the topic?
- Do I need to add something?
- Should I take something out that isn't needed?
- Did I put events in the right order?

Group Evaluation

It is also important for children to participate in a group evaluation of selected writing (possibly writing examples of other children who are not in the class). The teacher puts these on an overhead projector and reads the work aloud, models how to evaluate the writing, and then the children evaluate subsequent pieces for both content and form.

Using a Writing Folder

Writing folders can be made of legal-size folders secured at both ends. The child's name is written on top and the child decorates the folder. All folders are kept together in a large box or storage file cabinet, allowing access to both children and teacher. Children store their writing ideas and pieces of writing, including both finished compositions and work in progress. Pieces should be dated so a record of progress is developed. Writing folders can also store self-evaluation checklists, lists of writing process steps, or any other aids. Although it is important to children to take their writing home, many of these compositions can be duplicated so the folder contains representative samples of their writing.

Advantages of writing folders are many. They facilitate class routines by providing a process for storing, collecting, organizing, and retrieving pieces of writing. For children, they represent a tangible, concrete symbol of a rather abstract task. They feel a sense of ownership and pride as they see their writing accumulate and look back to see evidence of improvement throughout the year. The writing folder also encourages self-evaluation. Teachers find these folders useful as an ongoing record of student progress and a handy tool in evaluation. The teacher can quickly find evidence of the children's writing abilities. The teacher can point to signs of progress and set goals for future work. These folders are handy for use at writer's conferences and parent interviews.

Word Processors: A Tool in the Writing Program

With increasing access to computers in schools, there is a growing realization of their unique potential benefits to writers. Textbooks about teaching writing using computers (Balajthy, 1986; Clements, 1985; Knapp, 1986; Rude, 1986; Solomon, 1986) present a number of persuasive arguments for using the computer as a word processor in teaching different aspects of writing. For example, Clements argues that young children using word processors are less worried about errors, compose lengthier writings, revise more, correct spelling and punctuation, experience fewer problems with fine motor control, and take special pride in their print-outs because of the neater, more professional look. He suggests that poorer writers may get the most benefits from computer-aided writing.

Observing the effect of using a word-processing program on grade 1 children, Phoenix and Hannan (1984) concluded that the computer freed the children to write, especially those children who had limited printing and spelling ability. Solomon (1986, p. 5) states, "For many children and adults alike the physical task of writing is an obstacle to creating work of good quality." In her view, children can concentrate on their ideas rather than on the neatness of the writing, so the writing is more spontaneous and creative.

Experienced teachers vary in their opinions as to the importance of teaching keyboard skills to young children. Although young children will develop their own keyboard style quickly and are not unhappy with the slower pace of it, keyboard skills can be introduced early using keyboarding programs.

If the word processor is used frequently in writing activities, it is helpful for the children to have their own disk for saving compositions, thus providing easier access to earlier writings for revising.

Teaching Handwriting

Educators have varying opinions concerning the amount of formal teaching that should be given to handwriting. Most, however, would agree that it is a skill that needs to be taught through preplanned, directed group lessons; daily informal individual help; and practice that occurs when the children use writing to communicate with others. There is no one agreed-upon correct form for handwriting. Indeed, children develop their own style as they mature. Educators, however, do agree that handwriting should be legible so that it can be read easily both by the author during composing and by the readers. Handwriting should also become as fluent as possible so that it does not detract from the child's desire to compose. Thus legibility and, to a lesser extent, fluency are the standards by which the teacher can assess a child's progress in handwriting.

Emerging Handwriting

Before coming to school, most children have made some attempts at handwriting. Children do not follow a lock-step progression through stages as they learn to write. Instead they move freely between drawings and writings. When children come to school, the teacher can expect to see children at many different stages of this writing development. Some can easily execute any symbol, others have difficulty drawing a straight line and are not yet ready to see differences among letters such as *h, n,* and *m.*

In the beginning, there should be many activities where children use small-muscle coordination and visual perception as well as opportunities to develop an awareness of the function of handwriting. Thurber and Jordan (1987) recommend such diverse activities as tracing, paper folding, water play, stringing beads, lacing, cutting with a pair of scissors, and manipulating gadgets. Teachers need to modify activities to meet the needs of individual children. For instance, with paper cutting, help may be given to some when cutting detailed shapes or activities may be designed for those who have not yet had much experience with cutting. Within the context of class theme activities, practice distinguishing among different shapes and sizes results from various sorting and classification activities. Also, the teacher makes sure that the children see him or her modeling handwriting while writing functional messages. Children can dictate captions for pictures, which are printed as they watch. All these activities foster children's handwriting and can also be used to assess the children's abilities as they participate in the activities.

When children show a preference in handedness, they should be encouraged to continue using their favored hand and be shown proper paper placement for writing with it. According to Sloan and Triplett (1978), right-handed children predominate (85-90 percent), with few left-handed children (10-15 percent), and a smaller number of children who are ambidextrous.

Materials for Handwriting

Standard in most early-childhood classrooms is a long wall chart of either manuscript (printing) or cursive (longhand) alphabets to help children remember letter formation. Models of letters can also be taped to children's desks. Frequently a card with the child's first name is taped to the desk. Labels, posters, charts, and chalkboard all model printing and are placed in positions easily seen by children.

Medium soft pencils, crayons, felt-tip markers, chalk, modeling clay, and so on are writing tools available for children to use in a classroom. Although traditionally very young children were given "fat" pencils and crayons as aids in writing and drawing, there is no research evidence to show that these really help. Children should choose what size pencils to use.

A variety of surfaces are available for children to write on besides paper, such as individual chalkboards as well as the large chalkboard, large chart paper, boxes, and sand trays. Traditionally, many young children begin their formal writing training using wide-lined paper. These wide lines require the children to make large letters and may make the task of writing more difficult as they laboriously adhere to filling up the big space with the letters. Today many children begin their formal handwriting lessons using a variety of paper, including unlined paper, just with teachermade folds, and paper with closer lines divided by a midline. The D'Nealian Handwriting Program for writing manuscript letters (Thurber and Jordan, 1987) suggests a one-half inch ruled paper with a midline for use through third grade.

Methods of Teaching Handwriting: Formal and Informal Approaches

The superiority of any single method of teaching manuscript or cursive writing is not supported by research (Koenke, 1986). In most approaches, a specific amount of time is allocated to the preplanned, direct teaching of handwriting skills. Teachers can help children with various components, such as letter formation, spacing between letters and words, consistent slant, size and proportion, legibility, and neatness. After group lessons, children practice the skills during meaningful writing activities. At these times, the teacher can give individual help to children who need it with their handwriting. An important point to remember is that the primary goal of handwriting instruction is for the child to develop handwriting that is legible and easily executed.

To teach manuscript writing, traditionally children were asked to look at letters as made up of circles and sticks. Letters were formed with two or more independent strokes. An example of a commercial program that teaches manuscript letter formation in this way is the Zaner-Bloser Writing Program (1989) (see Figure 5-3).

A newer manuscript writing program, D'Nealian Handwriting (Thurber and Jordan, 1987) uses an untraditional style of printing. Letters are formed in continuous strokes and are slightly slanted (see Figure 5-4). This program can be

FIGURE 5-3 • *Zaner-Bloser Manuscript and Cursive Alphabets*

Zaner-Bloser Manuscript Alphabet

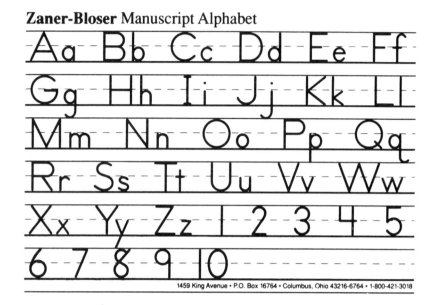

1459 King Avenue • P.O. Box 16764 • Columbus, Ohio 43216-6764 • 1-800-421-3018

Zaner-Bloser Cursive Alphabet

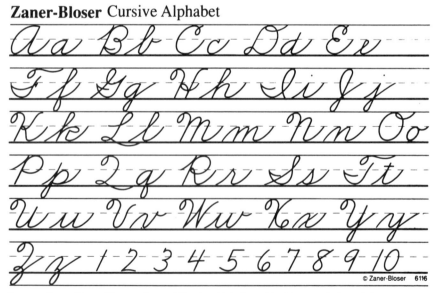

© Zaner-Bloser   6116

Source: Zaner-Bloser Manuscript and Cursive Alphabets. Used by permission of the publisher.

FIGURE 5-4 • *D'Nealian Handwriting Program*

Source: D'Nealian Handwriting Program. Thurber, D. N., and Jordan, D. R. © Copyright 1987. Reprinted by permission of Scott, Foresman and Company.

seen as an attempt to facilitate an easier transition between manuscript and cursive writing.

In teaching manuscript printing, many teachers group letters and then teach those with similar formations. For instance, the teacher might group *a, d, o, g,* and *c,* which are letters formed similarly. Some teachers like to have small groups of children work at the chalkboard or on individual chalkboards practicing letters. Dictating a caption for a picture and then tracing over what the teacher has written is frequently used with younger children. Meaningful copying (recopying a group story or group letter to take home, copying a favorite riddle or song and illustrating it) can provide effective practice in writing. For children who are struggling with handwriting, adjustments in length of assignments should be made.

In most North American classrooms manuscript writing is taught before cursive writing, with children making the transition to cursive in second or third grade. Children who have learned to print using the D'Nealian method will find the change relatively easy, as the slanting and continuous strokes are also common to cursive writing.

For many children, cursive writing is perceived as "adult writing," and they are very motivated to begin. Many have been practicing their name in cursive letters since they became aware of it. Again, the teacher provides group lessons in cursive letter formation, consistency of slant, appropriate alignment of letters, and so on. These are followed by practice using cursive writing in meaningful settings with individual help from the teacher when needed. Most children will gradually make a shift to cursive writing, sometimes using a combination of both in transition. Some children will continue to prefer to use manuscript print. They can write as fast and legibly as others using cursive writing. These children should be allowed to use whatever form and style of writing suits them. However, children who choose not to use cursive writing still need to be able to read cursive writing.

Clay (1975) describes a more informal approach to teaching handwriting. For one period a week the teacher gives a group lesson on letter formation along with daily individual help on this skill. The children learn to print as they—

- *drew pictures and the teacher wrote dictated captions;*
- *traced over the teacher's script;*
- *copied captions;*
- *copied words around the room;*
- *remembered word forms and wrote them independently;*
- *invented (generated) word forms, often correctly; and*
- *got a copy of unknown words from the teacher (p. 1).*

Developing naturally in the context of other writing, the children began to print in their first year of school. Clay maintains that their gain in handwriting skills "did not appear to differ significantly" from other schools that had a more formal handwriting program.

Teaching Spelling

The following section of spelling research and teaching strategies is taken from Tarasoff (1990).

> *English is not a phonetically regular language because its spelling represents not just speech but also word origins and meanings. For example, the spelling of sun and son relate to meaning rather than strict orthophonological relationships. The "peculiar" spelling of words such as night can be traced back to how it was spoken in the fourteenth century. Often it is stated that English spelling is so irregular that one should not point out spelling rules to children. In that case it would seem that writers must rely on visual memory rather than on the sounds of words. Indeed, teaching letter/sound relationships as rules and in weekly spelling lists does not seem to help children spell correctly in their daily writing. However, analyzing and generalizing sound/symbol and symbol/meaning patterns can be a meaningful activity in teaching spelling. It is helpful to know that there are letter/sound patterns (oi, oy, ou, ow), common letter sequences (-ight, -ture, -tion), and an underlying structure to the language.*

Helping Children Learn to Spell

An effective way to view the teaching of spelling is to begin with the following premises that acquiring spelling skills —

1. is a developmental, cognitive process;
2. is facilitated by the child's curiosity about print and words;
3. is part of the writing process;
4. is facilitated by learning a variety of strategies;
5. involves not memorizing letters and spelling;
6. requires problem-solving and thinking skills (an active process of making sense of the sound, symbol, and meaning relationships).

As part of the writing process, standard spelling enables writers and readers to read what is written more fluently, focusing on comprehension rather than on decoding. Peters (1985) stated, "Bad spelling is like mumbling over a telephone" (p. 3). Teaching spelling helps children become more competent, fluent authors.

As with any learning, too much attention on one aspect is inhibiting and too little may not encourage awareness and skill development. If only standard (correct) spelling is accepted, then the beginning writer may become dependent on a more competent speller for transcription or become unwilling to express even his or her simplest ideas on paper. A child in this situation will not develop a concept of self as an independent writer. On the other hand, if standard spelling receives no attention, the child, in effect, learns that spelling does not matter in the writing process.

The teacher therefore, needs to understand how to facilitate composing and transcribing by knowing what spelling strategies and knowledge to teach and deciding when and when not to provide direct instruction (Tarasoff, 1990).

There is no one sure way to teach spelling, and the approach used will vary depending on the child's developmental level, knowledge of spelling and strategies, and previous experiences with writing and spelling.

Developing Spelling (Stages and Strategies)

Learning to speak, listening to spoken language, and exposure to written language read out loud are the foundations for the child's beginning in writing and spelling. A young child before and during the first years in school develops ideas about how the writing system works, gradually applying new understandings to what was already known about letters, sounds, and words. Various stages in this process have been described by Read, and Beers, Beers, and Grant (both cited in Hodges, 1982). Others have redefined the stages and labeled them differently (Cochrane, Cochrane, Scalena, and Buchanan, 1984; Gentry, 1987; Henderson and Templeton, 1986; Parry and Hornsby, 1985). The names of the stages differ but the pattern of development is the same (Tarasoff, 1990). As children become interested in letters, they draw wiggly lines and letterlike shapes indicating the initial discoveries. Sometimes this stage is referred to as precommunicative or prealphabetic (Gentry, 1987; Parry and Hornsby, 1985), indicating that the children are becoming aware of letters. When children offer to "read" what they have written, this signals that they are becoming aware that writing has a meaning and purpose. At this stage the children's growth is facilitated by watching others write and read print and then attempting to do the same. By pointing out one or two features when responding to the message, the children's awareness of letters and spelling can be enhanced.

As children continue to experience writing, both by watching and by participating in language activities, they focus on more refined features of print, such as letter shapes, letter sequences, directionality, speech/print relationships, spelling of "special" words, word concept, and letter/sound relationships.

Early attempts at spelling using recognizable strings of letters (sometimes referred to as the *alphabetic stage*) indicate the child's awareness of the linearity of print. At this stage, discussing the print and showing its relationship to speech (e.g., pointing while reading or speaking the words as they are written with the child watching) reinforces this. Acknowledging the genuine attempts and attending to the child's desire to communicate in print is important. The child can also be led to awareness of even more details during individual conferences and through group lessons. According to Hodges (1982):

> *An effective environment in which to learn to spell is one that provides numerous and varied opportunities to master the patterns, generalizations, and anomalies of the writing system. Spelling instruction cannot be restricted to the relationship of letters with sounds but demands an active involvement with both spoken and written language. The maxim that instruction should start where the learner is has no more fitting application than in spelling instruction and that starting place is the phonetic knowledge that young children entering school already possess. (p. 4)*

Using the child's emerging writing, teachers can:

1. develop the child's confidence in his or her own ability to write by recognizing the child's effort and discussing what the child can do;
2. enhance the child's willingness to write by providing choices, variety, and positive, genuine response;
3. encourage the child to use a variety of strategies and teach strategies when appropriate (e.g., letter/sound relationships, similarities among words, unusual spellings); and
4. model curiosity about words and spelling strategies.

Children can use their knowledge of letters and sounds to move from writing random letter sequences to representing speech by sequences of letters, which is sometimes referred to as the semiphonetic stage (Gentry, 1987; Parry and Hornsby, 1985). During this stage, various strategies incorporating what the child knows about words are used to construct spellings. The following list provides some examples.

1. At first a child may use the knowledge of letter names related to speech sounds: e.g., *p r t = party, c = see.*
2. As a child becomes aware of how the mouth and tongue move when saying letter names (articulation cues), the letter sounds may be related to the letter whose name is articulated in a similar way (e.g., short *e* sound is written as the letter *a, p* as b, v as *f).*
3. As a child refines his or her knowledge, the child becomes aware that a letter can represent a sound unrelated to its name or articulation. This indicates an awareness of sound/symbol relationships and words are then written using correct initial, final, and/or medial consonants.
4. When the child becomes aware of words and spaces, dots, dashes, or spaces will appear between words in the writing.
5. Also, the child may begin to use other strategies, such as visual memory, to remember spelling of a particularly meaningful word or words used frequently (e.g., *Mom, the, was, dinosaur*).
6. Sometimes the child becomes aware of words seen in books or around the classroom and makes lists or copies sections of the text.

Strategies that the teacher can focus on with beginning writers are:

1. developing the child's confidence and concept of self as a writer and speller;
2. encouraging risk taking and viewing invented spelling as a way to get words down on paper, which later can be proofread and corrected;
3. using a child's knowledge of phonics and pointing out relationships between speech sounds and initial and final consonants, between words that rhyme, sounds of letter sequences;
4. helping the child to use articulation and letter-name cues;
5. teaching how to use rhyme and oral spelling to help remember letter sequences;
6. encouraging the child to remember more than one letter at a time when copying words and teaching the child how to visualize spellings;
7. providing instruction and frequent writing activities so that the child becomes able to print letters easily from memory; and
8. encouraging the child to read what has been written and find words that may need changing. (Tarasoff, 1990)

This is an excellent opportunity to discuss different strategies — pointing out spelling relationships and anomalies. As spelling competency increases, more emphasis can be put on proofreading for standard spelling.

Beyond the initial stage of awareness, the child gradually becomes able to spell words that approximate more closely the standard spellings. This is often referred to as the phonetic and transitional stages (Gentry, 1987; Parry and Hornsby, 1985). There is an increasing awareness and refinement of spelling knowledge and strategies. Not only does the number of correct letters in words increase, the number of words spelled correctly increases. Printing becomes more fluent, confidence develops, and children become more able to edit and proofread their own work.

Combined with other developing vocabularies (listening, reading, and speaking), the writing vocabulary increases. Also, as as result of experience, guidance, and practice, children's spelling competency increases. The predominant spelling strategies change from reliance on sounds and articulation to reliance on visual memory. The children develop more awareness of the relationships between letter sequences and sounds and of analogies among words. Also, having frequent opportunities to write develops automatic motor patterns in printing and handwriting and thus facilitates spelling memory.

Studies of spelling development in older students (Hodges, 1982, p. 11) reveal "a shift among better spellers from reliance upon phoneme/grapheme strategies used in early school years toward a strategy of spelling words by analogy to other known words." Radebaugh (1985, cited in Tarasoff, 1990) states that poor spellers in third and fourth grade tended to rely on phonetic (phonic) strategies, whereas better spellers used visualization strategies to recall the spelling of easy and difficult words.

Teaching spelling to children beyond these beginning stages involves teaching and reviewing spelling strategies and knowledge, such as:

visualizing spellings
noting and studying spelling/meaning relationships
observing common letter sequences
word building (endings, prefixes, suffixes)
becoming aware of syllables
noting relationships between meanings and derivatives
maintaining a curiosity about words and continuing to develop an awareness of spelling strategies
using mnemonic devices (memory aids)
enhancing proofreading competency
improving handwriting skills
developing a bank of easily spelled words

Approaches to Teaching Spelling

Teaching spelling strategies and knowledge involves both formal and informal approaches. Both can be used with the whole class, a small group, or one-on-one. A formal approach will involve studying spelling patterns or strategies during a teacher-guided lesson, followed by further study and practice. An informal approach involves pointing out spelling patterns or strategies as they arise in language activities and taking advantage of the immediate interests or needs of the child. In both cases, the teacher is aware of what knowledge or strategy is being used and what is the most effective to teach next. Children also can learn to help each other study. In pairs they can discuss strategies and ask each other to spell the words being focused on. In writing activities, they can provide the spelling of words for each other.

Choosing strategies to be taught will depend on the previous experience and developmental level of the children, their knowledge of spelling, the preferred strategies already in use, whether the children can learn more effective strategies, and so on.

Choosing Words to Study

Choosing the word patterns or word to be taught will again depend on the child's developmental level and present competency in spelling. However, some general guidelines can be given:

1. Choose words that are the most frequently used in writing. For example, eight words (*a, of, is, the, and, to, in, you*) account for 18 percent of the words found in the writing according to word frequency counts (Sitton, 1989) and 100 words account for 49 percent. This is a good place to start. Sitton suggests that 4–5 words be presented each week and a preview-study-test method be used along with other activities that relate the words to reading and writing activities in the classroom. Each child should then become responsible for proofreading his or her own work, particularly for these words.

2. Choose words that demonstrate particular letter sequence patterns (e.g., *ight, oi, ture, ick*). Discuss, study, and relate the words to reading and writing activities. Proofread especially for these patterns. If a preview-study-test method is used, include more than one kind of pattern (e.g., *ck* and *ke*) so that the child must discriminate which pattern to use and when testing use words different from, but similar to, those studied (Tarasoff, 1990).

3. Choose words that you know the students are having difficulty with in their writing and that are from the list of high utility words.

4. When focusing on a theme, brainstorm the theme-related words that the children may want to use in writing on that topic. Post these words in alphabetical order (as a reference chart) in the classroom. The children can then refer to the chart when they are writing (Sitton, 1989). Memorizing a list of 15–20 theme-related words each week is not the most effective spelling program. It tends to be a test of the student's short-term memory, because many of the words will not be used in the child's writing once the theme changes so they will soon be forgotten. Better to ensure the student is learning to spell high utility words that they are likely to want to use in their writing. This does not mean that the spelling of theme-related words is not discussed and used to point out spelling patterns and strategies (relationships between spelling and meaning, affixes, endings, letter-sequence similarities between words, etc.). Nor does it mean that they will never be added to the list of words for focused study. But they should not comprise the bulk of the words focused on if the child has not learned to spell the most frequently written words.

Summary

As the knowledge and experiential base increases and predominant strategies change, the child can become aware of visualizing; proofreading; word elements (derivations, affixes, syllables); relationships among words; letter-sequence patterns; and so on. This is done in the context of writing activities in an environment of curiosity about words, supportive of risk taking, and focused on a continuum of learning.

Teaching spelling involves ongoing assessment, evaluation, and instruction while the child is actively involved in writing. How children spell words and the strategies they use indicate not only what the children know but also what to focus on next for instruction (Tarasoff, 1990). For example a child who is using only initial consonants would most likely benefit from focusing on final consonants more than vowel sounds. A child whose spelling indicates a command of a phonic strategy (i.e., the words are easily read with a phonetic approach) could perhaps benefit from focusing on some visualization strategies.

Learning about spelling continues throughout a child's schooling and, actually, on into adulthood. What effective spelling programs provide are the belief that one can learn to spell, a curiosity about words, awareness of many useful spelling patterns, the opportunity to learn a variety of spelling strategies (including proofreading), the chance to use and practice spelling in meaningful contexts, and an awareness of how one can continue to learn independently.

Conclusion

This chapter describes how children begin developing written language abilities prior to beginning formal schooling. These writing abilities develop concurrently with the other literacy behaviors — oral language, listening, and reading. Each area of language arts, in turn, fosters and supports the other three. A nurturing home environment where writing is an integral part of daily life and is modeled frequently by adults and older children is seen as very important to the development of writing in young children. Here children learn writing, handwriting, and spelling through active use in real, functional situations. They explore, experiment, take risks, and grow in their understanding of these processes. In preschool, kindergarten, and primary classrooms, the teacher's role is to continue to foster and develop this emerging writing by creating this same nurturing, print-rich, literacy environment where children can engage in writing, handwriting, and spelling activities that are functional and meaningful. The teacher structures the classroom so children will not only have a number of successful experiences with writing but also intervenes occasionally to help children grow in their understanding of these processes. This child-centered program will, in the author's opinion, not only help children to write well, but also encourage children to value and enjoy writing throughout their lives.

References

Anderson, P., & Lapp, D. (1988). *Language skills in elementary education* (4th ed.). New York: Macmillan.

Balajthy, E. (1986). *Microcomputers in language and reading arts.* Englewood Cliffs, NJ: Prentice-Hall, Inc.

Britton, J. (1970). *Language and learning.* New York: Penguin.

Clay, M. (1976). *What did I write?* London: Heinemann Educational Books.

Clements, D. (1985). *Computers in early and primary education.* Englewood Cliffs, NJ: Prentice-Hall.

Cochrane, O., Cochrane, D., Scalena, S., & Buchanan, E. (1984). *Reading, writing, and caring.* Winnipeg: Whole Language Consultants.

Davies, A. (1988). *Children learning to write their own names: Exploring a literacy event in playschool.* Unpublished doctoral dissertation, University of Victoria, Victoria, British Columbia.

Ferriero, E., & Teberosky, A. (1982). *Literacy before schooling.* Exeter, NH: Heinemann Educational Books.

Freeman, Y. S., & Whitesell, L. R. (1985). What preschoolers already know about print. *Educational Horizons, 64*(1), 22–24.

Gentry, J. P. (1987). *Spel . . is a four letter word.* Ontario: Scholastic.

Grabe, M., & Grabe, C. (1985). The microcomputer and the language experience approach. *The Reading Teacher, 38*(6), 508–511.

Graves, D. (1983). *Writing: Teachers and children at work.* Portsmouth, NH: Heinemann Educational Books.

Harste, J. C., Woodward, V. A., & Burke, C. L. (1984). *Language stories and literacy lessons.* Portsmouth, NH: Heinemann Educational Books.

Henderson, E. H., & Templeton, S. (1986). A developmental perspective of formal spelling instruction through alphabet, pattern, and meaning. *The Elementary School Journal, 86*(3), 305–316.

Hillocks, G. (1987). Synthesis of research on teaching writing. *Educational Leadership,* 71–82.

Hodges, R. E. (1982). *Learning to Spell.* Urbana, IL: National Council of Teachers of English.

Hogan, P. (1984). Peer editing helps students improve written products. *Highway One, 7*(3), 51–54.

Knapp, L. R. (1986). *The word processor and the writing teacher.* Englewood Cliffs, NJ: Prentice-Hall.

Koenke, K. (1986). Handwriting instruction: What do we know? *The Reading Teacher, 40*(2), 214–216.

Parry, J., & Hornsby, D. (1985). *Write on: A conference approach to writing.* Portsmouth, NH: Heinemann.

Peters, M. L. (1985). *Spelling: Caught or taught?* London: Routledge & Kegan Paul.

Phoenix, J., & Hanna, E. (1984). Word-processing in the grade one classroom. *Language Arts, 61,* 804–812.

Proett, J., & Gill, K. (1986). *The writing process in action: A handbook for teachers.* Urbana, IL: National Council of Teachers of English.

Read, C. (1970). *Children's perceptions of the sound of English.* Unpublished doctoral dissertation, Harvard University, Cambridge, MA.

Rude, R. T. (1986). *Teaching reading using microcomputers.* Englewood Cliffs, NJ: Prentice-Hall.

Sitton, R. (1989). *Increasing student spelling achievement.* Bellevue, WA: Bureau of Education and Research.

Sloan, C. A., & Triplett, D. (1978). *Parents' and teachers' perceptions of handwriting.* Alexandria, VA. (ERIC Document Reproduction Service, ERIC Report No. ED 155 723).

Solomon, G. (1986). *Teaching writing with computers: The power process.* Englewood Cliffs, NJ: Prentice-Hall.

Sulzby, E. (1989). Forms of writing and rereading example list. In J. M. Mason (Ed.), *Reading and writing connections.* Boston, MA; Allyn & Bacon, 51–63.

Tarasoff, M. (1990). *Spelling: Strategies you can teach.* Victoria, British Columbia: M. V. Egan Publishing (available from M. V. Egan, Box 6275, Victoria, British Columbia V8P 5L5).

Thurber, D. N., & Jordan, D. R. (1987). *D'Nealian handwriting, teacher's edition, Book 1.* Glenview, IL: Scott, Foresman and Company.

Vygotsky, L. S. (1978). *Mind in society: The development of higher psychological processes.* Cambridge, MA: Harvard University Press.

Zaner-Bloser. (1979). *Creative growth with handwriting.* Columbus, OH: Zaner-Bloser, Inc.

CHAPTER SIX

Language and Literacy for the Limited English Proficient Child

Advance Organizer

Increasing numbers of limited English proficient (LEP) children are entering school, and they represent a variety of language and cultural backgrounds. Teachers are presented with the challenge of offering these young children instructional experiences that build upon their previous knowledge and support the development of oral and written language. In this chapter we deal largely with the question of how teachers can plan effective classroom environments, activities, and teaching strategies for LEP students.

We first present an overview of the strategies children are likely to use in learning a second language and offer examples of physical and social features of classroom environments that support second language acquisition. We discuss the potential of informal as well as planned activities as means to language and literacy development for LEP students. Activities that demonstrate oral and written language uses in real contexts, such as sociodramatic play, thematic units, story reading, and writing based on personal experiences, are emphasized.

Objectives

After studying this chapter, the reader should be able to —

- describe how the classroom environment and interaction patterns influence young children's acquisition of English as a second language;
- identify appropriate classroom activities to support the oral language and literacy development of young limited English proficient (LEP) students;

Graphic Organizer

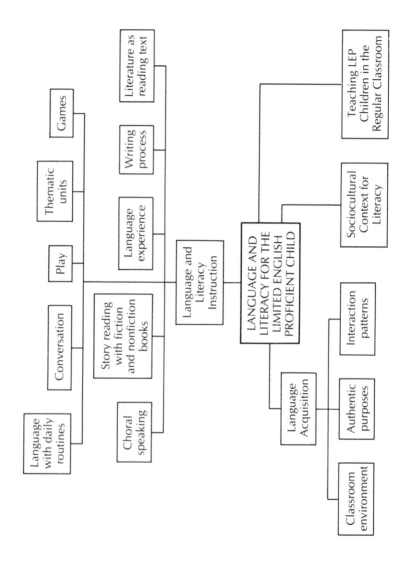

- describe how social and cultural contexts affect the language and literacy development of young LEP students;
- identify appropriate techniques for teaching young LEP students in a regular classroom setting.

Introduction

With the growing cultural and linguistic diversity in North America, it is increasingly likely that at some point in their careers most classroom teachers will teach children whose first language is not English. What information about second language acquisition is needed to plan effective classroom environments, activities, and teaching strategies for these children?

While first and second language learning processes are not identical, there are a number of basic commonalities that are reassuring to the early childhood teacher who teaches children whose native language is not English. As with all other language and literacy learners, limited English proficient children develop *communicative competence*. That is, they learn ways that listening, speaking, reading, and writing are used naturally in an interrelated manner to communicate meaning. All LEP students come to the classroom with many skills in their native language. In many cases, these skills are well developed. This means that as language learners they have already worked out systems for dealing with the diversity of language. They can use language for many culturally appropriate purposes and in a variety of contexts involving many different participants and focusing on many different topics. These strategies can transfer to learning a second language used in similarly authentic communicative situations.

First and second language learners use some common strategies to figure out how the complex and abstract system of language is used to communicate meaning. They seldom try to imitate and store specific pieces of language for later use. Instead, language learners tune in selectively to the language around them, noticing regularities and patterns in talk and writing. Based on these observations, they creatively construct their own individual versions of language based on their personal experiences of the world. This active understanding of language is never explicitly modeled, described, or taught, but rather it is constructed, tried out, and confirmed in the many contexts of individual children's ongoing experiences with the everyday world (Urzua, 1989; Ventriglia, 1982).

Like preschool-aged first language learners, LEP students can begin to acquire literacy at the same time as they continue to develop oral language when they are exposed to an environment rich in print as well as oral language (Hudelson, 1984). Studies of older LEP students show that many of these students have a concept of reading and writing that focuses on decoding and spelling individual words to an extent that interferes with comprehension and composition (Hatch, 1979; McLaughlin, 1987; Rigg, 1989). These findings demonstrate the importance of focusing on language as a communicative activity that conveys meaning from the earliest encounters with literacy. An interactive view of literacy assumes that both readers and writers use strategic processes. The reader coordinates cognitive processing of meaning based on relevant past personal experience with perceptual decoding of visual aspects of the text. The writer coordinates the selection and organization of language to express the intended ideas with the mechanics of transcribing those ideas on paper.

Language Acquisition: Ways Teachers Can Help LEP Children

The teacher can do many things to help LEP children learn English at the same time as they are becoming familiar with the social and instructional life of the early childhood classroom. Most important for second language development are: (a) a classroom environment filled with materials and activities that invite, encourage, and support language use; (b) a range of authentic purposes for language use; and (c) a variety of teacher/student and student/student interaction patterns to meet the individual needs, abilities, and prior experiences of LEP students.

Classroom Environment

Since children develop language best by observing and engaging in authentic communication, the most effective classroom environment to support development for both native speakers and LEP students is one in which language is used in situations that are meaningful and purposeful to children. Teachers can help children with limited English proficiency by providing many language-oriented materials and language-productive activities that emphasize meaningful communication rather than correct form (Allen, 1986; Lindfors, 1989).

A particularly important part of meaningful language use for young LEP students is the opportunity to receive what Krashen (1982) has labeled *comprehensible input*. Comprehensible input is language that contains an understandable message that is interesting and relevant to the student. Teachers can do several things to increase the chances that classroom language will be meaningful to LEP students. Using visual aids to illustrate accompanying oral or written language is one effective technique to increase the comprehensibility of input (Enright, 1986). For example, while giving directions for completing an art activity, the teacher can hold up each type of material and piece of equipment to be used as it is named and described (color, texture, shape, function). During story reading activities, reading of the text can be interspersed with discussion of the illustrations, with the teacher pointing to key objects and events as they are mentioned. Connecting concrete, familiar objects with their unfamiliar English labels in this way allows children to build vocabulary by tapping their existing networks of skills and concepts developed in their first language.

Another way to increase the comprehensibility of input is by combining speech or writing with gestures, movements, or facial expressions that will clarify the meaning of the language (Chaudron, 1988). For example, during a cooking activity, the teacher or a child could demonstrate such actions as pouring, scooping, stirring, and spreading as the class previews the steps of a recipe on a group experience chart. The teacher or aide supervising center- or small-group activities could supply descriptive language to fit children's activities: e.g., "You're adding enough weights to balance the scale." Children could also be encouraged to talk about what they are doing as they work together in small groups with math or other manipulative materials, providing another meaningful context for vocabulary development.

Language can be made more meaningful and understandable for LEP children by using simple adaptations. For example, the teacher may use slightly exaggerated pauses and changes in intonation and volume to focus the children's attention on key vocabulary terms: e.g., "Now we're going to put on our *coats* and *hats* to go *outside.*" The teacher may also speak a little more slowly, using more basic vocabulary in simply structured sentences to reduce the amount of information LEP students must process to understand the complete ideas expressed (Kleifgen, 1985). Repeating key vocabulary terms and concepts in slightly different sentence constructions and in both oral and written contexts gives LEP students many opportunities to communicate in English. These adaptations are especially effective when paired with the use of gestures, motions, facial expressions, or other sensory aids.

Authentic Purposes

Many functions and forms of language that will be useful to children as they become fluent in English can be taught through daily interactions with adults and age peers in the context of meaningful classroom activities. The structure of early childhood classrooms includes a variety of functional uses of English: regulation of the behavior of self and others, requests to meet personal wants and needs, reports of information, and entertainment through sharing of real and imagined experiences (Tough, 1985; Wallace, 1988). For example, the teacher can show how behavior is regulated by highlighting the oral and written language used in directions and commands during transitions and routine activities, such as collecting lunch money, taking attendance, announcing time to switch centers, or lining up for recess. LEP students can also observe and experiment with short phrases that their classmates use to control each other's behavior, such as "Stop that!" or "I'm next" or print signs such as "Don't touch" on a block construction or a name on a list of students wanting a turn at the computer.

Adults and children in the classroom can serve as models for LEP students in their use of oral language (e.g., asking for the hall pass to the restroom, asking for a turn to take the soccer ball to the playground, or volunteering to pass

out napkins for snack). Native speakers can assist LEP students in the classroom by using language in direct relationship to the objects requested and by
initially accepting rough approximations of correct forms as the LEP students
try these requests. The role of written requests can be demonstrated when the
teacher shares with children the note sent to the office to ask for more thumb-
tacks to display children's work on the bulletin board or involves a group of
children in dictating a letter to the local dairy asking for pictures of the equipment they will see on an upcoming fieldtrip.

Many authentic opportunities to use language for reporting information
and entertainment are also possible in the classroom. Children can be given interview questions to use at home with family members to gather information to
be used in class to create graphs or charts. Information individual children
found significant from fieldtrips can be dictated onto group experience charts
or written individually and combined into class books to remember the event.
Newsletters can be written to distribute to the families to keep them informed
about important classroom events. Language can be used for entertainment by
sharing favorite stories and poems through writing, reading, and telling.

Interaction Patterns

As with children whose native language is English, children learning English
as a second language will have a wide range of individual differences in ease
and rate of acquisition. Children will understand much more English than they
will be able to produce, especially early in the learning process. Some children
will need a relatively long "silent period" before they feel comfortable and confident enough to express themselves in the new language. A child who says little
or nothing during this period may appear to the teacher not to be learning very
much; however, much progress may be made in understanding the new language, a prerequisite to expression for fluent language use. Other children will
be much more willing to take risks and experiment, often in playful ways, with
the current version of the language they have constructed (Wong-Fillmore,
1979). Teachers can help meet a range of learning styles by planning a variety of
classroom interactions that support children's active participation with whatever language skills they currently control.

Opportunities to interact with both adults and age peers in the classroom
setting are important to the language development of LEP students, since they
are likely to gain different kinds of assistance from these two types of language
partners. Both adults and children can support the LEP student's language development by *scaffolding* language interactions with them—that is, arranging
the language situation so the LEP student moves from known to unknown,
from simple to complex, from concrete to abstract, always starting where the
child is competent and moving gradually to the unfamiliar. One aspect of scaffolding is that language partners include LEP students in highly contextualized
speech and literacy interactions with the expectation that they will understand

An age peer helping to record a story for an LEP student

at least the gist of the meaning expressed. The English proficient partner should also act on, expand, and extend the LEP student's minimal language production as if it were the full form that will eventually develop to model and maintain communication.

Teachers and other adults are the primary sources of the informational language needed to understand the content being taught in the classroom. Teachers can help LEP students develop this cognitive aspect of language through demonstrations with concrete objects that illustrate new vocabulary for content areas being taught. Coordinating concrete objects and observable actions with the language that describes them will help LEP children bridge familiar concepts with new vocabulary labels. Combinations of oral and written language for labels, lists of materials, and sequences of steps in directions will give LEP students opportunities to use all their available sensory modalities to understand meaning. LEP students will be better able to understand if the teacher limits the amount of new information presented in any one lesson and ties new information to concepts and language already familiar to LEP students (Wong-Fillmore, 1985).

Teachers also control the procedural language used to manage classroom routines and instruction. They can support LEP students' understanding of the structure of everyday classroom events by clearly marking the boundaries of lessons with changes in location, types of props used, and formulaic cues to lesson beginnings and endings. Within individual lessons or activities, teachers can maximize student participation by allocating many turns for each student and inviting a variety of types of responses tailored to meet the different levels of language skill of individuals in the group. Adults can also model the form and content of questions that children can use to get further information needed to understand new concepts.

English-speaking age peers can provide a different kind of input and feedback for the second language learner, since peer interactions usually focus on the social rather than the cognitive aspects of language (Ventriglia, 1982). Other children in the class can serve as models of the language used in different activities throughout the school day. "Listening in" to English-speaking peers provides LEP students with chunks of language in meaningful contexts that can be used "as is" or in new combinations later. Peers can also provide safe opportunities for LEP students to take the risks of trying out whatever language they currently have to communicate. They may do this at first by using

An LEP student reading his story to an interested peer

imitated formulaic chunks of language to join a group or by attempting to participate in groups by roleplaying and using gestures. Other children in these groups can support the language learner by including them in ongoing conversations, which most often relate to the objects and actions at hand.

Language and Literacy Instruction for LEP Students

In keeping with the integrated language arts perspective of this chapter, the acquisition of written and oral language is viewed as a reciprocal process of constructing meaning through which skills are acquired. Literacy is an integral part of language acquisition for both young native English-speaking (NES) and limited English proficient (LEP) children (Rigg and Allen, 1989). There are a number of activities that are especially successful in assisting young LEP children in acquiring language and literacy in this manner. These activities, with suggestions for how to integrate them into the total curriculum, are described. Each of these activities provides a vehicle for developing the child's oral and written proficiency in English in a meaningful context.

Language with Daily Routines

Surrounding the everyday routines of the classroom with language builds receptive and expressive vocabulary that can be used by LEP students to become active members of the classroom community. Because of the repetitive and concrete nature of these activities, LEP students will have many opportunities to see and hear the same words and phrases and attach them in a meaningful way to objects and events in the classroom. The structure of many routines will allow LEP students with very limited English proficiency to initially participate by using known single words or memorized chunks of language. Taking attendance can develop language by creating a chant with individual names or by having children sign in on an attendance sheet using their personal script or moving their name card from the home to the school pocket chart. Filling in dates and the weather daily on the calendar can allow LEP students to first participate by counting in chorus with other children the dates in the month up to the current one, or by holding up a number card with today's date and placing it in the correct space on the calendar. On a weather calendar, the teacher can review the names of the weather symbols by guiding the class to count or graph the number of days that have been sunny, rainy, or snowy before asking a child to name the symbol that fits with today's weather.

LEP students with more advanced language skills can participate in group oral brainstorming of possible topics to include in the "daily news" before some students dictate actual sentences for the teacher to write. Oral brainstorming allows LEP students to be part of the group process with whatever language they currently control: words, phrases, or sentences to express ideas important to them. A daily schedule of important events can be posted on a chalkboard or a chart with a movable pointer that children can use to show the current activity in relationship to what has already occurred and what is still to come. Highlighting the pattern of the day with regular and special activities can help children feel secure in what to expect during the day. Verbally previewing where the class is going and what they will be doing as they leave the classroom can also increase LEP students' confidence in attaching appropriate language labels to directly experienced events. Daily menus for snack and lunch can be posted and read each morning by the teacher, the whole class, or interested individuals. If a daily snack is provided by the school, menus can be planned by the class for the following week. If children bring snacks from home, names of the different foods can be charted as a way to help LEP students attach labels to significant items in the environment.

Conversation

Many classroom activities can be planned for groups of 2–5 children that provide a setting for children to converse with each other as they work. Talking with age peers can be especially beneficial to LEP students because the focus is

Working in an informal group setting allows for frequent low-risk conversation

on communicating meaning rather than on using correct forms that may be beyond the students' capabilities. Experimenting with new language forms can occur in these informal settings, which are lower risk environments than the whole-group lessons with an academic focus. For example, lunch or snack can be served at tables seating 4–6 children, allowing children to talk quietly to anyone else at the table. Limited English proficient students and native speakers are likely to share similar, age-related interests and, in this informal setting, can express their personal opinions about topics such as the food they are eating, important family events, or incidents with classmates during the morning.

Small groups can also be set up in the classroom to support the language that meets program objectives. Art projects or activities using manipulatives can be organized at small tables or at collections of 4–6 desks, with the materials and equipment needed to complete the project in the center of the space for the group to share. This arrangement will naturally encourage the use of functional language to request needed materials, to comment on how the work is going, and to offer informal suggestions and assistance. Assigning tasks for pairs of students to work at the computer will give a meaningful and concrete context to use the language of directions and problem solving for an LEP student with a more language proficient partner.

Another way to stimulate conversation in the classroom and link it to written language uses is to plan the first 10 minutes of the day for small groups of children to work informally in selected centers at self-selected tasks (e.g., the reading or writing centers). A small library corner stocked with several cushions and a notebook of reviews of favorite books can set the stage for informal conversation among children wanting to know what book to select next. Children may write or draw in journals to record important ideas or events. This time will also allow the teacher to circulate among all children to hear personally important stories from home and establish a comfortable beginning to the day.

Play

Both sociodramatic play and games with rules offer many opportunities for LEP children to develop and expand their oral and written language. For children just beginning to learn English, observing and listening in on other children's play before actively participating can be a risk-free way of figuring out how to enter the group, how to take turns, and what rules must be followed to play. In play activities, LEP students can demonstrate their understanding and desire to become a part of the classroom culture with a combination of whatever English they currently can use and appropriate gestures, sound effects, and movements.

Sociodramatic play offers many opportunities to learn oral and written English. Building upon the sociocultural context of the LEP child, sociodramatic play provides concrete props and familiar situations to bridge home experiences and native language to school experiences and English. A home center, block center, or centers organized around current curriculum themes automatically encourage interactive play and oral language. The objects and activities in these centers provide opportunities for comprehensible input, vocabulary development, bridging new concepts familiar to native language and culture, and practice with oral and written English.

Contextualized Print in Sociodramatic Play

By adding print to the sociodramatic play center through labels, signs, and logos, the LEP child is exposed to print in a natural environmental context. The same words seen in the child's everyday environment are repeated in a meaningful context in the classroom, providing the LEP child with meaning for both the written word and the concept. Through gradual exposure over time, the children learn to recognize these words out of context and in regular print. This process of decontextualization emerges from repeated opportunities to read and write words in their natural, meaningful context and fosters reading with understanding rather than simply decoding words for which they have no meaning (*word calling*). It also builds upon the child's home experiences with print, in which reading and writing are used as a part of daily living with no special pedagogical intent. For the LEP child the home print experience may be somewhat different from that of the native speaker. It is important for the teacher to draw upon the LEP child's print experiences, allowing for a natural emergence of literacy for these children (Wallace, 1988).

Attempts at Writing in Sociodramatic Play

The sociodramatic center also lends itself to opportunities for writing. Writing implements can be added naturally to most centers: for example, order pads in a restaurant, bills in a shop, paper work in an office, tickets at the airport. Initial writing attempts will probably be scribbling or copying of words in the center. Eventually both the LEP and native English-speaking children will attempt to write words on their own using letterlike symbols, strings of actual letters and numerals, phonemic (invented) spelling, and then correct spelling (Heald-Taylor, 1986). Incorporation of writing and reading with oral language in centers and other classroom activities provides a natural whole language environment for the LEP child to gain fluency in English in a meaningful context.

Games

Games with rules also offer many opportunities to support use of limited language with concrete actions. The repetition of many words in typical directions for games gives LEP students a chance to see and hear instructional language in a meaningful and concrete context. Since games with rules usually give the players many chances to use the same language and actions, LEP students have opportunities to observe peers model the approved actions and experiment with their own actions a number of times before the game is over.

Games also offer concrete and immediate feedback to the LEP student about the appropriateness of both the language and actions used. Board games will typically use much of the same vocabulary that is used in many teacher-directed lessons or in the directions for many published materials used as independent work in many classrooms. Most board games can be structured to be cooperative rather than competitive.

Thematic Units

Thematic units can be developed around a topic, an event that is personally meaningful to a particular group of children, or a book that stimulates special interest. The teacher and students can begin a thematic unit together by orally brainstorming a planning web, a graphic diagram showing the relationships of concepts, objects, descriptions, and actions. The web will indicate what the children already know about the topic and what experiences could extend their knowledge. LEP students can participate in this group brainstorming by contributing orally, with gestures and movements, or through pictures or drawings of their unique experiences related to the topic. Thematic units can be used to create a microcosm of the real world in the classroom through hands-on experience with a topic. The children become actively involved in the topic using language in realistic ways. By incorporating activities into a thematic unit, the vocabulary and language patterns are repeated in other activities, such as story reading, dramatization, and art projects. Thus, the thematic unit provides practice with oral and written language in a variety of interconnected activities reinforcing the LEP child's acquisition of oral language and literacy.

Webs resulting from this process can include a wide variety of oral and written language activities; experiences with books; hands-on activities; and expressive activities (art, music, drama, movement) designed to present content in a language-rich context (Enright and McCloskey, 1988; Heald-Taylor, 1986). Related experiences included in the unit to develop LEP children's oral and written language might include trips; classroom visitors and displays; audiovisual materials; roleplaying; cooking; and construction activities (woodworking, block building, sand table, art, needlework). Many books lend themselves to inclusion in a thematic unit of instruction integrating language with the content areas and fine arts (Hudelson, 1989a). For example, reading *Swimmy* (Lionni, 1963) might lead to a unit on fish. *The Runaway Bunny* (Brown, 1972) might be included in a unit on families. Appendix A gives an example of a unit for young LEP children developed around *The Gingerbread Boy* (Galdone, 1975) using many of the techniques discussed in this chapter.

Choral Speaking

Some stories lend themselves to choral speaking activities in which children recite parts of the story individually or in groups. Language with strong rhythm and/or rhyme lends itself to this activity. After some modeling, the LEP children will join in, giving them practice in English articulation, syntax, rhythm, and expression (Heald-Taylor, 1986). Choral speaking activities often are accompanied by movement, music, or sound effects (clapping, rhythm instruments). They may also be used in story dramatization, for example with puppets or flannelboard characters. The teacher reads the verse or narration and the children chant or sing the chorus or refrain. Excellent sources for choral reading activities with LEP children are—

nursery rhymes;
poems for primary grade pupils: e.g., *A Light in the Attic* (Silverstein, 1981);
folk songs: e.g., *Go Tell Aunt Rhody* (Aliki, 1974); and
stories with refrains: e.g., *"Fire! Fire!" Said Mrs. McGuire* (Martin, 1970).

Story Reading with Fiction and Nonfiction Books

Well-written, well-illustrated books for young children provide a natural focus for both oral and written language acquisition (Allen, 1989; Lindfors, 1989). Oral fluency, listening comprehension, vocabulary, concepts, contextual understanding and use of language, story structure, print concepts, sociocultural use of text, oral language/print connections, storytelling, word recognition, science and social studies content, and creative and written responses to text are easily incorporated into a story reading activity. And, reading stories together is fun for both limited English proficient and native English-speaking children!

The Story Reading Process

As a part of the daily planning for the class, including at least one group story reading session every day assists LEP students to expand their oral vocabulary, develop listening skills in English, gain cultural information and background needed for success in North American schools, and acquire print and story concepts to be applied in reading and writing. Select interesting books with good illustrations and varied use of language. (See Huck, Hepler, and Hickman, 1987; Johnson and Louis, 1987; Taylor and Strickland, 1986; Trekase, 1989 for suggestions of good literature for young children.) Especially effective for limited English proficient children are books that are predictable or that have repeated refrains. For example, *Ask Mr. Bear* (Flack, 1968) in which the pattern of the story (the boy asking each animal for a suggestion for a birthday present for his mother) is repeated with each animal or *The Very Hungry Caterpillar* (Carle, 1969). The predictable and repeated language allows the LEP child to begin to join in orally with the rest of the group using chunks of story language, meaningful in that context, before the individual words are meaningful. A list of suggested books with predictable, repeated text is given in Box 6-1. The story reading session consists of prereading language activities, interactive story reading, and postreading language activities.

BOX 6-1 • *Predictable Books*

Aliki. (1974). *Go tell Aunt Rhody.* New York: Macmillan.
Bang, M. (1983). *Ten, nine, eight.* New York: Greenwillow.
Baum, A., & Baum, J. (1962). *One bright Monday morning.* New York: Random House.
Berenstain, S., & Berenstain, J. (1971). *Bears in the night.* New York: Random House.
Brown, M. (1976). *One, two, three.* Boston: Little Brown.
Brown, M. W. (1942). *The runaway bunny.* New York: Harper & Row.
Brown, M. W. (1974). *Goodnight moon.* New York: Harper & Row.
Burningham, J. (1970). *Mr. Grumpy's outing.* New York: Puffin.
Carle, E. (1969). *The very hungry caterpillar.* Cleveland: Collins.
Charlip, R. (1969). *What good luck, what bad luck.* New York: Scholastic.
de Reginers, B. (1972). *May I bring a friend?* New York: Atheneum.
Emberley, B. (1974). *Klippity klop.* Boston: Little Brown.
Flack, M. (1932). *Ask Mr. Bear.* New York: Macmillan.
Hutchins, P. (1968). *Rosie's walk.* New York: Macmillan.
Martin, B. (1970). *Brown bear, brown bear: What do you see?* New York: Holt, Rinehart & Winston.
Mayer, M. (1975). *Just for you.* New York: Golden Press.
Mayer, M. (1973). *What do you do with a kangaroo?* New York: Macmillan.
Miller, J. P. (1978). *Do you know colors?* New York: Random House.
Preston, E. M. (1976). *The temper tantrum book.* New York: Viking.
Quackenbush, R. (1975). *Skip to my lou.* Philadelphia: Lippincott.
Scheer, J., & Bileck, M. (1964). *Rain makes applesauce.* New York: Holiday.
Sendack, M. (1962). *Chicken soup with rice.* New York: Scholastic.
Seuss, Dr. (1957). *The cat in the hat.* New York: Random House.
Skaar, G. (1972). *What do the animals say?* New York: Scholastic.
Slobodkina, E. (1940). *Caps for sale.* New York: Scholastic.
Speir, P. (1961). *The fox went out on a night.* Garden City, NJ: Doubleday.
Weisgard, L. (1940). *The county noisy book.* Chicago: Harper.
Viorst, J. (1975). *Alexander and the terrible, horrible, no good, very bad day.* New York: Atheneum.
Zemach, M. (1965). *The teeny tiny woman.* New York: Scholastic.
Zolotow, A. (1971). *Wake up and good night.* New York: Harper & Row.

Prereading activities   During the prereading stage, the book is introduced with an oral discussion to focus the children's attention on the topic or concept of the story. Use of a key illustration for that topic aids the LEP children in attending to the topic and in comprehending the oral language. Questions are used to help them predict what the topic of the book might be and what they think might happen in the story. These questions can also be used to tap into the children's background experiences, relating the topic and illustrations to familiar experiences in their lives. Relating to their lives is especially important for LEP children, whose sociocultural context may be very different from that of the school and the other children. For example, children familiar with snow will easily relate to *The Snowy Day* (Keats, 1962). However, children from a climate where it does not snow will not be able to predict what might happen in the story. They will have had experience with rainstorms, however, which could serve as a link to snowstorms. By relating this new concept to the child's prior experience, the child's cognitive and linguistic development is fostered.

Bridging or *webbing* is a special technique for helping the LEP child make these connections. After previewing the pictures in the book and hearing the title read, the children brainstorm about the topic, giving related ideas, concepts, objects, descriptions, and actions. Initially, the LEP children will give limited responses, but gradually with modeling from the teacher and native English-speaking children in the class they will join in the discussion. The ideas generated can be drawn into a web diagram showing the relationship of the topic at hand to other topics familiar to the children. For example, *Swimmy* (Lionni, 1963) might be used to make a web about fish, swimming, colors and shapes, and things that are different. A sample web is given in Figure 6-1. The web serves to build a bridge between the child's prior experiences and the vocabulary and concepts of the new language. Bridging is used to link the child's experiences and the text through discussion of the experiences related by the teacher to the text to be read. This technique is also useful for enhancing reading comprehension, especially when children are taught to make the bridge independently (Au. 1979).

For young LEP children the bridge will be most effective when based upon a concrete experience. If actual, concrete experiences are not possible (e.g., a real snowy day), visuals such as pictures, models, or filmstrips and videos may be used. Abstract descriptions are too difficult for young children and generally are not effective in helping the young child acquire a new concept or even a new label (in their second language) for an existing concept (Gonzales, 1981). Nonfiction picture books as well as picture storybooks provide a special help for young children acquiring English: e.g., concepts books such as *Push Pull, Empty Full: A Book of Opposites* (Hoban, 1972) or *Is It Red? Is It Yellow? Is It Blue?* (Hoban, 1978). The concrete illustration of abstract and/or unfamiliar concepts provides an additional context for the child. This context may help trigger past experiences and concepts, which can now be associated with English vocabulary.

Interactive story reading   During interactive story reading, arrange the children so that they all can see the illustrations in the book. For LEP students pointing to the relevant print, illustration, or item within the picture is particularly important in order to direct their attention to the object being labeled or described (Heald-Taylor, 1986). Interactive story reading is a technique in which the children and the adult interact with the story as it unfolds. By asking questions, highlighting illustrations, and predicting what happens next, the child's linguistic and literacy acquisition is shaped. The process of scaffolding can be used in this manner. In *The Runaway Bunny* (Brown, 1972) the child can be asked to identify the bunny and mother, giving appropriate labels. Then on each page the child can be asked to predict what the mother will become if the bunny changes himself. For example, when bunny becomes a goat, what

FIGURE 6-1 • *Sample Web: Fish*

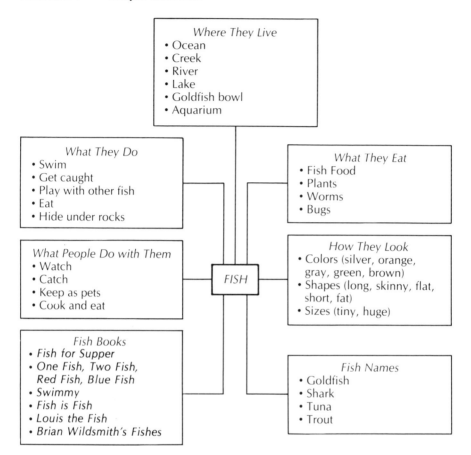

might the mother become? Using the child's responses, extend the child's language to build the vocabulary and concept of a *goat herder*. This sample dialogue illustrates the use of scaffolding:

Teacher: Now what is bunny going to be?

Child: A goat

Teacher: What do you think mother will become?

Child: A mother goat

Teacher: Good! A mother goat takes care of baby goats. Who else might look after goats?

Child: (*no response*)

Teacher: Who takes care of cows?

Child: Farmer

Teacher: A farmer who lives in the mountains and looks after goats is called a *goat herder.*

This process builds on the child's language and concepts, adding new vocabulary and using the context of the story and illustrations to relate the concepts to the child's experiences.

Postreading activities   Postreading activities following the oral reading of the story present an opportunity to return to the initial questions asked during prereading. What did happen in the story? Were the original predictions accurate? Why did the specific characters act as they did? How did they feel? Use of these open-ended questions allows for discussion and response to the story, expansion of the child's oral language concepts, understanding of the story structure (important to reading), and relation of the story and language to the LEP child's background experiences.

Story Reading Follow-up

Follow-up or extension activities provide opportunities for review of the story and language experienced during reading and discussion. They also provide opportunities for including written language and other means of expression. Follow-up activities might include small-group rereading of the story, retelling of the story, or listening to a tape of the story.

Small-group rereading of the story   When books are read to a small group of children, they can sit on either side of the adult and look at the print as the story is read. By watching as the adult runs a finger under the line of print being read, the child begins to acquire a number of print concepts. Attention is drawn to the portion being read (not the picture or the blank spaces) and to the directionality of reading (left-to-right and top-to-bottom in English). Frequently repeated words may be noted and remembered. The division of the print into words and the use of capital letters and punctuation may be noticed. All of these print concepts are important in acquiring reading and writing; some of which differ in English from the children's first language (e.g., Chinese, Hebrew, Arabic). For primary grade students who have begun to read on their own, small-group story reading provides reinforcement of word and phrase recognition, especially grammatical function words used in context (e.g., *the, is, of, are*). It is often difficult for teachers to find time to read stories to small groups of children. The use of aides and volunteers (parents, grandparents, older children in the school) is one way to ensure that LEP children have this opportunity to become familiar with books and concepts about print.

Retelling of stories   Children love to hear the same story read over and over again. Not only do they enjoy the humor, excitement, and events, but they also enjoy anticipating what they know comes next. This is true for all children, but more so for LEP children who need repeated hearings to grasp the language and concepts necessary for understanding the story. In hearing stories read and reread, they begin to acquire the story language, developing a cognitive framework for all narrative text. They acquire an expectation for the traditional beginning of stories; look for the setting (time and place) and characters; expect dialogue and the expression of feelings; and anticipate the sequence of problem, climax, and resolution followed by a traditional ending. This narrative structure will be used extensively in their writing and reading comprehension. After repeated hearing of a story, the LEP child will be able to tell the story, especially with the pictures as props. This initial story "reading" is, of course, memorization, but gradually the child begins to recognize certain words within the context of the book. Limited English proficient children frequently have different experiences with stories and narrative structure from their native language and culture (Heath, 1983). A part of acquiring proficiency in English involves acquiring English narrative structure and language. Hearing and retelling stories is an effective way to do so.

Taped books   A variation on repeated reading of stories is for the child to listen to a tape of the story while following along in the book. A listening center with story tapes provides an opportunity for LEP children to listen to stories independently as frequently as they wish. Gradually they begin to repeat the story — especially the refrains and predictable phrases. Soon they can "read" the story just by looking at the pictures, and later they begin to recognize words within the story context. Special benefits for the LEP child accrue from the use of language in context accompanied by concrete pictures and the simultaneous oral/written language presentation. Of further benefit is the limitless possibility for repetition not present in most other language situations.

Language Experience

A very effective bridge from the LEP child's oral to written language is through the child's dictation of stories or events recorded by the teacher. The story is then read aloud by the teacher and by the child. It may be followed by reading instruction (word recognition, comprehension, sequence); illustration; publishing; and reading to an audience. Box 6-2 outlines the steps in using the *language experience approach* with young LEP children. This technique, when based upon the child's actual experiences, provides meaningful links between the experience and oral language and then between oral and written language. Students find it much easier to read and understand their own language than that of unfamiliar texts because they use vocabulary, language patterns, and contexts already familiar to them. It is important to record their oral language exactly as given, even if it is not standard English. If the oral language is changed, the child will not recognize what has been written and will read it as it was stated, not as it is written. After reading has begun, some stories dictated by children may be selected for publication. These stories can be edited by the child and teacher together as a part of the publishing process. When recording, however, the teacher should use correct spelling, capitalization, punctuation, and penmanship, thus providing a written language model for the LEP children.

BOX 6-2 • Language Experience Approach Outline

Plan an activity that allows active participation by each child with ample opportunities for oral and written language.

Making Gingerbread People

1. *Experience:* Use a simple recipe printed on a chart or a mix to prepare gingerbread dough. Involve the children in reading and discussing each step as they assist in preparing the batter, emphasize (both orally and on the recipe) the labels for ingredients, descriptive words for textures and smells, measurements, and action words. Decorate and bake.

2. *Discussion:* While the cookies are baking or the next day, discuss the activity, eliciting key words that will be used in the story. Emphasize one or two types of language (e.g., labels, descriptions, actions); body parts (eyes, nose, legs); ingredients (flour, sugar, raisins); smells and tastes (spicy, sweet, yummy); sequence ("first we mixed the dough, next we rolled the dough, then we cut out the gingerbread cookies"); action words (*stir, roll, cut, bake*); measurements (1 teaspoon, 2 cups, 12 raisins); responses ("I liked mixing the dough. I liked eating the cookie"). As words are elicited, write them on the board for use in dictation.

3. *Dictation:* Have the children dictate a story about the experience, which the teacher records on a chart. Use good manuscript printing; correct spelling, capitalization, and punctuation; and the children's *exact* language (vocabulary and syntax). Using the ideas generated in the oral discussion, have the children dictate a story about making gingerbread cookies. The story might be about making the cookies (ingredients, measurements, actions); the sequence followed; the five senses (how the cookies looked, smelled, and tasted); or what the children liked about the experience. For beginning readers, put the children's names on their sentences to ease recognition of their language.

4. *Reading:* Read the completed story. First the teacher reads the story aloud; then the teacher and children read it together. The teacher runs a marker (ruler or sentence strip) under the print as it is read, pointing to key words. Then the children take turns reading their sentences and/or the whole story.

5. *Follow-up:* Follow up print activities. Select some aspect of the story to emphasize in follow-up activities. Write the action words, descriptions, or sensory words on cards. Have the children match these cards to the words in the story and read the sentence.

- Write the sentences in a sequence story on strips. Distribute and have children come up with the sentences in correct sequence.
- Read the story to verify sequences.
- Write each child's sentence on a strip. Have children match their sentence on the chart and read it.
- Find repeated words (or one category of words) in the story and underline them (e.g., "Find *liked* each time it occurs or find all the body part words—*eyes, arms, nose, legs, mouth, body, head*").
- Type or print the story and make a copy for each child.
- Have the children illustrate the story. For a short story, type in the bottom one-third of the page and illustrate it above. For a longer story, type sections on several pages, illustrate, make a cover and staple into a book.
- Continue rereading the story periodically over the next several weeks to reinforce and enjoy the literacy skills and language involved.

Experiences used as background for dictation include group and individual activities (trips, art, cooking, experiments); stories heard; films or television programs viewed; and personal or family experiences. The activity may be especially planned for the language experience activity (e.g., make popcorn and then write a story about the sights, sounds, smells, and tastes experienced) or may follow a spontaneous experience (e.g., school assembly, a severe windstorm, or a popular children's television program).

Class-composed charts written by the teacher provide models of written language and allow for use of repeated text. The class discusses the topic together and dictates sentences that the teacher records on a chart. For example, the class might each contribute a sentence to a favorite food chart: e.g., "I like chocolate cookies. I like pizza. I like peanut butter sandwiches." Another example is a class survey recording children's favorite fruits: e.g., "We like apples" (Jose, Lihn, Mei-ling, Eric); "We like bananas" (Tom, Maria, Susan, Tshepo, Aaron). The language experience approach is an ideal setting for language acquisition as it provides a total communication experience within a meaningful context. Thus it is very effective for introducing limited English proficient students to reading and writing while expanding their oral language performance (Dixon and Nessel, 1983; Enright and McCloskey, 1988; Hamayan and Pfleger, 1987; Heald-Taylor, 1986; Rigg, 1989).

Bookmaking

As a follow-up to both story reading and language experience, LEP children enjoy making books about the story. These may be individual or group efforts and may present the story sequentially or just the highlights. Children illustrate a page and dictate or write an appropriate text for the illustration. Books may be typed and bound for permanency ("published"), although a simple cover with the title and author(s) tied with yarn is effective. When the books are completed, create opportunities for the children to share them with others by reading them aloud. The authors may also tape-record their book to be listened to while looking at the book. By using the LEP students' own language in creating the book, the children are able to read and comprehend the text more easily, relating the new language to their experiences. (See Appendix B.)

Dramatization

Many stories lend themselves to dramatization as plays, and puppets or masks can be used. After hearing the story several times the LEP children can dramatize the action using appropriate oral dialogue, especially using repeated phrases or refrains. For older children, a narrator can read the descriptions and settings while the children paraphrase the dialogue. The flannelboard is a simple means of dramatizing stories for young children. The children move figures and objects on the flannelboard as the story is read. Felt figures may be purchased for many stories and nursery rhymes. They may be cut from flannel or felt, or a second copy of the book may be cut up (glue a piece of velcro on the back of the laminated pictures) for use on the flannelboard. The children can make masks for the characters in the story. Use heavy paper or lightweight posterboard; cut holes for the eyes, nose, and mouth; and glue on to a tongue depressor so children may hold the masks in front of their faces. Items from the dress-up corner, paper hats, or even squares of nylon net placed on top of the child's head (a "magic net" that transforms the child into the fox, caterpillar, beanstalk, or old woman) are effective props for dramatization by young children. Once again, this literature extension provides a vehicle for use of oral and written language in a meaningful context enjoyed by LEP and native English speakers alike. Stories with a lot of action and particularly with repeated sequences (e.g., *The Three Bears* or *The Three Billy Goats Gruff*) lend themselves particularly well to dramatization.

Illustration

Another enjoyable follow-up to story reading and language experience involves illustrating the story using a variety of art media (Franklin, 1989). Children may make a mural, collage, or painting of the story as a whole or they may use sequential pictures to tell the entire story. Oral language is involved in the group project as the mural or picture is planned. Written language may be used in titles, captions, or balloons for dialogue. The concrete context for the language assists the LEP student in making links between prior experiences and new language stimuli. Each child might illustrate a favorite part of the story or a favorite character, or children might illustrate the entire story to emphasize the beginning, sequential events, and ending of the story. Crayons, markers, poster paint, colored pencils, colored construction paper, scraps (e.g., bits of string, ribbon, felt, sequins, material), and finger paint are possible media. Three-dimensional illustrations may be made with clay, play dough, Legos, bristle blocks, small plastic or wood figures of people and animals, and cut-out illustrations. These hands-on activities are as important for primary grade LEP children as they are for prekindergarten and kindergarten LEP children. To be effective for the LEP child, these activities should be accompanied by oral discussion of the story, illustrations, art media, and written captions, titles, or labels.

The Writing Process

LEP children can also be involved in all phases of the writing process while they are acquiring control of oral language. Classroom teachers can support their development by providing a meaningful, print-rich environment, modeling the process of composing for a variety of purposes and audiences, and encouraging LEP students to participate in all the steps of the writing process.

Environmental print can be used throughout the classroom to demonstrate that written language can convey information important to children. Classroom locations, materials, and equipment used every day can be labeled to support children's independent use of them. Children's names can be used to label personal possessions, show responsibility for daily jobs in the classroom or membership in small groups or center activities, and allow children to participate actively in such classroom routines as attendance, lunch count, and checking out library books.

Teachers can model the composing process for children by drawing their attention to the many times in the school day when they use writing to communicate. Examples of a variety of purposes for writing could include writing notes to the school secretary to request supplies, filling out forms for the office, sending the lunch count to the cafeteria staff, writing announcements for the next PTA meeting, or requesting special books for the upcoming dinosaur unit from the librarian.

Children can also be involved in all steps of the writing process from the first day of school. Children can experiment with writing materials in a writing center. LEP children can use whatever oral language they have to participate in group brainstorming with the rest of the class to decide what ideas to include in a group story about a class fieldtrip. Opportunities to draft ideas on scrap paper or in journals without immediate concerns for the conventions of writing are especially important for students still developing control of the vocabulary and syntactic patterns of English. Individual or class books on themes important to children will allow LEP children to participate in the feelings of success that accompany publishing writing in forms for others to enjoy.

Writing Folders and Journals

Both native speakers and LEP children benefit from daily opportunities to write (Edelsky, 1989). When writing is kept in a folder or journal, children are encouraged to continue with a composition, revising and adding to it on subsequent days. Both handwritten compositions and computer-generated (word processor) writing is helpful. The use of the computer makes the physical act of writing easier for young children with immature fine motor coordination. It also offers opportunities for correction and revision, which are difficult and time-consuming by hand.

Interaction with the Teacher

For writing to be effective, the LEP child needs to read the composition to the teacher during a conference. By reading what has been written, the child is able to hear the language used, note omissions and places that are not clear, and spontaneously make changes and corrections. The teacher is able to intersperse skill instruction, noting that a space here or a question mark there would make the composition easier to read and understand. Holistic scoring of these compositions directs attention to the ideas being communicated by the students rather than to the mechanics of the composition. (See Chapter 9 of this book for an example of a holistic scoring guide useful for young LEP and NES children.) Mechanics may be addressed in the editing process for works selected for publication. Such works may be illustrated, published, and shared with an audience as described with language experience writing. (See Figure 6-2 for both handwritten and computer-generated samples of a young LEP child's writing.) At first LEP children with some first language literacy skills may write completely or partially in their native language. Hudelson (1989c) recommends encouraging these efforts as a transition into writing in their second language.

Literature as Reading Text

Young LEP children's oral and written language acquisition is facilitated by hearing stories read and observing the printed page as the story is read aloud or on tape. The same fiction and nonfiction picture storybooks can be used as

FIGURE 6-2 • *Sample of LEP Kindergarten Child's Handwritten and Computer-generated Stories over a Period of 4 Months*

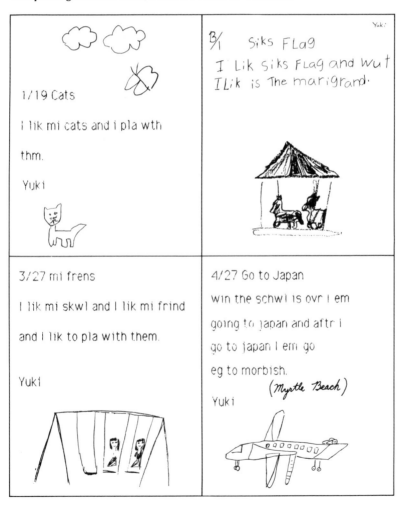

texts as the child's reading develops. Whether using large sized (big) books with a small group of children or regular sized books with an individual child, the use of real texts for reading increases the probability of the LEP child's success in reading and understanding the text. The pictures, stories familiar to the child from experiences or reading aloud, and interesting natural language patterns all facilitate comprehension. Using meaningful reading materials is especially important for LEP children in order to avoid their simply mastering letter/ sound relationships leading to decoding words for which they have no meaning (*word calling*).

Big Books

The use of large sized versions of picture storybooks helps a small group of LEP children to focus on the relevant pictures and print. This technique of shared reading (Heald-Taylor, 1986; Holdaway, 1976; Johnson and Louis, 1987) allows the teacher to point to the print as the story is read aloud. Using the story reading techniques described above, the teacher aids the LEP child to connect oral language and print while enjoying the story. The large size makes it easy to point to, underline, or highlight specific words or phrases as well as to match words and phrases written on strips of posterboard to those in the big book. Vocabulary, word recognition, print concepts, and story schema are all fostered in a meaningful context. The children memorize phrases and the structure of the story and soon are able to read the big book as a group and independently.

Individual Storybooks

The big book technique can be used with individual children using regular picture storybooks. The teacher first reads the book to the child and then encourages the child to read it aloud to the teacher. By using real texts meeting the criteria for good narrative and expository texts rather than basal readers with controlled vocabulary and artificial language patterns, LEP children experience written language similar to the oral language they are hearing and learning (Hudelson, 1989b). Vocabulary is easier to learn as it is presented in a meaningful context; comprehension is more likely as the text makes sense and is augmented by illustrations; natural oral language patterns and rhythms can be applied to reading the written texts. With primary grade students, these individual storybooks may be used for independent reading in sustained silent reading (a daily period of 10–15 minutes when everyone in the room reads a book) and in regular teacher/child reading sessions when the LEP child reads aloud to the teacher during the time designated for reading instruction.

Sociocultural Context for Language Literacy

Written language as well as oral language are acquired within the context in which the young child lives. For LEP children this context may be very different from that of the school and of the native English-speaking children's homes. Nevertheless, the LEP children have rich experiences with language and print in their homes and communities. They will have observed adults reading and writing at home, in the community, and in places of worship. The books, newspapers, sacred texts, and letters may be in a different orthography with a different set of print conventions from English. Print will have a special significance as it is used both for the purpose of communication and to preserve the family's cultural heritage. Unfortunately, schools often use print and text without any context and thus without any real communicative purpose. This use creates confusion for all children, but especially for young LEP children (Schieffelin and Cochran-Smith, 1984; Wallace, 1988). The integrated language arts approach presented in this text helps to overcome this problem by using real language (both oral and written) in real contexts within the classroom as the primary language for instruction. Careful study of the communities represented, both English and non-English-speaking, and their use of print will help schools become sensitive to the sociocultural context for literacy familiar to each child.

A large number of non-native English-speaking children will be acquiring English in classrooms taught by monolingual English-speaking teachers. Many of these children will be continuing the acquisition and use of their native languages and cultures at home and in their communities. Some of them will also be acquiring native language literacy at home or in schools organized by their community (e.g., Japanese language schools, Pakistani religious schools, or Eskimo summer schools). These children will be able to maintain their native language and culture and to acquire native language literacy while simultaneously acquiring proficiency in English. They will have the advantage of being both bilingual and bicultural. In some schools where there is a majority of one language represented (e.g., Spanish), bilingual education within the school is possible. If bilingual teachers are available, the child can acquire English and Spanish language fluency and literacy at the same time. The benefits of a strong native language literacy program include the connection of reading and writing with previous oral language and experiences; the development of a literacy background upon wihch English literacy can be built; and validation of the children's native culture and community (Hudelson, 1987). To succeed in North American society, it is necessary to become fluent in English. Therefore, bilingual education must provide children with opportunities to become fluent and literate in both their native language and English. Nevertheless, the opportunity to become bilingual as well as bicultural provides children with both educational and career opportunities not available to monolingual persons. The critical issue is quality—instruction must lead to a high level of literacy in order to be effective.

Teaching LEP Children in the Regular Classroom

The oral and written language methods and materials suggested in this chapter for use with young LEP children are equally valid and effective for young native English-speaking children (Rigg and Allen, 1989). For both LEP children and native English-speaking children, the activities described begin with each individual child's level of acquisition of language and build upon it. The language acquisition of LEP children is fostered through interaction with English-speaking adults and children, especially using the literacy techniques described above (Hough, Nurss, and Enright, 1985). Special instruction in a self-contained or resource room is provided for beginning students in many school districts. However, even resource room instruction is likely to be available for only an hour or two per day, leaving the child in the regular classroom the rest of the day. In districts with small numbers of LEP children, they may be placed in the regular classroom for the entire day. Fortunately the early childhood classroom is uniquely suited to instruction appropriate for these children. The interactive, concrete materials and activities are natural vehicles for oral language acquisition. Story reading, taped books, and writing centers are an integral part of the classroom along with thematic unit-based instruction and sociodramatic play. Thus, inclusion of LEP children in these activities is natural. Special attention does need to be given to making certain that every activity — teacher-directed and independent, group and individual — includes opportunities for using meaningful, natural language, both oral and written. By so doing, comprehensible input within a meaningful sociocultural context can be ensured for both LEP and NES children.

References

Aliki. (1974). *Go tell Aunt Rhody.* New York: Macmillan.

Allen, V. G. (1986). Developing contexts to support second language acquisition. *Language Arts, 63,* 61–66.

Allen, V. G. (1989). Literature as a support to language acquisition. In P. Rigg & V. G. Allen (Eds.), *When they don't all speak English: Integrating the ESL student into the regular classroom* (pp. 55–64). Urbana, IL: National Council of Teachers of English.

Au, K. (1979). Using the experience-text relationship method with minority children. *The Reading Teacher, 32,* 677–679.

Brown, M. W. (1972). *The runaway bunny.* New York: Harper & Row.

Carle, E. (1968). *The very hungry caterpillar.* New York: World.

Chaudron, C. (1988). *Second language classrooms.* Cambridge, England: Cambridge University Press.

Dixon, C., & Nessel, D. (1983). *The language experience approach to reading (and writing): Language experience approach for English as a second language.* Hayward, CA: Alemany Press.

Edelsky, C. (1989). Putting language variation to work for you. In P. Rigg & V. G. Allen (Eds.), *When they don't all speak English: Integrating the ESL student into the regular classroom* (pp. 96–107). Urbana, IL: National Council of Teachers of English.

Enright, D. S. (1986). Use everything you have to teach English: Providing useful input to young language learners. In P. Rigg & D. S. Enright (Eds.), *Children and ESL: Integrating perspectives* (pp. 115–162). Washington, DC: Teachers of English to Speaker of Other Languages.

Enright, D. S., & McCloskey, M. L. (1988). *Integrating English: Developing English language and literacy in the multicultural classroom.* Reading, MA: Addison-Wesley.

Flack, M. (1968). *Ask Mr. Bear.* New York: Macmillan.

Franklin, E. A. (1989). Encouraging and understanding the visual and written works of second-language children. In P. Rigg & V. G. Allen (Eds.), *When they don't all speak English: Integrating the ESL student into the regular classroom* (pp. 77–95). Urbana, IL: National Council of Teachers of English.

Galdone, P. (1975). *The gingerbread boy.* New York: Clarion.

Goffstein, M. B. (1976). *Fish for supper.* New York: Dial Press.

Gonzales, P. C. (1981). Beginning English reading for ESL students. *The Reading Teacher, 35*(2), 154–162.

Hamayan, E., & Pfleger, M. (1987). *Developing literacy in English as a second language: Guidelines for teachers of young children from nonliterate backgrounds.* Washington, DC: Center for Applied Linguistics.

Hatch, E. (1979). Reading a second language. In M. Celce-Murcia & L. McIntosh (Eds.), *Teaching English as a second or foreign language* (pp. 129–144). Rowley, MA: Newbury House.

Heald-Taylor, G. (1986). *Whole language strategies for ESL primary students.* Toronto, Canada: Ontario Institute for Studies in Education.

Heath, S. B. (1983). *Ways with words: Language, life, and work in communities and classrooms.* Cambridge, England: Cambridge University Press.

Hoban, T. (1972). *Push pull, empty, full: A book of opposites.* New York: Macmillan.

Hoban, T. (1978). *Is it red? Is it yellow? Is it blue?* New York: Greenwillow.

Holdaway, D. (1976). *Foundations of literacy.* Auckland, New Zealand: Ashton-Scholastic.

Hough, R. A., Nurss, J. R., & Enright, D. S. (1986). Story reading with limited English speaking children in the regular classroom. *The Reading Teacher, 39*(6), 510–514.

Huck, C. S., Hepler, S., & Hickman, J. (1987). *Children's literature in the elementary school* (4th ed.) New York: Holt, Rinehart & Winston.

Hudelson, S. (1984). Kan yu ret an rayt en Engles: Children become literate in English as a second language. *TESOL Quarterly, 18,* 221–238.

Hudelson, S. (1987). The role of native language literacy in the education of language minority children. *Language Arts, 64*(8), 827–841.

Hudelson, S. (1989a). "Teaching" English through content-area activities. In P. Rigg & V. G. Allen (Eds.), *When they don't all speak English: Integrating the ESL student into the regular classroom* (pp. 139–151). Urbana, IL: National Council of Teachers of English.

Hudelson, S. (1989b). Working with second-language learners. In L. W. Searfoss & J. E. Readence (Eds.), *Helping children learn to read* (pp. 397–421). Englewood Cliffs, NJ: Prentice-Hall.

Hudelson, S. (1989c). *Write on: Children writing in ESL.* Englewood Cliffs, NJ: Prentice-Hall.

Johnson, T. D., & Louis, D. R. (1987). *Literacy through literature.* Portsmouth, NH: Heinemann Educational Books.

Keats, E. J. (1962). *The snowy day.* New York: Viking.

Kleifgen, J. A. (1985). Skilled variation in a kindergarten teachers' use of foreigner talk. In S. M. Gass & C. G. Madden (Eds.), *Input in second language acquisition* (pp. 59–68). Cambridge, MA: Newbury House.

Krashen, S. (1982). *Principles of second language acquisition.* Oxford, England: Pergamon Press.

Lindfors, J. W. (1989). The classroom: A good environment for language learning. In P. Rigg & V. G. Allen (Eds.), *When they don't all speak English: Integrating the ESL student into the regular classroom* (pp. 39–54). Urbana, IL: National Council of Teachers of English.

Lionni, L. (1963). *Swimmy*. New York: Pantheon.

Lionni, L. (1970). *Fish is fish*. New York: Pantheon.

Martin, B., Jr. (1970). *"Fire! Fire!" said Mrs. McGuire*. New York: Holt, Rinehart & Winston.

McLaughlin, B. (1987). Reading in a second language: Studies with adult and child learners. In S. R. Goldman & H. T. Trueba (Eds.), *Becoming literate in English as a second language* (pp. 57–70). Norwood, NJ: Ablex.

Rigg, P. (1989). Language experience approach: Reading naturally. In P. Rigg & V. G. Allen (Eds.), *When they don't all speak English: Integrating the ESL student into the regular classroom* (pp. 65–76). Urbana, IL: National Council of Teachers of English.

Rigg, P., & Allen, V. G., (Eds.), (1989). *When they don't all speak English: Integrating the ESL student into the regular classroom*. Urbana, IL: National Council of Teachers of English.

Schieffelin, B. B., & Cochran-Smith, M. (1984). Learning to read culturally: Literacy before schooling. In H. Goelman, A. A. Oberg, & F. Smith (Eds.), *Awakening to literacy* (pp. 3–23). Exeter, NH: Heinemann Educational Books.

Seuss, Dr. (1968). *One fish, two fish, red fish, blue fish*. Westminster, MD: Random House.

Silverstein, S. (1981). *A light in the attic*. New York: Harper & Row.

Taylor, D., & Strickland, D. S. (1986). *Family storybook reading*. Portsmouth, NH: Heinemann Educational.

Tough, J. (1985). *Talk two: Children using English as a second language in primary schools*. London: Onyx Press.

Trelease, J. (1989). *The new read-aloud handbook*. New York: Penguin.

Urzua, C. (1989). I grow for a living. In P. Rigg & V. G. Allen (Eds.), *When they don't all speak English: Integrating the ESL student into the regular classroom* (pp. 15–38). Urbana, IL: National Council of Teachers of English.

Ventriglia, L. (1982). *Conversations of Miguel and Maria*. Reading, MA: Addison-Wesley.

Wallace, C. (1988). *Learning to read in a multicultural society: The social context of second language literacy*. New York: Prentice-Hall.

Wildsmith, B. (1968). *Brian Wildsmith's fishes*. New York: Watts.

Wong-Filmore, L. (1979). Individual differences in second language acquisition. In C. J. Fillmore, D. Kempler, & W. S. Wang (Eds.), *Individual differences in language ability and language behavior* (pp. 203–228). New York: Academic Press.

Wong-Fillmore, L. (1985). When does teacher talk work as input? In S. M. Gass & C. G. Madden (Eds.), *Input in second language acquisition* (pp. 17–50). Cambridge, MA: Newbury House Publishers.

Yorinks, A. (1980). *Louis the fish*. New York: Farrar.

CHAPTER SEVEN

The Classroom Environment: A Living-in and Learning-in Space

Advance Organizer

In this chapter, we discuss the classroom context, where much of young children's early literacy development takes place. The early childhood classroom environment can be used to stimulate and promote young children's literacy growth. We examine the characteristics and effects of both the social-emotional environment and the physical environment. Then we discuss effective practices for promoting children's social interactions, positive self-concepts, motivating children, and encouraging play and hands-on learning. Finally, we describe several types of learning centers and provide questions for evaluating the classroom environment.

Objectives

After studying this chapter, the reader should be able to —

- define the term *classroom environment,*
- identify the possible effects the classroom environment can have on young children's behavior and learning,
- describe the characteristics of effective classroom environments,
- explain how a teacher can organize the classroom environment to promote children's social interactions,
- describe ways of encouraging and motivating young children,
- describe how a teacher can foster young children's positive self-concepts while recognizing their individual needs,

Graphic Organizer

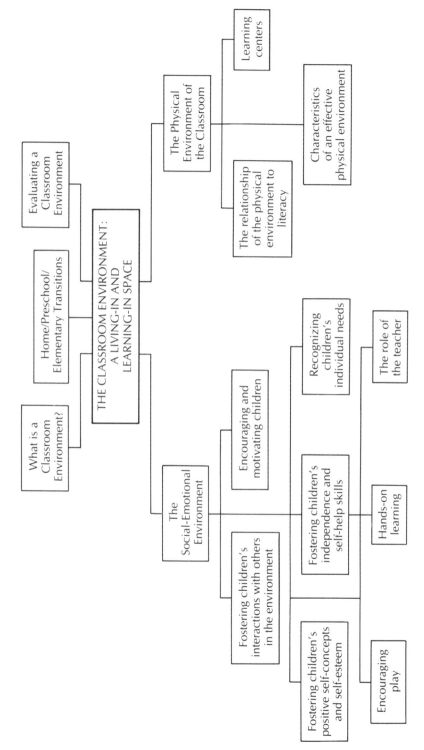

THE CLASSROOM ENVIRONMENT: A LIVING-IN AND LEARNING-IN SPACE

- What is a Classroom Environment?
- Home/Preschool/Elementary Transitions
- Evaluating a Classroom Environment

The Physical Environment of the Classroom
- Learning centers
- The relationship of the physical environment to literacy
- Characteristics of an effective physical environment

The Social-Emotional Environment
- Encouraging and motivating children
- Fostering children's interactions with others in the environment
- Recognizing children's individual needs
- Fostering children's independence and self-help skills
- The role of the teacher
- Hands-on learning
- Fostering children's positive self-concepts and self-esteem
- Encouraging play

- describe how a teacher can promote and encourage play and hands-on learning,
- explain the relationship between the physical environment and children's learning and literacy development,
- name the typical learning centers found in early childhood classrooms and describe how each promotes children's literacy development,
- evaluate a classroom environment using suggested questions.

What Is a Classroom Environment?

Think of the preschool and primary classrooms you've observed. Some of these environments were attractive, comfortable and full of activities and materials to foster emergent literacy. They looked like fun, friendly places for both children and teachers. Other classrooms you have observed may have conveyed the message that these were not particularly "child-friendly" places. They may have been dark and dreary or so formal that one's overall impression was "Look, but do *not* touch." These classrooms were not the types of environments in which you would want children — or yourself — to spend a lot of time. The classroom environment is an essential component of the total early childhood program. It not only supports the curriculum but directly influences children's behavior and learning.

Classroom environment is a rather abstract concept and can include social-emotional and cognitive aspects as well as the physical features of a classroom. Gordon and Browne (1989) have defined *environment* as "the sum total of the physical and human qualities that combine to create a space in which children and adults work and play together" (p. 236). The total environment conveys messages to the children about the program and teachers from the child's very first encounter with the classroom. As one child remarked to his mother when first entering my kindergarten classroom years ago, "Kindergarten looks neat! I think I'll stay."

This chapter will focus on two aspects of the early childhood classroom environment: the social-emotional climate and the physical arrangement of the classroom. We will examine each aspect in the context of being rich literacy environments for preschool and primary children. The social-emotional environment should be a child-friendly one that helps foster children's positive self-concepts and their desire to learn and participate actively in the program while facilitating learning. The physical environment should reflect, support, and extend the curriculum and be an interesting, attractive, developmentally appropriate learning and living space for young children.

Children spend a great many of their waking hours in a classroom. A child will spend up to 7,000 hours in this environment by the end of elementary school and up to 15,000 hours by the end of high school (Fraser, 1986). It is part of the teacher's role to provide a classroom environment that is rich, relevant, and rewarding.

Home/Preschool/Elementary School Transitions

The classroom environment impacts on young children in many ways. Moving from home to preschool to elementary school usually means moving to increasingly more institutional settings. For many young children, this can be a problem. Parents have told me that their children are frightened by large institutional buildings (some children associate school buildings with going to the hospital or the dentist). For some children, entering a public school is the first time they will be in a large, multistoried building that isn't a department store! Young children are affected by the size and scale of the school building and its contents, arrangements, and organizational patterns (Cleve, Jowett, and Bate, 1982). Educational facilities for young children should be scaled to their needs (Esbensen, 1990).

Although the school building itself may be intimidating to young children, the classroom environment can be made more homelike, attractive, and welcoming. A classroom environment that says to them, "This space is designed for you and this is a space where you can live and learn comfortably" reduces their stress and anxiety and thus facilitates learning. Such an environment is planned and implemented with the children's needs — both group and individual — in mind.

The Social-Emotional Environment

Young children respond, both positively and negatively, to the social-emotional environment of the classroom. *Social-emotional environment* refers to the "feel," climate, tone, or atmosphere of the classroom as it relates to interpersonal relationships and learning. Young children have developmental needs that can be fostered by a supportive, appropriate, caring environment. Learning is easier and more pleasant for young children in a positive social-emotional environment.

Recall your previous experiences with preschool and primary classrooms and think of some adjectives that describe those you think were good social-emotional environments for young children. Probably many of your adjectives are the same as those included in reviews of the research. For example, some commonly used descriptors are *warm, supportive, pleasant, fair, democratic, personal, congenial,* and *understanding* (O'Neill, 1988). Another frequently used descriptor of early childhood environments is *nurturing,* which refers to a secure and stable place where children are free to communicate, make choices and decisions, take risks, and feel some control of their lives (Regan and Weininger, 1988).

Even young children can describe what is, to them, a good environment:

- "This school is different from my last one. It doesn't look and feel like a dungeon."
- "Even the principal's office makes you feel she cares about kids."
- "I wish our room was like the one across the hall. That teacher makes it look like a nice place to come into."
- "Our teacher? She likes to hear our ideas." (Jacobs, 1984, p. 68)

The following are characteristics of good social-emotional environments for young children:

1. Interactions with others and the development of social skills are fostered.
2. Children are encouraged and motivated.
3. Children's positive self-concepts and self-esteem are fostered.
4. Independence and self-help skills are promoted.
5. Children's individual differences and needs are recognized.
6. Play is facilitated and encouraged.
7. Hands-on learning is central to the curriculum, including the use of realia (real objects), resource people, and fieldtrips.
8. The teacher plays an active role in fostering a positive social-emotional environment that encourages young children's literacy development.

Fostering Children's Interactions with Others in the Environment

Learning and language are cumulative processes. We learn from and use language when interacting with other people and can thereby learn even more. As discussed in previous chapters, a rich, supportive environment for young children will foster such interactions and help promote children's literacy development. The interactions can involve other people, materials, and the physical environment.

There are many language and literacy activities during the typical week in an early childhood program where the teacher can encourage and facilitate children's interactions with each other, with older children, and with adults in the environment. At the beginning of the school year, the teacher can have the children play a name game or use a song to help them learn each other's names.

The teacher can also encourage children to play with other children in pairs, small groups, or larger groups (a well-arranged physical environment can help to facilitate this). For example, the teacher could teach two or three children how to play a game, such as Snakes and Ladders, Spill and Spell, or a lotto game; and when the children seem to be able to play the game, bow out of the game and ask another child to take his or her place and request that the original children teach the game to the new player. Not only can the children work on the concepts and skills related to a particular game (e.g., matching, rhyming, initial consonants, etc.), they can use language to explain the rules to a new player as well as to discuss any "interpretations" of the rules.

Children can benefit from their interaction with older children and adults. With many families in North America now having only one or two children, many children have not had experience interacting with an older sibling. One activity that can facilitate this is a buddy program (or cross-age tutoring), where an older child regularly reads to and talks with a younger child (see Chapter 4 for a description of this). Young children should also have opportunities to interact with adults outside of their families. Parents have told me that one of their major objectives for their child in attending an early childhood program is not only to socialize with other children but also to interact with other adults (Mayfield, 1989).

In many early childhood settings, there are other adults in addition to the classroom teacher who are available to interact with the children. For example, a nursery school may have parent volunteers; a daycare center may have several staff members; and a kindergarten or primary class may have regular contact with the school librarian, learning assistance teacher, teacher's aide, or principal. A classroom teacher can provide opportunities for young children to relate to adults on an individual basis, in small groups, and as a large group several times during the week: for example, trips to the local public or school library to hear the librarian tell stories, volunteers in the classroom reading to the children or playing games with them or acting as scribes.

A teacher of young children needs to try and find time each day to talk to each child on an individual basis. It means a great deal to a child if you ask him or her, "Is your Grandma still visiting with you?" or "What did you decide to name your new puppy?" This tells children that you see them as individuals and that you care about them and their lives. It is also a good opportunity to encourage oral language and to do some informal assessment of the children's language.

Encouraging and Motivating Children

It is not difficult to encourage and motivate most young children to learn. They are eager to try and make sense of their world and are continually interacting with it in a variety of ways. But children's motivation for literacy can vary.

One of the key generalizations about reading set out in *Becoming a Nation of Readers* is "Reading requires motivation" and "is one of the keys to learning to read" (Anderson, Hiebert, Scott, and Wilkinson, 1985, p. 14). Teachers of young children typically use a variety of motivators because not everything is equally motivating to all children, and what is motivating now may not be as motivating for a child in six months or even six days. The two general types of motivation are intrinsic and extrinsic.

With *intrinsic motivation*, "the reward for the activity seems to be part and parcel of the activity itself — there is no reward separate from the spontaneous feelings and thought that accompany the activity. . . . Curiosity, exploration, and play are examples of this type of activity" (Deci and Ryan, 1982, pp. 71–72). Most teachers of young children are generous with verbal praise and encouragement of children's efforts and try to reinforce children's developing literacy behaviors. A smile from the teacher is important to and valued by young children. Also, learning to do something new is motivating.

On the other hand, *extrinsic motivation* involves "working toward some external reward. . . . The behavior tends to be a means to some end rather than a part of the end" (Deci and Ryan, 1982, p. 72). For young children, extrinsic motivators might include stickers, happy faces, stars, extra time for a special activity such as a computer game, and so forth. According to Harris and Smith (1980), "One of the most fascinating challenges for the teacher is to combine the intrinsic and extrinsic forces that keep a child moving toward fluency and competency in reading. . . . There should be an interaction between internal and external forces" (p. 20).

There are many interesting activities that can motivate and encourage young children to engage in literacy experiences. One stimulating and motivating early literacy activity is to take children on a "reading walk" where they identify signs, logos, or print in the environment that they can read. Then take a Polaroid picture of some of these examples for display in the classroom or for the children to take home. Doing a class newsletter with the children's written stories to take home is another way of encouraging reading and writing. Some classrooms and schools have developed programs with certificates, school or peer recognition, or free books to foster children's reading and writing.

In Chapter 4, several ideas for encouraging literacy, such as sustained silent reading, teacher modeling of reading behaviors, and shared or buddy reading were described. Teachers can also use brief "book talks," during which they and/or the children show and describe books that may be of interest to others. Retelling stories, reading books, or sharing their own writings with another group of children or with each other on a regular basis can provide encouragement. Attractively displaying children's drawings and stories (written or dictated) in the classroom will send the message that their work has value and encourage them to read and write. A literacy center with varied and purposeful activities can also encourage young children to participate in reading and writing activities (see details later in this chapter). Providing children with the time to browse and learn about the local public library and the school library can help to promote interest in books.

Fostering Children's Positive Self-Concepts and Self-Esteem

Children's self-concepts are an integral part of the learning process. How children feel about themselves can influence how they learn, their attitudes toward new experiences, as well as their literacy abilities (Deeds, 1981). *Self-concept* can be defined as "the perceptions, feelings, and attitudes that a person has about himself or herself" (Marshall, 1989, p. 45). According to Briggs (1970), *self-esteem* "is a quiet sense of self-respect, a feeling of self-worth. When you have it deep inside, you're glad you are you" (p. 3).

The development of self-concept and self-esteem is a lifetime process; it begins at birth and continues to develop with life experiences. How a person feels about himself or herself results from an accumulation of experiences and feedback from people with whom he or she comes into contact (Beaty, 1988). Children's perceptions of themselves influence what they try to do or are willing to try.

A teacher needs to create an environment for young children that is a secure and comfortable one, where children know they can try things and say things and people will not put them down or call them names if they are not successful. Continued exposure to a negative environment can damage children's self-esteem (Kostelnik, Stein, and Whiren, 1988). A positive environment is where children are encouraged to try new experiences and, if not totally successful the first time, to try again, knowing that the people around them will be supportive, encouraging, and will value their efforts.

Many literacy activities can be used to foster young children's self-concepts and self-esteem. One such activity is to have the children draw or paint pictures of themselves and their families, followed by dictating or writing about their picture, and then perhaps sharing this with the entire group. Birthdays and missing teeth are two occasions when young children can be given recognition by the group and an opportunity for oral language if the child describes the experience to the rest of the children and the group then compares experiences. Some teachers have a "Special Day," which features one child. A similar activity is for the children to describe or write what they like best about each other. Their stories can be assembled and bound in book format.

A daily or weekly helper chart, where the children's names are posted next to jobs to be done in the classroom (e.g., help with snack, feed the fish, water the plants, take messages to other classrooms, distribute materials), assist the child in learning to read his or her name and those of the other children while providing an opportunity to take responsibility for a specific task and to receive positive reinforcement when the task is accomplished.

Labeling a child's cubby, locker, or desk with his or her name tells the child that he or she has ownership of space in the environment. By using an attendance chart, each child can find his or her name card (a picture and the child's name can be included for those less experienced with print) and place the card in a pocket chart first thing in the morning. The same procedure can be used to designate learning center choices.

Creative drama activities not only foster listening and speaking but can also be opportunities to discuss feelings of other people and themselves (e.g., "How do you think the three bears felt when they came home and saw what Goldilocks had done to their house? How would you feel if you were Momma Bear?"). Teachers' daily interactions with children can do much to foster positive self-concepts and increase self-esteem.

Fostering Children's Independence and Self-Help Skills

Young children derive pleasure and satisfaction from being able to say, "I can do that myself." Their gradually developing independence and self-sufficiency, in turn, reinforces their self-esteem and encourages them to try new tasks. Teachers can help foster this developing independence and self-sufficiency by teaching children strategies and skills they need to know to function more efficiently and effectively in the classroom environment. Even children as young as 3 years of age can be taught how to use an attendance check-in chart and how to operate a cassette tape player in a listening center. Older children can become proficient in the use of word-processing programs on a computer.

Arranging the classroom environment with the needs and abilities of the children in mind can help promote independence and self-help skills. Such a classroom will permit children to function as independent learners as much as is possible. If Alfredo wants to listen to a taped story on the cassette player, he is more likely to do so if the listening center is easily accessible and if he knows how to operate the cassette player by himself. If he has to ask for permission and for the materials and then wait for someone to operate the equipment for him, he'll be much less likely to listen to the cassette stories.

Recognizing Children's Individual Needs

Not all 4-year-olds are alike, nor are all 8-year-olds. Children of the same chronological age can be at different levels of development, and individuals can have different strengths and weaknesses. For example, Terri may have excellent fine motor skills and do beautiful drawings but may not have the level of social interaction skills that her peers do. Mikio may be reading much more fluently and independently than his classmates but his large motor skills may not be as well developed and he may be reluctant to particpate in playground games with his peers. Although knowledge of age-appropriate behaviors is important, knowledge of what is individually appropriate for each child is also important (Bredekamp, 1987).

The teacher's role is to be aware of each child's developmental levels and individual needs and to use materials and methods appropriate for that child at that time. This is not an easy task. There are many ways in which you can get to know about the children with whom you work. Some of the most frequently used methods are observation, talking with the children, questioning, and informal evaluation in the course of daily classroom activities. (Chapter 9 describes a variety of assessment strategies to identify children's abilities and needs.)

Encouraging Play

It is a truism in early childhood education that play is the way children learn. Play is a natural and normal activity of young children. It is pleasurable and self-sustaining, providing opportunities for children to practice skills and to learn new ones. Much that young children learn is acquired through play. Foster and Cissi may look as though they are not "really learning" much when they play in the sandbox, but much learning is happening. For example, they can be learning about sharing and turn-taking; the physical properties of sand and how this can change when water is added; new vocabulary (e.g., *funnel, sift, sieve, grains*); and relating stories of their personal experiences at the beach.

Sally, Maria, and Pierre, three grade 2 children, are playing in the dramatic play center set up as a bakery (the class is studying community helpers). During their play, the children read recipes from cookbooks, find ingredient containers, read labels, measure, take orders, design and decorate bakery boxes and bags, create advertisements, write receipts for purchases, and so forth.

Researchers have found that play is related to children's development of oral language (see Chapter 3); written language (Isenberg and Jacob, 1983); problem-solving (Cheyne and Rubin, 1983); creativity (Pepler, 1986); use of symbols (Pellegrini, 1985); prosocial behavior/social participation (Smith, Daglish, and Herzmark, 1981); and cognitive competence (Almy, 1968). After reviewing the literature on play, Rogers and Sawyers (1988) concluded that "the research clearly indicates that play can facilitate healthy development. Play may even provide the best context in which children grow and learn" (p. 71).

Teachers can do much to facilitate children's play. One thing teachers can do is to provide children with a variety of appropriate play materials, sufficient materials, and to see that these materials change frequently. In my experience, when children are no longer using a particular material or a particular learning center, it means that they are tired of it or have outgrown it and it is time for a change. The types of materials will also influence children's play. For example, including human figures with blocks may encourage children to make up more elaborate stories about their block constructions. Likewise, writing materials may encourage children to record information, make signs, detail their observations, write notes to each other, and so forth.

Another thing teachers can do is arrange space for children to play. The arrangement of space and materials affects children's play (Christie and Johnsen, 1987). It is difficult for children to make a road or a town out of building blocks or Legos when there is not enough space. Insufficient space is sometimes the cause of conflicts among children.

A third way in which teachers can facilitate children's play is to provide time for this activity. In many early childhood classrooms, there is a large block of time called *free play*. This typically refers to a time when children can self-select their own activities and materials and have sufficient time to use these materials to develop some of the complex play situations that are so stimulating for language development. An example of such an activity that you may have observed is children playing in a dramatic play center or with blocks.

A fourth way in which teachers can facilitate young children's play is to actually play with the children. A teacher can encourage children to participate, model language and play behaviors, support and encourage their efforts by questioning and positive comments, provide props, and so forth. The teacher's role is really one of facilitator and resource. Research has shown that this can be a very effective technique and can increase the complexity and quality of children's play (Smilansky, 1968).

Play is an important part of the school day for young children. While more play occurs at the preschool level than at any other level of school (Christie and Johnsen, 1987), children continue to play throughout elementary school (King, 1987). Play can provide many opportunities for meaningful and authentic literacy experiences and therefore "opportunities for children to engage in literacy-related dramatic play should be considered an essential component of early childhood language arts programs" (Christie, 1990, p. 545).

Hands-on Learning

Young children learn by doing and by manipulating materials in their environment. Children's learning is an interactive process. The use of materials and activities that are concrete, real, and relevant to children's lives facilitates their learning (Bredekamp, 1987). Hands-on experiences also lay the foundation for children's later learning and help them to understand the meaning of symbols, such as letters and numbers.

This learning is facilitated by providing real objects for children to manipulate (e.g., sand, battery-operated telephones, regular-size plates and pots for

Hands-on learning with real objects at the exploration center

the dress-up corner, etc.) as well as providing opportunities for children to experience the community in which they live through frequent neighborhood walks and fieldtrips (e.g., public library, zoo, museums, shopping mall, parks, recreation centers, post office, clinic, grocery store, fire station, farm, children's theater). Much language learning can result from fieldtrips, from the planning stage to the reporting stage (the language learning on one fieldtrip was described in Chapter 1).

It is not always possible to take children to places related to the current curriculum. Another option, however, is to invite resource people to come and talk with the children. The children's parents can provide much knowledge and experience, which can enrich the early childhood curriculum. Often family members are willing to come to school and talk about their jobs or demonstrate a craft (e.g., pottery, wood carving, cooking an ethnic dish, etc.); read to a small group of children; or act as scribes in recording stories dictated by individual children (see Chapter 10 for more information on parent participation). People in the community (e.g., nurses, dentists, cashiers, veterinarians, truck drivers, engineers, computer programmers) are also potential resource people.

The Role of the Teacher

The teacher plays an active role in facilitating and fostering a positive social-emotional environment that encourages literacy development. Effective teachers can facilitate a positive social-emotional environment by both modeling and instruction. In language arts, they can do this by reading to the children, letting the children see them read, being scribes for the children's stories, and using writing during the day for jotting notes to the children and to themselves. They also model listening and speaking behaviors, such as listening attentively and courteously to a child, using good grammar, emphasizing fun new vocabulary words, and calling children's attention to new words in stories that they read or are read to them. Good teachers also model curiosity, love of learning, and interest in one's surroundings. They demonstrate respect for and sensitivity to each individual child and encourage children's independence, self-help skills, and risk taking: e.g., for some children, reading a story they have written to the class or participating in a creative dramatics activity for the first time are risk-taking activities. Such teachers also encourage children to use language to make known their wants and to resolve problems; for example, "Whose turn it is to feed the hamster? Whose turn is it to use the computer?". Teachers can create an atmosphere conducive to sharing thoughts and feelings in a variety of developmentally appropriate ways through literacy activities.

The Physical Environment of the Classroom

The physical environment of the classroom is an important part of the total early childhood program. It is the setting for the program and the place where children spend a considerable part of their days. The physical environment should be an interesting, attractive, developmentally appropriate learning and living space for young children.

The physical environment directly affects young children's behavior and learning (Taylor and Vlastos, 1975). The size and arrangement of the classroom space can affect children's behavior by conveying subtle messages to children about what is appropriate or not and what is expected of them. For example, materials stored on low-level, open shelves tell children "Help yourself." Materials stored in tall cupboards behind closed doors say "Don't touch. Ask an adult if you need something."

Researchers who have looked at the size of early childhood classrooms report that in crowded classrooms, children are less involved and show more aggressive behaviors (Shapiro, 1975; Smith and Connolly, 1976); were less attentive (Krantz and Risley, 1972); and teachers used more controlling behaviors toward the children (Perry, 1977). The National Association for the Education of Young Children Information Service (1989) suggests 35 square feet per child (3.25 m²) as the minimum amount of indoor space and recommends 40–50 square feet per child (3.7 m² to 4.65 m²). The size of an individual area within a classroom can also affect children's behavior. Smaller enclosed areas can encourage quiet activities and interaction among a small group, while larger spaces allow for large-group activities, more boisterous play, and higher noise levels (Phyfe-Perkins, 1980). However, even small areas should be large enough to accommodate not only individuals but small groups of children in order to promote social interaction, cooperative play, and collaborative learning.

The type of classroom space as well as the amount of space influence the children's behavior and interactions. Different classroom areas tend to encourage different types of behavior. For example, there is typically more cooperative and dramatic play in a housekeeping corner and more solitary and parallel play with puzzles (Phyfe-Perkins, 1980). Different learning centers can also elicit different types of language functions (Pellegrini, 1983).

The physical environment also affects children's choices of activities (Morrow and Weinstein, 1982, 1986; Phyfe-Perkins, 1980; Weinstein, 1977). Choice is dependent on what and how much is available in the environment and how it is displayed. Children interact with different materials in different ways and for differing lengths of time.

The Relationship of the Physical Environment to Literacy

An effective physical environment can help promote young children's literacy development. As discussed in previous chapters, children who spend their time in a print-rich environment, whether at home or in school, are being exposed to reading and writing in a natural, nonthreatening, nonpressured manner. Literacy activities are found throughout the classroom in many learning centers, not just in the book corner. For example, the inclusion and use of writing materials in a housekeeping corner encourages taking telephone messages, noting down grocery lists, penning invitations to parties, making a For Sale sign, copying a recipe, and so forth. Similarly, the inclusion of writing materials in the science center encourages older children to make notes and drawings of their observations and experiments. If we wish to help children develop literacy, they must have access to literate environments (Hall, 1987).

Characteristics of an Effective Physical Environment

Although there is no one best way to arrange an early childhood classroom, the following are some general characteristics of effective physical environments:

1. There are well-defined areas.
2. The setting and materials are appropriate for young children.
3. The classroom is attractive to children and comfortable for them.
4. The space is flexible and usable in a variety of ways.
5. The physical environment reflects the curriculum and the children's interests and needs.
6. A variety of materials are available and accessible.

Well-defined areas   To help young children organize their activities and see relationships, materials are usually grouped together and placed in an area designed for those materials. Such an arrangement helps children focus on what they are doing with more active involvement, better concentration, and less distraction. A well-defined area also conveys to the children information about where and how these materials may be used and thus affects children's behavior. Continued contact with a well-organized, well-planned environment can help children become more independent and productive.

I remember observing a boy make a valentine in a grade 1 classroom. First, he went to the shelf and took a piece of red construction paper, then he went across the room to get a pencil and some crayons, which he took back to the table where he chose to work. After he sat down, he noticed that the pencil needed sharpening so he got up and walked to another part of the room to sharpen the pencil. Before he actually began to write a message on his valentine, he decided he needed a ruler, so he got up and walked over to yet another area of the room to look for a ruler in a drawer. When he couldn't find it there, he looked on a nearby shelf and then gave up and asked the teacher. Because all of these materials were not conveniently located in one area (e.g., the writing center), this child spent more time looking for the materials he needed than he spent writing his valentine.

Areas of the classroom can be made visually significant for children in numerous ways. Bookcases or shelves positioned perpendicularly to a wall help define an area as well as provide additional display space on the back of the unit. A piece of carpeting can be used to define an area; this is particularly useful in a block center, as it helps the children keep their block structure in bounds as well as muffling the noise of falling blocks. Colored electrical tape can also be used to mark out a space for a particular area (a science area or a parking lot for the wheeled toys).

Areas appropriate for young children   When planning a physical environment for young children, the needs and characteristics of the children must be considered. Child-sized furniture and developmentally appropriate materials are essential if children are to be able to manage without adult help. The space must also be safe for children. This includes the arrangement of clear and safe traffic patterns in the classroom as well as clear sight lines (so adults are able to see easily all areas of the room and be aware of what each child is doing). Hazardous objects and materials (e.g., cleaning solutions) should be placed in spaces not accessible to children.

In addition to having materials and furnishings that are appropriate for the children, there should be a sufficient amount of materials and a variety of materials, which are stored and displayed in such a way as to be readily accessible to the children (the contents of individual areas is discussed later in this chapter and the selection of materials is discussed in Chapter 8). The availability and accessibility of materials also influence children's behavior and learning. Accessible shelves provide children with the opportunity to select their own toys quickly and get down to their play sooner (Montes and Risley, 1975). Fewer materials for the children to share can result in both more sharing (Rohe and Patterson, 1974) as well as more aggressive behavior and stress (Smith and Connolly, 1980). Also, arrangements that restrict children's access to materials increase the supervisory duties of the teachers (Pollowy, 1974). Availability and placement of materials and equipment can be one of the most effective predictors of program quality (Kritchevsky and Prescott, 1969).

Attractive and comfortable space   Both children and adults appreciate spending their time in an environment that is pleasant. Children like an environment that is visually interesting and stimulating without being overly stimulating. Young children are responsive to color and like the primary colors (Adams, 1987; Utzinger, 1970). This does not mean that the classroom should be painted orange, purple, pink, and red, as was suggested by one group of 9-year-olds (Anderson, 1971). The usual advice is that "wall surfaces should be light in tone and subdued, though not drab" (Smith, Niesworth, and Greer, 1978, p. 134). Bright colors can be used effectively for accents and can also be used to code areas or sets of materials that belong together. If all the storage containers in one learning center are the same color, it is easy for the children to know where to return materials.

Other environmental considerations when planning a physical environment for young children include adequate natural and artificial lighting without glare; a comfortable level of heat, especially at the floor level where many

Materials should be available and easily accessible on shelves.

young children prefer to work and play; and good ventilation and air circulation to prevent that stuffy, sleepy feeling in the afternoons. The floor covering should be warm, attractive, and easy to keep clean. There should also be a variety of surfaces: for example, wall-to-wall carpeting for part of the room; vinyl flooring for the art and messy areas; and smaller carpets to help delineate areas such as the literacy center or the block area. Textures can also be used with colors, surfaces, levels, and lines to create visual interest (Campbell, 1984).

The addition of noninstitutional furniture and furnishings, such as rocking chairs, floor pillows, and stuffed furniture, can add needed softness to many classrooms that are seen by children as being very institutional and not very warm and friendly. A reading corner with carpeting and big pillows to stretch out on seems much more inviting to a young child than a reading area equipped with the traditional library table and hard wooden chairs!

Flexible and usable space   Unfortunately, the space in the average classroom is finite: the teacher cannot expand it whenever he or she would like more space. There should be space available in the classroom for a variety of activities including whole-group activities, such as sharing or meeting time, creative drama, and music and movement. If such a space is not readily available, many times these activities are omitted. Rather than omit activities that are valuable in developing literacy skills and are enjoyed by the children, the teacher needs to plan a flexible and convenient arrangement that can provide a large space with relatively little effort (e.g., the children can help move a few tables and chairs while the teacher moves the heavier pieces).

The classroom arrangement should never be permanently "set." There should be flexibility to change and rearrange. Sometimes if there is a problem with traffic patterns or children are having conflicts because of inadequate or poorly arranged space, one can use the conflict as an opportunity for oral language and problem solving by having the children discuss what the problem is and what are some possible solutions. I have found that even quite young children have some very good ideas on arranging space more efficiently and attractively; after all, they are the ones who use the space on a daily basis.

Reflection of the curriculum and children's interests and needs   Ideally, it should be apparent upon entering an early childhood classroom for the first time what is being studied. Pictures, stories, children's drawings, and other displays reinforce the children's learning and provide literacy experiences for the children. A classroom should be a functional reading and writing environment (Harste, 1989). Examples of this functional environment could include experience charts related to the current or recent themes, children's drawings with their written or dictated captions or stories, a chart with that week's recipe for cooking, the daily schedule, charts and posters related to children's interests, directions for using audiovisual equipment, the daily "News Flash," or the joke-of-the-day.

The classroom environment should include sufficient display space so that the children's work can be displayed. This not only reinforces the concepts being learned but also tells the children that their work is important and that it is valued. A classroom that only has teachermade or commercial materials on display tells the children that nothing they do will ever be good enough to be shown. The display of the children's work adds to the aesthetics of the classroom, indicates their ownership of classroom space, and provides interesting materials for the children to read. These displays of children's work can be referred to during teaching; for example, "Let's take a look at the painting Jane did and see if there are more red ducks or more yellow ducks," or "Let's review Louisa's and Jeff's list of animals that hibernate."

A variety of materials   There should be variety in the types of materials to accommodate children's individual interests and abilities. For example, it is not unusual in a preschool or primary class to have children for whom English is a second language, children with limited experience with books and reading models, as well as children who can recognize a few words and children who are reading fluently. The same books and materials will not appeal to nor be appropriate for all these children.

There should also be sufficient materials, as young children typically use a wide variety of materials and participate in many activities in the classroom during the day. According to Rosenthal (1974), during a one hour, free play period, preschoolers averaged approximately 20 changes in activities, visited approximately half of 13 learning centers, and were idle for less than 3 minutes!

Learning Centers

What is a learning center? A *learning center* "occupies a defined area in the room and relates to a specific theme, topic, or skill. The learning activities instruct, reinforce, or enrich a child's knowledge in that particular area" (Norton, 1989, p. 600). A learning center may also be termed an *interest center, activity area, play center,* or an *activity zone.*

Most early childhood classrooms contain one or more learning centers. Some classrooms may have only a library corner and maybe an arts and crafts center, while other classrooms may have six or more learning centers. Ideally, "many learning centers are available for children to choose from. Many centers include opportunities for writing and reading, for browsing through books, reading silently, or sharing a book with a friend; a listening station; and places to practice writing stories and to play math or language games" (Bredekamp, 1987, p. 68).

An effective learning center will be attractive to children and encourage them to explore actively and use the materials in that center. A well-planned center has a variety of materials at differing developmental levels to permit several children of differing abilities to use the center at the same time in cooperative activities: for example, a dramatic play center set up as travel agency or an experiment sprouting seeds in the science center. Learning centers can provide opportunities for individualized instruction based on the instructional goals for and the individual needs of each child. They can facilitate independent work by allowing children to self-select and to develop their particular interests while at the same time fostering independence in learning.

Typical learning centers found in early childhood programs include (see Figure 7-1):

- literacy center
- dramatic play center
- manipulative toys and games center
- construction and modeling center
- art center
- music center
- exploration center
- other centers, such as a quiet place, sand, water, woodworking, and cooking.

Literacy center A *literacy center,* also called a *language center,* provides children with opportunities and materials to develop listening, speaking, reading, and writing. It typically includes a listening and viewing center, a library area, and materials for writing. This combination reflects the integrated nature of the language arts and their place in the curriculum. It has been suggested that "the literacy center can occupy at least one quarter of the wall space in a classroom" (Morrow, 1989, p. 173).

As with other learning centers, the literacy center should be attractive for children and equipped with sufficient materials to accommodate children's individual needs and interests. A well-designed, appealing literacy area can in-

FIGURE 7-1 • *Floorplan for an Early Childhood Classroom with Learning Centers*

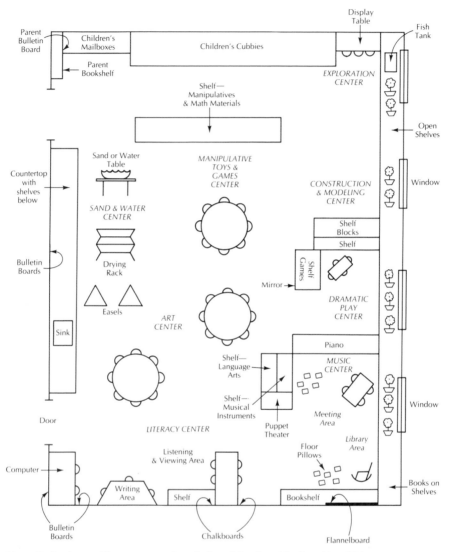

Note: Desks clustered in groups may be substituted for the tables for older children.

crease the numbers of children who choose to use that area (Morrow, 1987; Morrow and Weinstein, 1986), whereas a poorly designed literacy center is among the least popular areas (Morrow, 1982). Literacy centers should be spacious, well lighted, comfortable, and well organized. There should be tables and chairs for children to work at, shelves for displaying books and storing materials, electrical outlets for audiovisual equipment, display space for the children's work, posters about books and reading, a chalkboard, a puppet theater, a flannelboard, and soft furnishings (e.g., floor pillows, a sofa, an easy chair, and carpeting).

A key component of the literacy center is the library area. Researchers have found that children read more and are more interested in reading in classrooms with a library corner (Coody, 1983; Huck, 1976). The literacy center should have a good supply of a variety of children's books. According to Huck, Hepler, and Hickman (1987), "If we want children to become readers we must surround them with books of all kinds. We know that wide reading is directly related to accessibility; the more books available and the more time for reading, the more reading children will do" (p. 641).

The books should reflect a variety of topics, levels, and types (e.g., stories, poetry, nonfiction, etc.). It is also important to change the books frequently so there is always something new and exciting on the bookshelf as well as some old favorites (see Chapter 4 for suggestions). A classroom aide or parent volunteer can take a small group of children to the school and/or public library on a weekly basis to return books and select new ones. The children can take "orders" for books from the other children when it is their turn to return the library books. It is suggested that 25 books be replaced every two weeks (Strickland and Morrow, 1988).

The books should be displayed attractively on shelves with the covers facing outward whenever possible. Young children really do judge a book by its cover! In addition to trade books, the library area can include children's magazines (e.g., *Highlights, Owl, Chickadee,* etc.), child-made books, photo albums of class activities, catalogs, newspapers, big books, picture dictionaries and other reference materials (children enjoy looking at the pictures in National Geographic, Time/Life and Childcraft publications long before they can read the text).

A listening center is typically a small area, but one that pays big dividends in promoting children's interest in books and reading while developing their listening skills. The children can listen to cassette tapes of books (commercially available or recorded by the teacher and/or parent volunteers), music, instructions for activities, authors reading their own poetry, and recordings that the children make themselves. If there are multiple copies of the book, three or four children can use the tape or record at the same time. A listening center can include a cassette player, headsets and a jack, tapes, a record player and records. A near-by flannelboard with felt figures or puppets can be used for retelling the story, and accessible writing materials permit children to draw or write their ideas resulting from the tape. With the addition of filmstrips, a filmstrip projector, and a viewmaster, this center becomes a listening and viewing area.

Another key part of the literacy center is the writing materials. Children use this area to draw pictures, make greeting cards, write messages, make captions for their drawings, write stories or letters, and experiment with print and writing. (Children's writing development is discussed in Chapter 5.) A writing area could include—

- a variety of writing tools: e.g., pencils of differing diameters, fine and wide felt-tip markers, crayons, chalk and a chalkboard;
- a variety of paper: e.g., lined and unlined paper, newsprint, colored construction paper, computer print-out paper, typing paper, envelopes;
- a computer for word processing or a primary typewriter (children's typewriters are usually not sturdy enough for classroom use), magic slates, individual chalkboards, letter-stamp sets and ink pads, magnetic letters;
- materials for bookmaking: e.g., staplers, a hole punch, yarn, glue, a book of wallpaper samples for use as covers, paste, tape, scissors (see Appendix B for bookmaking instructions);
- other materials to assist children in their writing: e.g., key-word cards, sentence strips, pocket charts, labels from containers, picture dictionaries, childmade dictionaries, teachermade dictionaries or word lists, published dictionaries, bulletin board space to display their writing.

Some of these materials can be gathered together and placed in a small suitcase, bag, or a writer's briefcase for the children to take home overnight or over the weekend (Rich, 1985; Wrobleski, 1990). A class mailbox of individual mailboxes can encourage children to write while reinforcing the communicative function of print (Hayes, 1990) (see Figure 7-2).

Dramatic play center   The importance of children's play in their literacy development was discussed earlier in this chapter and Chapter 3. A dramatic play center is one effective way to promote children's play and literacy development. Some of children's best experiences with literacy are connected with dramatic play (Hall, 1987).

The traditional housekeeping corner contains items such as child-sized tables, chairs, mops, brooms, and kitchen appliances (the sink can have real taps and the stove real knobs for more authenticity), regular-sized dishes, pots, and pans. Dolls, stuffed toys, a mirror and dress-up clothes including jewelry, handbags, hats, and capes can also be included in a dramatic play corner.

The language potential of the traditional housekeeping corner can be increased and the area given new meaning for children with the addition of literacy materials (Schrader, 1989). These materials can include telephones (battery-operated if possible), magazines, paper and pencils (for grocery lists, notes, cards, etc.), empty food boxes and tins (recognition and reading of logos and directions, brand names, etc.), signs, price tags, play money, a cash register, paper grocery bags, coupons, cookbooks, recipe cards, a telephone directory, and so forth.

FIGURE 7-2 • *Classroom Mailboxes Made from Shoeboxes*

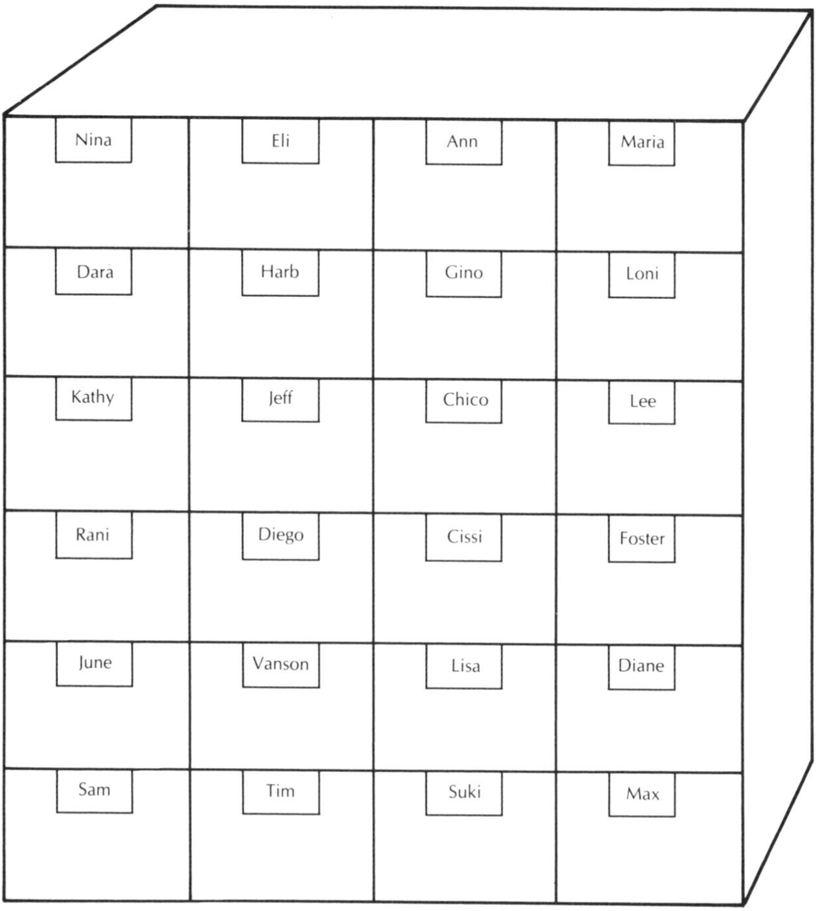

Nina	Eli	Ann	Maria
Dara	Harb	Gino	Loni
Kathy	Jeff	Chico	Lee
Rani	Diego	Cissi	Foster
June	Vanson	Lisa	Diane
Sam	Tim	Suki	Max

Note: Classroom mailboxes can also be made from cardboard tubing or milk cartons, which have been rinsed and dried.

The dramatic play center should change throughout the year and can become a grocery store, train station, bank, restaurant, post office, office, fix-it shop, beauty shop, hat shop, shoe store, space station, hospital (for people or dolls), flower shop, bakery, McDonald's, or a travel bureau. Many of these suggested centers are appropriate for use with primary level children as well as with preschoolers.

Manipulative toys and games center   The manipulative toys and games center also provides children with the opportunity and materials for social and literacy activities. Board games, such as lotto, and card games can be used to foster visual discrimination, vocabulary development, word recognition, or rhyming. Materials such as pegboards, beads, table games, and other materials also help to develop children's fine motor skills and eye-hand coordination. Many of the activities found in this center also lend themselves to cooperative play and collaborative learning. Typical materials include puzzles, posting box, geoboards, stacking/nesting boxes, abacus, sewing cards, magnetic shapes, dominoes, card games, board games, and so forth.

Construction and modeling center(s)   A construction and modeling center (or two separate centers) encourages children's creative play as well as the manipulation of different materials. These activities can foster children's imaginations, sensory awareness, fine motor skills, and use of multiple media and language as they plan, make, and discuss their creations and invent stories or perhaps incorporate the material they make (e.g., boats or hats) into their dramatic play. Children will also play cooperatively with much social interaction and oral language when building with blocks and will invent stories to accompany their creations. They will also use written language to write stories or make signs for their creations (e.g., Fire Hall, Expressway, For Sale, Do Not Touch). The addition of small wooden or plastic people, animals, and natural objects (e.g., small rocks, sticks, pieces of wood) can increase the amount and complexity of the children's language during block play.

Some materials typically found in the construction and modeling areas are: unit blocks, larger cardboard bricks, cuisenaire rods, unifix cubes, parquetry blocks, Lego/Duplo blocks, attribute blocks, play dough, plasticene, cookie cutters, rolling pins, popsicle sticks, child-safe knives, paper and fabric scraps, glue, tape, paper plates, yarn, string, small boxes and containers, cardboard rolls, egg cartons, and so forth.

Art center   Art is important in young children's development, not only in fostering their creativity and aesthetic awareness, but also as a contributor to their literacy development. A child who is drawing or painting is a symbol user, and there are developmental links between pictures, play, and print (Dyson, 1990).

While painting or drawing, children will often describe what they are doing or tell or write a story about their picture or a character or object in that picture. One 4-year-old child in my class invented an ongoing illustrated saga of the adventures of a nose! In addition, many of the strokes and marks children make while drawing and painting are the same or similar to the strokes used in conventional writing.

Children doing many art activities, such as cutting with scissors, are using the same fine motor movements that are needed for printing and writing. Many art activities are excellent for fostering the further development and refinement of fine motor abilities and eye-hand coordination as well a providing children with the opportunity to use oral and written language.

Some materials typically found in the art center include: crayons, felt-tip pens, colored chalk/pastels, assorted paper, scissors, paste, glue, tape, string, a stapler, two double-sided easels (for a class of 25 children), paint, brushes, pieces of sponge, objects for block printing, Q-tips, toothbrushes, pipe cleaners, and so forth. Many art centers also include reproductions or original artwork for the children to look at, stimulate their imaginations, reflect upon, and discuss or write about if they wish. In my experience, even children as young as 3 have some interesting ideas and comments on works by famous artists, such as Picasso. In many communities, the public library, art gallery, or school district will loan original works of art to classrooms. This is especially beneficial for the children if the artist is from that community and can visit the classroom and describe how he or she created that particular piece.

Music center　As with art, the music area can stimulate children's imaginations and provide opportunities to use language and develop vocabularies. Music helps develop children's listening skills (e.g., auditory discrimination, auditory memory, listening for enjoyment, listening to follow directions, etc.) as well as oral language when the children talk about or respond to what they have heard.

Some materials typically found in a music area include: rhythm instruments (e.g., triangles, tambourines, drums, rhythm sticks, sand blocks, maracas, gourds, bells, castanets); homemade instruments; Orff instruments; tone blocks; sound cans; kazoos; movement materials (e.g., scarves, streamers on a ring, etc.); big-book type songbooks; and song charts.

Exploration center　An exploration or investigation or science center provides young children with the opportunity to problem solve while discovering basic concepts through hands-on manipulation. This center helps children to understand the more abstract concepts related to science and math through observation, experimentation, and manipulation of concrete objects. As children are using this center, they will often ask questions of one another and comment on what they are doing. Judicious questioning by the teacher can also stimulate additional language and problem solving.

Some materials typically found in an exploration center include: magnets, iron filings, mirrors, magnifying glasses, a microscope, binoculars, prisms, a tuning fork, scales and weights, an eggtimer, a clock, touch-and-feel bags/boxes, rocks, shells, seeds, plants, measuring cups, a thermometer, calculators, an abacus, and a variety of collections for sorting and classifying (e.g., buttons, shells, marbles, coins). This center can also be the location for a terrarium, aquarium, or a class pet.

Other centers　Other centers that are often found in early childhood classrooms include a quiet area (i.e., a small, private space where a child can get away by him- or herself for a short period of time), a sand-and-water area, a woodworking center, a cooking center, and a puppet theater with a variety of puppets. Of course, the outdoors also provides a great many opportunities for learning.

Evaluating a Classroom Environment

Although the classroom environment does not make a successful program in and of itself, it is important for the teacher to be aware of, attend to, and assess the early childhood classroom environment. Changes in the environment can result in changes in children's and teachers' behavior (Weinstein, 1977), and thus these changes can be used as a teaching strategy to improve the program. The information in Box 7-1 may help you to plan and evaluate an effective classroom environment.

A physical environment that is thoughtfully planned and carefully arranged can do much to enhance a program. A good physical classroom environment does not just happen — it takes planning and attention to details. Such an environment will expose children to a variety of literacy experiences, provide lots of materials for them to work with, encourage oral and written language, and

---

BOX 7-1 · *Questions for Evaluating a Classroom Learning Environment*

After a classroom environment has been established, a good practice is to review the characteristics of effective environments to be certain nothing has been overlooked or been neglected. Then after the classroom environment has been in use for a while, a good idea is to evaluate the environment to find out how it can be improved. The following sets of questions are not meant to be a definitive list but are suggestions you might consider in assessing both the strengths and weaknesses of a classroom environment. The questions can be utilized by individual teachers or by a small group of teachers working together.

The Social-Emotional Environment

1. Do the children seem happy to enter the environment?
2. Are the children active and interacting with others throughout the day?
3. Is there mutual respect and tolerance between children and adults and among the children themselves?
4. Do the teachers support and encourage the children's endeavors without being interfering?
5. Are the children encouraged to cooperate with others in the environment and to work in small and large groups as well as on their own?
6. Do the teachers have goals and ideas for each child that are appropriate for that child's developmental level and accommodate that child's individual strengths and weaknesses?
7. Are children aware of the classroom routines and rules and have had input into their formation?
8. Do the teachers and other adults in the environment model appropriate behavior and language for the children?
9. Is the environment accepting and accommodating of a range of children's family, ethnic, and cultural backgrounds?

The Physical Environment

1. Is the classroom attractive, safe, clean and well organized?
2. Is the classroom arrangement and its contents appropriate for the children?
3. Does the classroom reflect the curriculum and the children's interests and needs?

4. Is the children's work displayed?
5. Are the various areas well defined and accessible?
6. Can the children move around the areas easily? Are the traffic patterns efficient and clear?
7. Can the teacher see easily all areas of the room?
8. Is there adequate space for the activities and centers?
9. Is it possible to rearrange the room as needed (i.e., versatility and flexibility)?
10. Is there sufficient space for the whole class to gather together at one time? Are there also smaller spaces?
11. Is the storage efficient, convenient, attractive, and well organized for children and adults?
12. Does the content of each center change frequently enough to keep the children's interest?
13. Are there both structured and open-ended materials and materials that foster the development of a range of skills and interests?
14. Is the room comfortable (e.g., heating, lighting, ventilation)?
15. Are the furnishings and equipment appropriate for the children?
16. Does each child have an individual storage space?
17. Is there a quiet space where a child can get away from the group?
18. Are quieter and noisier areas separated?
19. Are all of the areas of the room being used by the children? Which areas are used the most? The least?

The following sets of questions relate to the assessment specifically of the literacy center and the dramatic play center. The reader can develop similar sets of questions for use in assessing other centers.

Literacy Center

1. Is the area well defined, accessible, and well organized?
2. Is there a variety of materials (e.g., books, tapes, magazines, books written by the children, pictures, etc.) at a variety of levels?
3. Do the contents of the literacy center reflect, support, and extend the ongoing program?
4. Are the materials attractively and efficiently displayed and stored?
5. Is there a sufficient number and variety of books, writing materials, and other supporting materials?
6. Are the materials and equipment in good condition?
7. Can the audiovisual and other equipment be operated by the children without adult help or direct supervision?
8. Is the area well lighted and comfortable?
9. Is there sufficient, comfortable seating and space to work?
10. Is the center used regularly by all the children?

Dramatic Play Area

1. Is the area well defined, accessible, and well organized?
2. Is there a variety and sufficient amount of materials available?
3. Is there sufficient space for several children and the materials?
4. Is the center changed periodically to reflect the curriculum and the children's interest and needs?
5. Is the area attractive and comfortable?
6. Are the materials appealing to and used by both boys and girls?
7. Are the materials, equipment, and furniture appropriate for the children?
8. Do the available materials encourage imaginative play?
9. Are there materials incorporated into the dramatic play center that encourage literacy development?

thereby foster their overall literacy development. And although the environment of an early childhood classroom is an essential component, it is the teacher and children interacting with one another in the context of a good physical environment that creates an effective and desirable learning environment for young children.

References

Adams, R. J. (1987). An evaluation of color preferences in early infancy. *Infant Behavior and Development, 10*(2), 143–150.

Almy, M. (1968). Spontaneous play: An avenue for intellectual development. In M. Almy (Ed.), *Early childhood play: Selected readings related to cognition and motivation,* (pp. 8–21). New York: Simon and Schuster.

Anderson, R. H. (1971). The school as an organic teaching aid. In R. M. McClure (Ed.), *In the curriculum: Retrospect and prospect* (70th Yearbook of the NSSE, Part 1, pp. 271–306). Chicago: University of Chicago Press.

Anderson, R. C., Hiebert, E. H., Scott, J. A., & Wilkinson, I. A. G. (1985). *Becoming a nation of readers: The report of the Commission on Reading.* Washington, DC: The National Institute of Education.

Beaty, J. J. (1988). *Skills for preschool teachers* (3rd ed.). Columbus, OH: Merrill Publishing Company.

Bredekamp, S. (Ed.). (1987). *Developmentally appropriate practice in early childhood programs serving children from birth through age 8.* Washington, DC: National Association for the Education of Young Children.

Briggs, D. C. (1970). *Your child's self-esteem.* Garden City, NY: Doubleday & Company.

Campbell, S. D. (1984). *Facilities and equipment for day care centres.* Ottawa: Health and Welfare Canada.

Cheyne, J., & Rubin, K. (1983). Playful precursors of problem solving in preschoolers. *Developmental Psychology, 19,* 577–584.

Christie, J. F. (1990). Dramatic play: A context for meaningful engagements. *The Reading Teacher, 43*(8), 542–545.

Christie, J. F., & Johnsen, E. P. (1987). Preschool play. In J. H. Block & N. R. King (Eds.), *School play: A source book* (pp. 109–142). New York: Teachers College Press.

Cleve, S., Jowett, S., & Bate, M. (1982). . . . *And so to school: A study of continuity from preschool to infant school.* Windsor, Berkshire, England: NFER-Nelson Publishing Company.

Coody, B. (1983). *Using literature with young children* (3rd ed.). Dubuque, IA: William C. Brown Company Publishers.

Deci, E. L., & Ryan, R. M. (1982). Curiosity and self-directed learning: The role of motivation. In L. G. Katz (Ed.), *Current topics in early childhood education* (Vol. 4, pp. 71–85). Norwood, NJ: Ablex Publishing Corporation.

Deeds, B. (1981). Motivating children to read through improved self-concept. In A. J. Ciani (Ed.), *Motivating reluctant readers* (pp. 78–89). Newark, DE: International Reading Association.

Dyson, A. H. (1990). Symbol makers, symbol weavers: How children link play, pictures, and print. *Young Children, 45*(2), 50–57.

Esbensen, S. B. (1990). Designing the early childhood setting. In I. M. Doxey (Ed.), *Child care and education: Canadian dimensions* (pp. 178–192). Scarborough, Ontario: Nelson Canada.

Fraser, B. J. (1986). Determinants of classroom psychosocial environments: A review. *Journal of Research in Childhood Education, 1*(1), 5-19.

Gordon, A. M., & Browne, K. W. (1989). *Beginnings and beyond: Foundations in early childhood education.* Albany, NY: Delmar Publishers Inc.

Hall, N. (1987). *The emergence of literacy.* Portsmouth, NH: Heinemann Educational Books.

Harris, L. A., & Smith, C. B. (1980). *Reading instruction: Diagnostic teaching in the classroom* (2nd ed.). New York: Holt, Rinehart, & Winston.

Harste, J. C. (1989). *New policy guidelines for reading: Connecting research and practice.* Urbana, IL: National Council of Teachers of English.

Hayes, L. F. (1990). From scribbling to writing: Smoothing the way. *Young Children, 45*(3), 62-68.

Huck, C. S. (1976). *Children's literature in the elementary school* (3rd ed.). New York: Holt, Rinehart, & Winston.

Huck, C. S., Hepler, S., & Hickman, J. (1987). *Children's literature in the elementary school* (4th ed.). New York: Holt, Rinehart, & Winston.

Isenberg, J., & Jacob, E. (1983). Literacy and symbolic play. *Childhood Education, 59,* 272-274.

Jacobs, L. B. (1984). Thoughts on creativity. *Early Years, 14*(6), 68.

King, N. R. (1987). Elementary school play: Theory and research. In J. H. Block & N. R. King (Eds.), *School play: A source book* (pp. 143-165). New York: Teachers College Press.

Kostelnik, M. J., Stein, L. C., & Whiren, A. P. (1988). Children's self-esteem: The verbal environment. *Childhood Education, 65*(1), 29-32.

Krantz, P., & Risley, T. (1972). *The organization of group care environments: Behavioral ecology in the classroom.* Lawrence, KS: University of Kansas. (ERIC Document Reproduction Service No. ED 078 915).

Kritchevsky, S., & Prescott, E. (1969). *Planning environments for young children: Physical space.* Washington, DC: National Association for the Education of Young Children.

Marshall, H. H. (1989). The development of self-concept. *Young Children, 44*(5), 44-51.

Mayfield, M. I. (1989, July). *Parent participation in three early childhood programs.* Paper presented at the XIXth World Congress of the World Organization for Early Childhood Education, London.

Montes, F., & Risley, T. R. (1975). Evaluating traditional daycare practices: An empirical approach. *Child Care Quarterly, 4,* 208-215.

Morrow, L. M. (1982). Relationships between literature programs, library corner designs and children's use of literature. *Journal of Educational Research, 75,* 339-344.

Morrow, L. M. (1987). Promoting voluntary reading: The effects of an inner-city program in summer daycare centers. *The Reading Teacher, 41,* 266-274.

Morrow, L. M. (1989). *Literacy development in the early years: Helping children read and write.* Englewood Cliffs, NJ: Prentice Hall.

Morrow, L. M., & Weinstein, C. S. (1982). Increasing children's use of literature through program and physical design changes. *The Elementary School Journal, 83,* 131-137.

Morrow, L. M., & Weinstein, C. S. (1986). Encouraging voluntary reading: The impact of a literature program on children's use of library centers. *Reading Research Quarterly, 21,* 330-346.

National Association for the Education of Young Children Information Service. (1989). *Facility design for early childhood programs: An NAEYC resource guide.* Washington, DC: Author.

Norton, D. E. (1989). *The effective teaching of language arts* (3rd ed.). Columbus, OH: Merrill Publishing Company.

O'Neill, G. P. (1988). Teaching effectiveness: A review of the research. *Canadian Journal of Education, 13*(1), 162–185.

Pellegrini, A. D. (1983). *The effects of classroom ecology on preschoolers' uses of functions of language.* Paper presented at Annual Conference of the American Educational Research Association, San Francisco.

Pellegrini, A. D. (1985). The relations between symbolic play and literate behavior: A review and critique of the empirical literature. *Review of Educational Research, 55*(1), 107–121.

Pepler, D. (1986). Play and creativity. In G. Fein & M. Rivkin (Eds.), *Reviews of Research* (Vol. 4, pp. 143–153). Washington, DC: National Association for the Education of Young Children.

Perry, G. (1977). *Cross-cultural study on the effect of space and teacher controlling behavior.* (ERIC Document Reproduction Service No. ED 131 351).

Phyfe-Perkins, E. (1980). Children's behavior in preschool settings: A review of research concerning the influence of the physical environment. In L. G. Katz (Ed.), *Current topics in early childhood education* (Vol. 3, pp. 91–125). Norwood, NJ: Ablex Publishing Corporation.

Pollowy, A. M. (1974). The child in the physical environment: A design problem. In G. Coates (Ed.), *Alternative learning environments* (pp. 370–381). Stroudsburg, PA: Dowden, Hutchinson & Ross.

Regan, E. M., & Weininger, O. (1988). Toward defining and defending child-centered curriculum and practice. *International Journal of Early Childhood, 20*(2), 1–10.

Rich, S. J. (1985). The writing suitcase. *Young Children, 40*(5), 42–44.

Rogers, C. S., & Sawyers, J. K. (1988). *Play in the lives of children.* Washington, DC: National Association for the Education of Young Children.

Rohe, W., & Patterson, A. H. (1974). The effects of varied levels of resources and density on behavior in daycare center. In D. H. Carson (Ed.), *Man-environment interactions: Evaluations and applications* (Part 3, pp. 161–171). Stroudburg, PA: Dowden, Hutchinson & Ross.

Rosenthal, B. A. (1974). An ecological study of free play in nursery school (Doctoral dissertation, Wayne State University, 1973). *Dissertation Abstracts International, 34*(7-A), 4004–4005. (University Microfilms No. 73-31, 773).

Schrader, C. T. (1989). Written language use within the context of young children's symbolic play. *Early Childhood Research Quarterly, 4*(2), 225–244.

Shapiro, S. (1975). Preschool ecology: A study of three environmental variables. *Reading Improvement, 12*(4), 236–241.

Smilansky, S. (1968). *The effects of sociodramatic play on disadvantaged preschool children.* New York: Wiley.

Smith, P. K., & Connolly, K. J. (1976). Social and aggressive behavior in preschool children as a function of crowding. *Social Science Information, 16,* 601–620.

Smith, P. K., & Connolly, K. J. (1980). *The ecology of preschool behavior.* Cambridge, England: Cambridge University Press.

Smith, P. K., Daglish, M., & Herzmark, G. (1981). A comparison of the effects of fantasy play tutoring and skills tutoring in nursery school. *International Journal of Behavioral Development, 4,* 421–441.

Smith, R. M., Neisworth, J. T., & Greer, J. G. (1978). *Evaluating educational environments.* Columbus, OH: Charles E. Merrill Publishing Company.

Strickland, D. S., & Morrow, L. M. (1988). Creating a print rich environment. *The Reading Teacher, 42*(2), 156–157.

Taylor, A. P., & Vlastos, G. (1975). *School zone: Learning environments for children.* New York: Van Nostrand Reinhold Company.

Utzinger, R. C. (1970). *Some European nursery schools and playgrounds.* Ann Arbor, MI: Architectural Research Laboratory of the University of Michigan.

Weinstein, C. S. (1977). Modifying student behavior in an open classroom through changes in physical design. *American Educational Research Journal, 14*(3), 249–262.

Wrobleski, L. C. (1990). The writer's briefcase. *Young Children, 45*(3), 69.

CHAPTER EIGHT

Organizing for Teaching and Learning

Advance Organizer

There are a variety of ways early literacy instruction can be organized. How instruction is organized affects teaching and learning. Previous chapters have discussed the curricular areas related to early literacy development and the classroom environment. In this chapter, we examine patterns of classroom organization, scheduling, and the selection and use of literacy materials. Criteria for scheduling and sample schedules are provided. Criteria for selecting materials and the teacher's role in selecting and using literacy materials effectively are discussed. We describe teacher-made, child-made and commercial materials, including computer hardware and software, basal reading series, and classroom displays.

Objectives

After studying this chapter, the reader should be able to—

- name and describe the different patterns of organization used in early childhood classrooms and give examples of literacy activities for each type of grouping;
- discuss the implications of grouping in terms of the effects on pupils and instruction;
- describe the characteristics of a good schedule for an early childhood program;
- give examples of literacy activities that occur throughout a typical day in preschool, kindergarten, and primary programs;
- list general criteria for the selection of materials and equipment;
- describe the teacher's role in the selection and use of materials;

Graphic Organizer

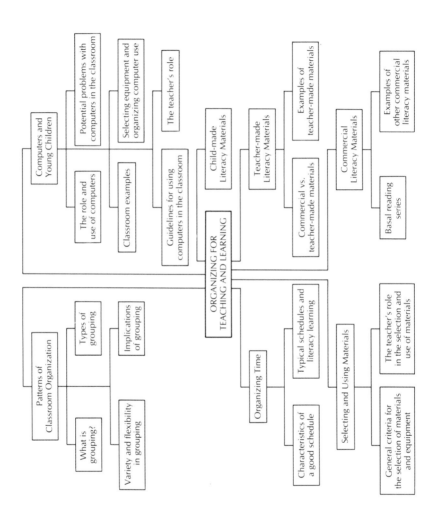

ORGANIZING FOR TEACHING AND LEARNING

Computers and Young Children
- The role and use of computers
- Potential problems with computers in the classroom
- Classroom examples
- Selecting equipment and organizing computer use
- Guidelines for using computers in the classroom
- The teacher's role

Child-made Literacy Materials

Teacher-made Literacy Materials
- Commercial vs. teacher-made materials
- Examples of teacher-made materials

Commercial Literacy Materials
- Basal reading series
- Examples of other commercial literacy materials

Patterns of Classroom Organization
- What is grouping?
- Types of grouping
- Variety and flexibility in grouping
- Implications of grouping

Organizing Time
- Characteristics of a good schedule
- Typical schedules and literacy learning

Selecting and Using Materials
- General criteria for the selection of materials and equipment
- The teacher's role in the selection and use of materials

- give examples of commercial, teacher-made, and child-made literacy materials;
- describe the role and use of computers in the classroom;
- list criteria for the selection of appropriate computer hardware and software for use with young children.

Patterns of Classroom Organization

There is no *one* magic way to organize children and instruction that will guarantee optimal teaching and maximum learning. Some organizational plans are more appropriate for some groups at some times than are others. This section describes some of the organizational arrangements most frequently used in literacy teaching and learning in early childhood classrooms.

What Is Grouping?

Grouping has been defined as "a flexible kind of classroom organization for adjusting the curriculum to the needs and abilities of class members. It is not a method of teaching reading, writing, mathematics, science, or any other subject. It is essentially a phase of classroom management. It is a means to an end, not an end in itself" (Wrightstone, 1967, p. 14). The preceding sentence is an important one. The ultimate purpose for grouping is to facilitate teaching and the children's learning. Sometimes it is most efficient and effective to present an activity to the entire group; at other times, a small-group activity or an individual conference is more appropriate. Most teachers use grouping, and a variety of grouping arrangements are possible (Petty, Petty, and Salzer, 1989). Grouping patterns vary depending on the objectives for the children, the needs of the children, the task, the teacher, and the available resources.

Variety and Flexibility in Grouping

A key to the effective use of grouping is flexible use of a variety of types of grouping. Some of the characteristics of flexible grouping identified by Unsworth (1984) are: (a) there are no permanent groups, (b) groups are changed and rearranged as needed, (c) group size can vary, (d) sometimes children are taught in one large group, and (e) group membership varies according to need and purpose.

Flexible grouping can enhance children's self-esteem because (a) children belong to and interact with several groups in the classroom; (b) not every group is determined on the basis of ability, so a child is not a permanent member of the "dumb" group; and (c) children are given the opportunity to sometimes select their own groups based on interest, friendships, or other special characteristics and therefore can be leaders of a group from time to time (Cecil, 1987). Also, there is research evidence that suggests that "children whose teachers use varied grouping patterns achieve more in reading than children whose teachers use only one kind of group" (Spiegel, 1981, pp. 31–32).

Types of Grouping

In the preceding chapters, some of the activities mentioned were whole-group activities (e.g., creative drama and storytelling); others were small-group activities (e.g., paired reading and listening center activities); and still others were individual activities (e.g., doing a puzzle and recreational reading). Several factors can influence the choice of organizational pattern. For example, because of their developmental level, toddlers typically engage in solitary or parallel play or one-on-one interaction with an adult, not in whole-group activities (Bredekamp, 1987). Much of a 4- and 5-year-old's time typically is spent working and playing individually and in small, informal groups (Bredekamp). Because of primary children's increasing social, emotional, and cognitive development, they are able to function in a wider range of grouping arrangements, including whole group, small groups, mixed-age groups, and individual activities.

Cambourne (1988) suggests that in terms of literacy activities, having the whole group together is useful for (a) focusing the children's attention on common tasks, events, and organizational or housekeeping topics; (b) demonstrating literacy related skills, knowledge, and attitudes; and (c) communicating teacher expectations to the children. Some of these activities can include class discussions, sharing time, fieldtrips, the teacher reading a story to the children, creative drama, listening to a guest speaker, viewing and then discussing a film, reviewing the format of a letter before writing an introductory letter to a new pen pal, making a chart of safety rules before going on a fieldtrip, and putting together a class newspaper. Of course, many of these activities (e.g., sharing time, creative drama) can be done in small groups as well.

On the other hand, there are many times when a small-group organizational pattern is most appropriate and efficient. For example, four or five children for whom English is a second language may benefit from the increased participation possible in a smaller group. A widely used, small-group activity in the primary grades is a reading group (Petty et al., 1989), and these are usually established on the basis of children's abilities (Jongsma, 1985).

Ability or achievement groups   Teachers often find that organizing a small group of children with similar abilities and needs is effective for teaching skills (Morrow, 1989). This organizational pattern allows the teacher to focus on an objective that is appropriate for all of the children in the group as well as to provide increased opportunities for child participation and teacher observation. Once the particular objective is achieved, the group is disbanded and another one may be formed to meet the specific needs of that group of children (some of whom may also have been in the previous group).

Although small groups based on ability can be an effective organizational pattern, there are potential problems and misuses. The report, *Becoming a Nation of Readers* by Anderson, Hiebert, Scott, and Wilkinson (1985, p. 92) cautioned that "grouping by ability may slow the progress of low-ability students." Research has indicated that ability grouping can (a) adversely affect children's self-esteem, (b) result in fewer learning opportunities for the lower-abillity group, (c) promote differential treatment of the groups by teachers, (d) benefit high-ability groups more than low-ability groups, and (e) factors other than ability may influence teachers assigning children to these groups (Harp, 1989; Hiebert, 1983; Jongsma, 1985; Peterson, Wilkinson, and Hallinan, 1984; Slavin, 1987; Sorenson and Hallinan, 1986; Wilkinson, 1988).

Interest groups   Another type of small-group organization used frequently in early childhood classrooms is the *interest group.* This is a group "formed on the basis of a common interest or a particular problem that is to be worked out. Such a group is often composed of children at different ability levels who have a common purpose but who are using books and other materials suited to their individual abilities" (Wrightstone, 1967, p. 17). Examples of interest group activities are an oral report to the entire class by two or three children who learned about one type of dinosaur, a mural depicting life on the moon, posters designed to promote the books of a favorite author, or a combined collection of shells or seeds.

This type of group forms and reforms as children's interests change and grow. The fact that the children share a common interest is motivation for them to work together and to share materials and ideas. In preschool, this kind of group is often formed on an ad hoc basis by the children themselves and can result in elaborate block structures, dramatic play on a particular theme, or cooperative play in the sandbox. In primary grades, such groups tend to be of relatively short duration and are disbanded when the purpose has been achieved (Schickendanz, York, Stewart, and White, 1990).

Social groups   An important part of early childhood education is providing opportunities for the development of children's socialization. *Social grouping,* which is basically grouping by friendship patterns, is one way to do this. Children, like adults, often prefer to work with their friends. Some literacy activities appropriate for social groupings might be performing a puppet play for the rest of the class, reading orally to each other to practice fluency and expression, or listening to a tape and following along in a book at the listening center.

Cooperative learning   Some of the small-group activities suggested above are also examples of *cooperative* or *collaborative learning.* This type of learning "refers to instructional methods in which students work cooperatively in small, mixed-ability teams. These teams of 2–5 students are heterogeneous with respect to sex, race, background, personal characteristics, and achievement" (Kozey, 1989, p. 57). Cooperative learning can be used both in classrooms where children are approximately the same age as well as in mixed-age class-rooms where the children are a year or more apart in age. Mixed-age class-rooms were common in the days of small rural schools and have been used for years in some schools in North America and Europe (Katz, Evangelou, and Hartman, 1990).

Some of the benefits reported for cooperative learning have been increased exchange of ideas among children, development of increased interpersonal and social skills, reduction of competition, improved achievement and attitudes to-ward learning, wider acceptance of other children, increased collaboration and cooperation for problem solving, less teacher-centered instruction, improved peer relationships, increased learning, and development of positive interdepen-dence (Arends, 1988; Harp, 1989; Johnson, Johnson, Holubec, and Roy, 1984; Katz et al., 1990; Kozey, 1989; Madden, 1988; Mason and Au, 1990). Children in grades 1 and 2 reported that collaborative learning provided them with com-pany while they worked, made them happy when asked for help by their peers, helped them learn from one another, made them feel good to be able to share their knowledge, provided a way to make new friends and to maintain existing friendships—and it was fun (Crouse and Davey, 1989). Some literacy activities that can be done cooperatively include children retelling a story they have just read to a partner, helping each other to review and edit a piece of writing, help-ing each other look for pictures or information in magazines, and peer tutor-ing.

Cross-age tutoring/peer tutoring/buddy program   In *cross-age tutoring,* typ-ically the older children tutor or assist the younger children. However, the tutor and the tutee can both be the same age but functioning at different levels (peer tutoring).

One literacy activity that utilizes this pairing is a "buddy" reading program in which older children (typically in the late primary or intermediate grades) read books on a regular basis to younger children in early primary grades or kindergarten. Some teachers also use buddies to help the younger children with their writing or to act as scribes for children who are at the dictation stage. Also, peers can read and write with one another. According to Topping (1989), "all the major research reviews on the effectiveness of peer tutoring in reading have shown that the tutors accelerate in reading skill at least as much, if not more than, the tutees" (p. 489). Similar effects have been reported for cross-age tutoring (Labbo and Teale, 1990).

Implications of Grouping

Obviously grouping can assist the teacher in providing effective instruction for young children, particularly when a variety of types of grouping are used and the grouping is kept flexible. Grouping also affects children's "cognitive progress as well as their self-perceptions and social development" (Schickendanz et al., 1990, p. 72). However, grouping can be *misused* by keeping children in the same group for most activities all year long, labeling children by the ability group they are in, using only whole-class or ability grouping, or placing children in groups when they do not yet have the skills to function successfully in those groups.

Teachers need to consider a variety of factors in grouping children, such as individual children's needs, their developmental levels, social skills, communicative skills, experience with working with other children, the nature of the task, the number of children, and the availability of resources. Teachers can also assist young children to develop the interpersonal skills and work strategies they need to function as a member of a group.

Organizing Time

Organization of time is another aspect of organizing for teaching and learning. When I was teaching young children (and even today with university students), there never seemed to be enough time in the school day to accomplish everything I wanted to accomplish. I was always looking for a few more minutes to spend with a child who needed a bit of extra help on an individual basis.

Because there is so much to do and a limited amount of time to do it in, most teachers develop a schedule to help them plan and implement their programs. These schedules can be very open, with large blocks of time designated for a particular type of activity (e.g., free play, center time, project work), or they can be quite specific (e.g., 9:15–10:30 reading groups, 11–11:30 math, 10:15–10:30 snack). A schedule is important in providing continuity and balance in the daily program. It also provides children with security and familiarity of routine as well as gives them cues to appropriate behavior that they can initiate themselves and thus become more independent. For example, when the teacher announces that it is time to clean up after the morning free play time, the children know they are expected to put away their materials, wash their hands, and find a place at a table for snack. Or older children get ready for gym more independently and at their own pace if they know the day's schedule.

Characteristics of a Good Schedule

There are several key characteristics of an effective schedule. A good schedule—

- is flexible. The teacher takes advantage of unexpected opportunities. For example, watching the firefighters put out a fire across the street from the classroom is more important than having the scheduled sharing time. The children will really have something exciting to talk about if the sharing time is postponed to allow them to observe and ask questions about the fire.

- is developmentally appropriate and accommodates children's basic needs. Young children have specific developmental characteristics that must be considered in planning a schedule. For example, they typically have relatively short attention spans, and therefore it is inappropriate to plan long periods of time when they will sit and listen. The younger the child, the more time is spent on basic needs: for example, many preschool children nap in the afternoon.
- balances active and quiet activities, whole-group and small-group activities, child-selected and teacher-organized activities, child-initiated and adult-initiated activities.
- provides for transitions between activities and the use of routines. The transitions and routines are the glue that holds the schedule together. Smooth, effective transitions mean that children move quickly and easily between activities. It is important to establish routines for arrival, cleanup, toileting, snack and lunch, nap/rest, recess or outdoor play, departure, and so forth.

There are many times throughout the day when literacy experiences are possible and desirable. The next section will describe typical schedules for different levels of early childhood programs and indicate some literacy activities that might occur.

Typical Schedules and Literacy Learning

The preschool day   Early childhood programs for 3- and 4-year-olds can be either a half-day program in a nursery school or a full day in a daycare center (see Box 8-1).

Daycare program   The length of the children's day in a daycare center can vary. Some children may spend fewer than 5 hours and others may spend 12 hours (see Box 8-2).

Kindergarten program   Traditionally in North America, kindergarten has been a half-day program. Although the half-day program is still the most common schedule, many states/provinces, school districts, and private schools have initiated full-day kindergartens. Box 8-3 is an example of a schedule for a half-day kindergarten program.

Early primary grades   The type of program and local conditions determine how the elementary school day for children in grades 1 and 2 is organized. A primary program that follows an integrated model will have large blocks of time for work on the current theme or project. All of the typical subject areas will be subsumed under the theme. In a more traditional program, the schedule is divided into smaller, more subject-oriented headings. Obviously, there are many possible schedules, and teachers need to find a schedule that works well for their children, program, school setting, and themselves. The two schedules in Boxes 8-4 and 8-5 illustrate the differences and similarities between an integrated primary program and a more traditional program.

BOX 8-1 • *Nursery School Half-day Program*

8:50–9:10	Arrival: Children arrive and are greeted individually at the door. Some children share news with the teacher and then put away their belongings. Some parents stop in to ask a question or relay information about their child to the teacher.
9:10–10:00	Free play at the learning centers in the classroom: The children select where and with whom they would like to work. In some centers there may be a special project for that day (e.g., fingerpainting in the art center or a new game in the manipulative toys and games area). Many of the children's activities involve literacy experiences (e.g., looking at books, painting on the easel and then dictating a story about the picture, writing a "pretend" shopping list in the housekeeping corner, playing a lotto game, matching shapes, etc.).
10:00–10:10	Cleanup time: The children put away their materials and wash their hands for snack. The children talk with each other during the cleanup and sort and classify materials in the course of cleaning up (e.g., all of the same-shaped blocks are placed on the same shelf, all of the yellow beads are returned to the yellow container, etc.).
10:10–10:25	Snack: The children sit at the tables and the adults sit with the children in order to encourage and facilitate conversation.
10:25–10:40	Quiet time: While the staff are clearing and washing the tables, the children do quiet activities, such as work on a puzzle or look at books and perhaps discuss the story or the pictures with a friend. The teacher then reads the group a story and the children are encouraged to comment on the book.
10:40–11:00	Group activities: The children do a few finger plays and sing some of their favorite songs. Some of the action songs involve both large and fine motor skills. The children then share any news they wish with the other children. The teacher then initiates a brief discussion or activity related to the theme the class is currently doing. They might have a resource person related to the theme come in and talk to them or see a video or filmstrip.
11:00–11:30	Outdoor time: The children gather together their paintings and other things they wish to take home and then get ready to go out to the playground. Sometimes the children go for a walk, or if the weather is inclement, they will do games or other gross motor activities inside.
11:30	Departure

There are a variety of ways early literacy teaching and learning can be organized. And just as there is no one way to organize the early childhood classroom environment, there is no one way to plan a schedule or to group children. What is important is that the schedule and grouping arrangements facilitate the learning of all the children.

BOX 8-2 • *Daycare Center Program*

8:00–9:00	Arrival of children and staff: Typically, not all children arrive at the same time at a daycare center. Most centers open with one or two teachers and provide quiet activities from which the children may choose as they arrive. Most children have arrived by 9:00.
9:00–11:30	The daycare center program is similar to the half-day program (described in Box 8-1) during the morning hours.
11:30–12:30	Cleanup and lunch: The children come in from outdoors, remove their coats, wash their hands, and find a place at the table for lunch. After lunch, the children brush their teeth, use the toilet, and prepare for nap/quiet time.
12:30–3:00	Nap or quiet time: Not all young children take naps in the afternoon. For those children who do not nap, quiet play is permitted. As not all children need the same amount of rest or sleep, the children awaken at different times and join the other children in quiet activities (some of which are literacy activities).
3:00–3:15	Snack time: When all, or nearly all, of the children are awake, they wash their hands and prepare for afternoon snack. Again, the teachers share the snack at the tables with the children in order to encourage and facilitate conversation among and with the children.
3:15–4:30	Activity time: The children self-select indoor and/or outdoor activities. These activities might include water play, woodworking, drawing and painting, use of the playground equipment, or dramatic play. Some days they might go for a walk, go to the library for storytime, or go on a fieldtrip.
4:30–5:00	Cleanup and group time: The children clean up the materials and equipment both indoors and outdoors and then gather as a group for a story, some songs and finger plays, and a discussion of their day.
5:00–5:30	Departure: The children begin to be picked up by their parents at 5:00. As the number of children is reduced, the staff also begin to leave. The children who do not leave at 5:00 participate in quiet activities until their parents arrive. Everyone has gone home by 5:30.

Selecting and Using Materials

Materials and equipment do not make a program. The classroom can be beautifully equipped, but there can still be a terrible program for children. However, good materials of sufficient number and variety can facilitate teaching and learning. It is important for young children to have access to a variety of developmentally appropriate materials and equipment that foster their literacy development. According to Moffett and Wagner (1976), "materials should initiate and facilitate every language-related activity you and your coworkers can imagine that your students might have the ability and interest to do and benefit from" (p. 53). One of the key roles of the early childhood educator is the selection, organization, presentation, and evaluation of materials and equipment.

BOX 8-3 • *Half-day Kindergarten Program*

9:00–9:20   Arrival and opening: The children typically arrive at the same time, hang up their coats, find their name cards and place them in a pocket chart or write their names on the sign-in paper to record their presence. They then gather at the meeting area for their opening activities. These activities typically include a greeting from the teacher; the children sharing any news they wish; and calendar activities such as putting up the marker for the day and counting how many days it will be until a certain date such as someone's birthday, a holiday, or a class fieldtrip. The teacher may have the children dictate a group story, which could be based on the news of that day, or they could dictate a list of questions they would like answered about a topic related to the current theme or project. A poem for the day may be read and discussed and/or a big book read. This period finishes with the teacher discussing with the children what the various options are for their activity time, including any "must-do" jobs (e.g., plant the seeds for the plants the children will grow as part of a science unit), any new additions to the learning centers, any centers that are not available that day, and any special activities scheduled for that day (e.g., library, gym, a resource person, or a fieldtrip).

9:20–10:10   Learning center time: The children use the learning centers (as described in Chapter 7). They may participate in a variety of literacy activities: for example, journal writing, table activities that foster the development of fine motor skills, dictating sentences or stories about their drawings or paintings, working at the class computer, reading books, and so forth. The teacher may use this time to work with individuals or small groups of children.

10:10–10:20   Cleanup

10:20–10:35   Snack and quiet time: The children have a small snack (e.g., juice and a cracker) and then find a quiet activity to do, such as looking at a book or working on a puzzle. In some kindergartens, the children's older buddies come at this time once or twice a week to have snack with the children, and then each buddy reads a story to his or her kindergartner.

10:35–10:45   Movement activities: The children participate in large muscle activities, such as a game, music and movement, or exercises.

10:45–11:25   Group time: The children gather together as a whole group to discuss and do activities related to the current theme under investigation. These activities can cover all curriculum areas. Some literacy activities that may be included are storytelling, creative drama, listening games, discussions, story reading, language experience stories, poetry, and riddles.

11:25–11:30   Closing: After the children and teacher briefly review the morning session and any messages or notices to go home, the children depart.

General Criteria for the Selection of Materials and Equipment

Following are ten criteria for the selection of materials and equipment for an early childhood program:

BOX 8-4 • *Integrated Primary Program*

9:00–9:30 Opening: When the children arrive, they first meet as a group and do many of the same activities that are done in the other early childhood programs described (see Boxes 8-1, 8-2, and 8-3): e.g., sharing news, calendar work, poem-of-the-day, writing a language experience story, or listening to a story. The children and teacher then plan and discuss what they are to do that day. The teacher may assign any specific tasks that he or she wants individuals or the entire group to do.

9:30–10:15 Integrated theme time: The children participate in a variety of activities, such as those described in Chapter 1. Most of the activities revolve around the theme and cover a range of subject areas: for example, language arts, science, social studies, and fine arts. Literacy activities and materials are typically related to the theme. During this time the teacher may work with the whole group, small groups, and/or individuals. There are also many opportunities for the children to talk and listen to each other as well as read and write as they collaborate on projects or assist one another.

10:15–10:30 Recess

10:30–11:15 Integrated theme time (*continued*) or specific instruction: Some teachers will have whole or group lessons in a specific subject area in which the children need specific instruction that is not being provided in the current theme or project. For example, a teacher may focus on mathematics during this time if the theme does not provide enough opportunity for the children to use math or if the teacher wants to introduce a new math topic (e.g., subtraction or multiplication) to the children.

11:15–11:45 Physical education/library/second language/other: Most elementary schools have a schoolwide timetable for use of the gymnasium or the school library or for instruction in a second language by a specialist teacher. These times are usually scattered throughout the weekly timetable, and the rest of the schedule must be adjusted accordingly.

11:45–12:00 Story/literature time

12:00–1:00 Lunch

1:00–1:20 Sustained Silent Reading (see Chapter 4 for a description of SSR)

1:20–3:15 Integrated theme time: This is basically a continuation and development of what the children were doing in the morning block.

3:15–3:30 Review, planning, and departure: The teacher and children review what they did that day and what they think about what was done. They make some initial plans for the next day and then the children depart.

1. developmental appropriateness
2. safety
3. durability
4. adaptability and flexibility
5. attractiveness to children
6. cost
7. instructional quality
8. relevance to the goals and objectives of the program
9. reflection of the children's culture
10. support for values

BOX 8-5 • *Traditional Primary Program*

9:00–9:20	Opening: After the same types of opening activities that have been described in Boxes 8-1, 8-2, 8-3, and 8-4, the teacher instructs the children about what they are to do that morning. This can include explaining the board work connected with the morning's reading lessons, distributing tasks that are to be done during the morning, and any corrections that need to be made to the previous day's work. The children return to their seats and the teacher begins with the first of three reading groups.
9:20–10:15	Reading groups: The basic procedure is that the children in two groups are working on independent activities while the teacher works with a third group. This group then returns to their seats to work independently and the teacher works with another group, and so on.
10:15–10:30	Recess
10:30–11:15	Mathematics
11:15–11:45	Physical education/library/second language/other (see Box 8-4 for a description of this block of time)
11:45–12:00	Story and literature
12:00–1:00	Lunch
1:00–1:20	Sustained Silent Reading
1:20–1:50	Language arts: This time might include journal writing, spelling, listening activities, choral speaking, creative writing, or other literacy activities.
1:50–2:45	Social studies or science.
2:45–3:20	Fine arts: This includes art, music, and creative drama.
3:20–3:30	Review of the day, story, and departure.

The first six criteria are given frequently by professional groups as criteria for selecting materials. For example, these criteria are the ones suggested for toy libraries by national organizations in the United States, Canada, and Great Britain (American Library Association, 1977; Canadian Association of Toy Libraries, 1986; National Toy Library Association, 1984) and are used by the people who select and purchase toys and materials for toy libraries (Mayfield, 1988). The last four criteria relate specifically to educational settings and are typically recommended by early childhood organizations, such as the Association for Childhood Education International (Moyer, 1986). Each of these criteria will be discussed briefly, and examples of appropriate literacy materials will be given.

Developmental appropriateness   If the materials in the classroom are not appropriate for the children, they will not be used, or they will be misused. Because there is typically a range of developmental levels found in any group of young children, it follows that there will need to be a wide variety of levels of materials to accommodate these individual differences. For example, most early childhood classrooms contain puzzles, which are useful for developing children's perceptual-motor skills, figure ground, and fine motor skills. However, in just one group of 5-year-olds I taught, there were children who had difficulty doing 3- or 4-piece frame puzzles, and a few children who were doing 100-piece jigsaw puzzles. In a class of 7-year-olds, there can be children who are still at the picture book stage as well as those who are reading at a third- or fourth-grade level (Ekwall and Shanker, 1989). It is necessary to have materials available that are developmentally appropriate for all children.

Safety Safety is one of the foremost criteria in the selection of materials and equipment for young children. Many children are injured each year from unsafe toys and materials or improper use of these materials. No one wants children to be injured, especially by materials that are poorly made, have sharp edges or splinters, are painted with toxic paint, are flammable, do not carry a safety seal if electrical, or are not cleanable.

Durability Durability relates to both safety and cost. The more durable the material, the less likely it is to break and injure a child. More durable materials will last longer and, therefore, need to be replaced less frequently. Hardwood unit block sets last much longer than those made of soft wood. In one class where I taught, the unit blocks and some of the wooden frame puzzles were more than 40 years old and were still in good condition.

Adaptability and flexibility Materials that can be used by children and teachers in a variety of ways for a variety of instructional goals are more useful and valuable than materials with only one use. Materials such as paper, colored markers, and crayons can be used in a variety of ways for a variety of purposes by young children, whereas most battery-operated toys have a limited range of options and children quickly become bored with them. Open-ended materials encourage children to be creative and to use the materials to meet their needs and objectives. Think of all the things a group of young children could do with a large cardboard box!

Stories on tape can be used in a variety of ways to accommodate the literacy levels of children from preschool to late primary. The children can listen to the tapes, follow along in the accompanying book, retell a story heard on tape by using feltboard pieces or finger puppets, practice oral reading skills by reading along with the tape, or use the stories for written activities.

Attractiveness to children If the material is not attractive to the children, they will not use it. Materials need to be interesting to young children and appeal to their curiosity. Materials that are well designed, colorful, and well constructed are desirable. A game board that is not attractive or a spinner that does not spin easily will discourage children from using a game even though it is developmentally appropriate.

Cost A perpetual dilemma of educators seems to be that there is never enough money for everything they would like to have in their classrooms. The reality is that educational budgets for materials and equipment are limited, and cost is therefore a relevant criteria. In determining the cost/value ratio for materials, factors to consider are: (a) the amount of projected use, (b) the probable life of the materials, (c) the possibility of sharing the materials between two or more classrooms, (d) having the materials made easily and less expensively, and (e) the number of children who will benefit from these materials. Cost should not be a more important criteria than appropriateness or instructional value, but it is a factor.

Instructional quality In addition to materials that provide children and teachers with a range of possibilities for use, the materials need to be conceptually correct and teach what is supposed to be learned. Some toys and materials that are labelled "educational" are of questionable educational value. Others do not have adequate or accurate instructions to the children on how to play a game or do an activity page. Still others have stated objectives that are not congruent with the materials provided.

Relevance to the program goals and objectives The materials and equipment used in a program should support and facilitate the goals and objectives of that program. If one of your goals for the children is to foster their independence and develop their self-help skills, you would look for games that are self-checking, materials that are self-correcting, and equipment such as cassette players that the children can operate with a minimum of adult assistance.

Reflection of the children's culture The classroom environment and the materials that are a part of that environment should reflect the broader context of the community and society. Children need to see that the school and the teachers recognize and value their backgrounds. Materials that are produced for the mainstream North American culture may need to be supplemented with materials that reflect the children's specific cultural heritage and current environment. Including local materials, such as posters, photographs, child-made books, teacher-made games using local pictures, and realia, can help provide a necessary connection between the classroom and the community in which the children live.

Instructional materials should also be relevant to the children's lives. I once taught in an isolated school in a desert where one of the social studies "kits" in the cupboard was about an urban, high-rise apartment building in winter. The children had never seen snow, and there wasn't a building in the community over three stories high, so they could not relate to the content of that unit except with a kind of curious wonder and disbelief.

Support for values The materials and toys selected for children reflect the values teachers wish to foster, such as cooperation, nonviolence, and racial and sexual equality. For example, some programs model recycling and reuse by using "junk" such as scraps of fabric, cardboard tubes, pieces of wrapping paper, scraps of wood, boxes, yarn, carpet samples, plastic tubs, buttons, milk cartons, and sponge pieces for children's art and construction projects. Some programs do not use food for children's play or artwork (e.g., using sand not rice or beans in the sandbox and not using pasta pieces for art collages) because this could be considered an inappropriate use for food that could be used to feed the hungry.

Children themselves are an excellent source of evaluative feedback on how successful the selection of materials and equipment has been. Taylor (1989, p. 122) states: "The acid test of the value of toys and equipment is appeal over time." In my experience, if the children are not using a particular material or toy it is because it does not meet one or more of the above criteria and probably should be reconsidered.

The Teacher's Role in the Selection and Use of Materials

The teacher's role in the selection of materials includes researching the types of materials available, assessing the relative merits of different materials, comparing prices, and placing orders or sometimes actually purchasing the materials. There are many sources of information on instructional materials.

Early childhood and language arts/reading journals have regular columns that review books and other literacy related instructional materials, including computer software: for example, *The Reading Teacher, Language Arts, Young Children, Childhood Education,* and *Day Care and Early Education* (see Appendix D). Some professional journals also have special theme issues or parts of one issue each year on instructional materials: for example, "Notable Children's Trade Books for the Language Arts" in *Language Arts* and "Children's Choices" in *The Reading Teacher.* Two organizations that distribute information on children's books are the Children's Book Council and the Canadian Children's Book Centre (see Appendix D for their addresses) as well as professional library organizations. Additional sources of information on children's books include reference books such as *Children's Catalog, The Elementary School Library Collection,* and *Children's Books in Print* (usually available in the school library or local public library).

Professional conferences usually have exhibits of the latest children's books and instructional materials. Other teachers and persons in related professions are also an excellent source of information about instructional materials. Publishers and distributors of instructional materials issue catalogs on a regular basis and are usually pleased to add your name to their mailing lists.

The Association for Childhood Education (Moyer, 1986) provides an excellent summary of the types of materials and the quantities needed for preschool, kindergarten, and elementary school programs in *Selecting Educational Equipment and Materials for School and Home.* This is a particularly useful reference for someone setting up a program or ordering materials for the year as it gives criteria for selection, has a listing of materials, suggests the quantities needed for different size groups, and provides a useful suggested order of acquisition.

The teacher should also keep an up-to-date inventory of materials needed or desired either for immediate purchase or for purchase at a later date when money becomes available. The teacher is also responsible for the organization of the materials in the classroom. (In Chapter 7, the importance of organizing materials in an attractive, readily accessible, efficient way was discussed.)

The teacher must also determine how the materials are to be introduced to the children. Many materials can be simply added to existing materials and the children are left to discover these for themselves. Other materials require a specific introduction to the children (e.g., some board games or a computer software program). The children and teacher are jointly responsible for the care and maintenance of materials and equipment. Children should be instructed to inform the teacher if there are pieces missing from materials, if equipment is not working, and so forth.

Yet another role for the teacher is to observe, facilitate, and evaluate the children's use of instructional materials. The teacher can encourage the children to use new materials and support them in their attempts. Careful evaluation of children's use of materials and the results will aid future selection and use of materials.

Commercial Literacy Materials

The typical early childhood classroom contains a variety of instructional materials whose origins can be classified as commercial, teacher-made, or child-made. Commercial literacy materials include children's trade books, a reading series, board games, card games, dominoes, posters, writing materials, individual chalkboards, big books, computer software programs, stories on cassette tapes, filmstrips, and so forth.

Basal Reading Series

One of the most frequently found commercial literacy materials in primary classrooms is a basal reading series (also called a developmental reading series or a reading scheme). Indeed, basal readers have been an "integral part of reading instruction" (Aukerman, 1981, p. i) for scores of years (see Chapter 2 for a brief description of their history). It is estimated that basal readers are used in over 90 percent of classrooms in the United States (Anderson, et al., 1985; National Council of Teachers of English, 1989; Shannon, 1989). There is some controversy about basal readers and their use, however. This debate includes those advocates of a literature-only approach, those who primarily use a basal reading series, as well as educators in-between these two positions. Because teachers make instructional decisions including the materials to use, this chapter presents a description of a basal reading series and briefly presents some of the advantages and disadvantages of this type of instructional material. A *basal reading series* has been defined as:

> *a set of instructional materials that are carefully developed based on a philosophy of teaching reading. The materials include basal readers for the pupils, teacher's manual, student workbooks, teacher's manual for the workbooks, supplemental materials, and tests. These basal readers are developed in sequential fashion starting at kindergarten and ending with eighth grade. (Fox, 1989, p. 13)*

Characteristics of a basal reading series   According to Aukerman (1981), *most* basal reader series have the following components:

- a readiness program
- beginning picture books with short captions and short sentences (usually 3–4 paperback books, sometimes called *preprimers*), which precede the first hardcover reader
- use of the whole-word method to begin reading
- provision for word-identification instruction based on analytic phonics
- use of "an elaborate battery of comprehension questions" (p. 12)
- a variety of types of comprehension questions
- detailed lesson plans in the teacher's manuals
- a vocabulary teaching strand
- suggested remedial activities for children who have not mastered the presented material
- suggested enrichment activities for those children who need more of a challenge
- suggested related language arts activities
- a range of literary genres
- workbooks for practice of skills
- tests for initial and formative assessment of student progress

Directed reading lessons   A typical lesson in a basal reader usually follows a somewhat standard format. The major part of the lesson is a Directed Reading Activity (DRA) consisting of three stages: the Preparation Stage, the Reading Stage, and the Discussion Stage (Binkley, 1986).

The Preparation Stage presents the children with vocabulary and background information relevant to the story they are to read. The purpose of presenting "background activities should be to get students thinking about certain aspects of the upcoming story. Prereading activities should provide students with a framework for organizing events and concepts in the story so that many threads become interrelated and more memorable" (p. 11). However, "teachers should activate, or add to, students' background knowledge only what is essential for comprehension" (Durkin, 1989, p. 403).

In the Reading Stage (sometimes referred to as *guided reading*), the teacher sets a purpose and asks the children to read the story or a part of the total selection silently. Each section read is preceded by discussion and a purpose for reading and then followed by questions and discussion to check the students' comprehension of the story. Oral rereading of parts of the story are sometimes included as part of the guided reading. The practice of round-robin oral reading, however, is condemned by reading experts and educators. Some teachers ask each child in turn to read aloud several lines or a page of story text, sometimes without prior reading of the material in the mistaken belief that this is helpful in developing reading fluency. The improper use of oral reading can result in children perceiving reading as simply "saying words." Round-robin oral reading does not foster fluency or comprehension and often results in student boredom, inattention, and disinterest. There are many legitimate opportunities for oral reading throughout the school day that can be utilized more effectively for improving children's oral reading skills than round-robin oral reading.

The Discussion Stage (sometimes referred to as postreading activities) of the basal lesson typically includes: (a) an assessment of the children's comprehension of the story, which can be done by activities such as questioning, written tasks, and acting out the story; (b) direct instruction of skills (e.g., comprehension, word recognition, or vocabulary); and (c) follow-up activities, which the children do independently while the teacher is working with another reading group. These activities often take the form of workbooks and skill sheets. Educators and children are critical of these "purple monsters" because they are misused and overused and become busy work for the children. According to Shannon (1989), "most students recognize neither the purpose nor the payoff from completing seatwork assignments" associated with a basal reading series (p. 101). The Report of the Commission on Reading in the United States (Anderson et al., 1985) recommended that children spend less time completing workbooks and skill sheets and more time in independent reading and writing combined with more teaching emphasis on comprehension instruction. The report states, "Workbook and skill sheet activities should be pared to the minimum that actually provide worthwhile practice in aspects of reading" (p. 119). The directed reading lesson has been described as follows:

> . . . *at once one of the strengths and one of the weaknesses of the entire basal reader approach. Its strength lies in its elaborate array of directions and references to resources for each textbook lesson. Novices to teaching have found the directed reading lessons in the teacher's manuals to be valuable guides . . . Critics . . . point to its highly structured and rigid routine, which if followed explicitly, might negate teacher/pupil originality and/or creativity. (Aukerman, 1981, p. 327)*

Directed Reading-Thinking Activity   The Directed Reading-Thinking Activity (DRTA) was suggested by Russell Stauffer (1969) as an alternative to the Directed Reading Activity. In a DRTA, there are basically three stages. The first stage is setting the purpose for reading in which the children examine the titles, illustrations, and headings and try to predict what the story will be about. In the second stage, the children read the selection or a part of the selection for evidence to support their predictions. During the third stage of verifying their predictions through discussion and teacher questioning, the children present evidence and reread key sentences to prove or disprove the predictions. This cycle is then repeated until the story is completed.

Advantages and disadvantages of a basal reading series   A summary of the advantages and disadvantages of a basal reading series was presented in the August/September 1989 issue of *Reading Today* (the newspaper of the International Reading Association). Several educators, reading specialists, and a publisher were asked to respond to the question, "What should be the role (if any) of basal readers in the elementary reading program, and do current basal readers fulfill that role?" The respondents included "basal boosters," "basal bashers," and several in-betweeners.

The critics of basal reading series stated that the language and stories found in basals were not the language of good literature, that the vocabulary was simplified and restricted, and that the content did not necessarily match the children's backgrounds. Basal reading series were also criticized for promoting the idea that reading was a sequential and hierarchical process and that it should be learned in a series of steps as opposed to being learned as a whole using more relistic literacy activities involving "real" reading and writing. In addition to criticizing the pedagogical soundness of the basal reading series, the critics commented on their misuse, especially the over-realiance on the materials, the slavish adherence to published materials, the basal reading series becoming all or most of the reading curriculum, the excessive use of workbooks and skill sheets, the reliance on outside experts to determine which skills the children need and how these will be taught, and the minimal provision for individual differences.

Other respondents stated that there is a role for a basal reading series and that it had strengths. Some of the strengths cited were the recent improvements in the amount and quality of literature, especially in the anthologies; the improved provisions for building the children's background before reading; the increased variety in activities and literary genres; the increased emphasis on children's writing; the provision of a variety of materials from which the teacher may choose; the support and guidance basal reading series can provide for inexperienced or less able teachers; the reduction in the preparation time for teachers as compared to a literature-based program; the assessment and evaluation systems provided, which help the teachers to identify children's needs and monitor their progress; and the suggestions and materials for instruction in the children's areas of weakness. In the final analysis, as with any type of instructional material, it is the decision of the classroom teacher if and how materials will be used and it is the skill and understanding of the teacher that determines the effectiveness of instructional materials. Commercial materials and programs should be modified and adapted as necessary to meet the instructional goals for the class. With a basal reading series, the objectives for the lessons and activities need to be matched with the teacher's goals for individual children; the possible use, modification, or nonuse of materials and activities determined; and thought given to substitution or addition of other materials or activities.

Examples of Other Commercial Literacy Materials

Other commercial materials commonly found in early childhood classrooms that can be used to foster young children's developing literacy include—

- children's trade books, including fiction and nonfiction, books without words, alphabet books, pattern books, big books, and concept books (see Chapter 4 for specific suggestions);
- children's magazines and newspapers, especially those that publish children's writing (see Appendix C);
- children's reference books (such as *Childcraft*), picture dictionaries, children's encyclopedias, and word books;
- dramatic play materials and props;
- telephones or walkie-talkies;
- blocks and wooden figures to stimulate language;
- puppets of various types and a puppet theater;
- puzzles of various types and levels of difficulty (e.g., inset, frame, jigsaw, foam, 3-D, floor puzzles, etc.);
- fine motor and perceptual motor materials (e.g., beads, lacing cards, dressing frames, parquetry, pegboards, geoboards, stacking, nesting, building and sorting toys, etc.);
- drawing and writing materials;
- a cassette player, tapes and books for the listening center;
- board games (e.g., Candyland, lotto games, bingo, etc.);
- card games (e.g., concentration, dominoes, fish, etc.);
- dice games (e.g., Spill and Spell, etc.).

(See also descriptions of individual learning centers in Chapter 7 for additional suggested materials for fostering literacy development.)

Teacher-made Literacy Materials

Commercial versus Teacher-made Materials

Most early childhood classrooms contain materials that are purchased as well as those that are made by the teacher and the children. The decision to buy or make materials is often determined by cost (especially when considering a limited budget) and because it is not always possible to find "exactly" what one wants or needs. The advantages to teacher-made materials are that: (a) they can be tailor-made to the needs of the children; (b) they can be modified for the level of the children; (c) they may better reflect the children's cultural, ethnic, or language backgrounds; (d) "old favorites" can be adapted to new concepts and uses; (e) the children can often be involved in making the materials; and (f) the materials are usually less expensive than the commercial equivalent. The disadvantages include the amount of time it takes to make the materials, and the materials must be of a high standard and appeal to the children. Also, they must be durable or they will need constant repair.

Examples of Teacher-made Materials

Most early childhood teachers spend time making materials for their classrooms or recruit parent or community volunteers to help them. Many of the materials suggested in this chapter and the previous ones can be made by the teacher. For example, puppets, which are excellent for stimulating language and creative dramatics, can be made easily and fairly quickly (see Figure 8-1). Some puppets that can be made quite easily are bag puppets, stick puppets, wooden spoon puppets, and paper finger puppets. A bit more complex but still quickly done are sock puppets, styrofoam ball puppets, and hamburger or milk carton puppets. Felt pieces for use on a flannelboard are also made easily — especially as felt does not require hemming and the pieces can be glued or stitched on top of one another. Interfacing (i.e., the fabric used to give stiffness to clothing) can also be used to make pieces for use on the flannelboard. A puppet theater can be constructed from a large cardboard appliance box and a flannelboard from a thin piece of plywood, wallboard, or heavy corrugated cardboard covered with a piece of flannel.

There are many types of card and board games that teachers can make. Bingo cards, lotto games, concentration cards, dominoes, and fish card games can be made easily from cardboard tag and pictures cut from magazines, stickers, or even the paint sample cards from paint stores. The children can often help glue or paste on the pictures or stickers. Bingo and lotto cards can be made up without the pictures or words and then laminated. These can then be written upon using the current reading vocabulary, spelling words, or rhyming words and later wiped off and the words or pictures changed to meet new teaching objectives.

Simple cardboard puzzles can also be produced from large calendar pictures or illustrations from books and magazines, large photographs of the class (this is a popular one!), or from food boxes or labels (examples of print in the environment). The picture, photograph, box front, or label is glued onto a thick piece of cardboard, allowed to dry, and then cut into puzzle pieces. Sometimes the puzzles are laminated or coated with a thin layer of lacquer. Although these puzzles are not as durable as the wooden ones, they can relate directly to the theme or unit being studied. For example, if the children are studying food or nutrition, pictures and photos of food, recipes, or cereal boxes could be made into puzzles for use during the duration of that unit.

Another type of teacher-made material is a display including wall charts and bulletin boards. Some ideas for appropriate wall charts include songs, poems, chants, science experiments, reports, observations, child-generated writing, birthday charts, weather charts, reference charts (e.g., synonym, problem words, characteristics of fairy tales, etc.), and class rules (Cambourne, 1988). There is almost an unlimited number of wall charts that can be made and used in the early childhood classroom.

Another type of teacher-made material is the bulletin board. These should be used for instructional purposes and be meaningful for the children, rather than simply being a pretty decoration on the wall that the children look at once and then ignore. A bulletin board can also be a participation bulletin board, where the pieces can be moved around by the children and used to practice matching pictures that rhyme, matching upper- and lowercase letters, or sorting pictures of food into food groups. It is important to keep in mind that the classroom environment should be a teaching and learning environment. The

FIGURE 8-1   •   *Examples of Puppets and Flannelboard Pieces*

A. Simple felt hand puppet
B. Finger puppets
C. Stick puppet
D. Glove puppet (pompoms attached to glove fingers with snaps or velcro)
E. Paper bag puppet
F. Paper plate puppet
G. Handkerchief puppet
H. Spoon puppet

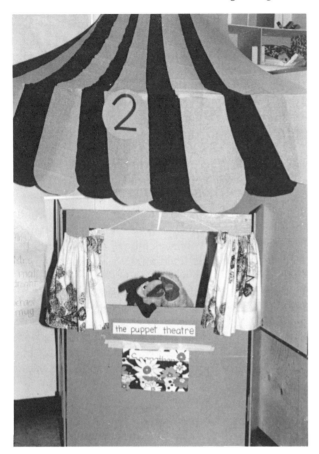

Puppet theater

bulletin boards should assist children's learning and the children should be involved in the construction of classroom displays.

Child-made Literacy Materials

Children can indeed create many of the displays in an early childhood classroom. These displays provide children with the opportunity to collect, sort, and share items related to a current project and can be referred back to by the children; they also demonstrate children's experience with the topic and provide a record of their work, and communicate their achievements to others (Katz and Chard, 1989).

The following are examples of literacy-related displays that can be done primarily by children. The children can find interesting words or pictures in magazines, cut them out, and then organize them into a display. A chart or bulletin board can also be used to display key words related to the children's reading or a unit being studied. A display can be made of photographs of logos, signs, words, and other print in the environment that the children read on one of their walks. Children's own drawings and writings should be prominently placed in the classroom and displayed in such a way that even the smallest child can see and read them. The children can record information on charts or bulletin boards (e.g., a diary of the incubation and hatching of chicken eggs, graphs summarizing the months of the children's birthdays or the number of people in their families, a diagram of the parts of a plant, etc.). Many of these displays can also be shared with other classes, teachers, administrators, and parents.

Additional examples of child-made materials in the classroom include child-authored books (either single author or anthologies), which have been bound and placed in the class library corner. The younger children can illustrate the charts written out by the teachers or the older children. Older children can do most of the work to produce a class newspaper or newsletter by writing and illustrating stories individually or collaboratively (see Appendix B for book-making instructions).

Example of child-authored/dictated book

Computers and Young Children

The Role and Use of Computers

The role of computers and computer literacy in early childhood education is a current "hot topic." Computers are becoming more common in schools across the United States and Canada (Tompkins and Hoskisson, 1991; Logan, 1989; Woodhill, 1987). Their increasing use is also reported in daycare and preschool programs (Goodwin, Goodwin, Nansel, and Helm, 1986). The support for computers in the classroom ranges from "enthusiasts who urge that young people from the very earliest school grades embark on a program of computer literacy" (Logan, p. 10) to the more tentative "only after a sound, basic program has been developed should preschools and kindergarten teachers consider buying a computer" (Anselmo and Zinck, 1987, p. 27).

Computers can be used to support, stimulate, and encourage young children in their development of literacy skills. They can be used by the children as an option during free-choice activity times, as instructional games for practice or reinforcement of skills, as a means of connecting pictures and words, and as a way of constructing and revising text, either through their own efforts using word-processing software or by dictating their ideas to a teacher, parent volunteer, or older child acting as a scribe.

Classroom Examples

In Ms. Diccicco's nursery school class for 4- and 5-year-olds, the computer is located in the writing center, and the children have access to it during the free play time. A parent volunteer or the teacher assists the children in the operation of the computer, although several of the more experienced children can turn on and load the software programs themselves. The adult works with the children individually or in small groups. The computer is equipped with a simplified keyboard with fewer and larger keys marked with pictures and simplified commands (e.g., GO instead of Enter). The programs used with the children have a gamelike format and the children press a key in response to a picture or simple word on the screen.

Most of Mr. Simon's class of 7- and 8-year-olds has had experience with computers in kindergarten and grade 1. For the few children who have not, Mr. Simon has asked the more experienced children to assist when needed. Although individuals or pairs of children are sometimes assigned to work on a specific software program to practice specific skills (e.g., word recognition, spelling, vocabulary), the computer is used primarily as a word processor. Each morning, the "Reporter of the Day" summarizes the news from sharing time and produces a one- or two-page newsletter complete with class title banner. After the newsletter is written and edited, a copy is printed for each child. The class and teacher then review the contents of the newsletter in the afternoon, and individuals are encouraged to write in any additional happenings from that day that they wish to share with their families. Mr. Simon has found that the daily newsletter is an excellent way for the children to apply literacy learning while at the same time keeping the parents informed about what the children are doing in school. The computer is used for other class projects as well as small-group and individual instruction, writing and assignments. There is a selection of quality educational games in the computer center for the children's use. The school has a computer lab, and the class has a weekly session with a computer specialist. Mr. Simon also uses the computer for class record-keeping, to record anecdotal notes about the children, for lesson planning, and to create instructional materials.

Guidelines for Using Computers in the Classroom

The general consensus of educators seems to be that the selective and judicious use of computers and appropriate software can help foster young children's literacy development, but that it is by no means sufficient in and of

Young writers composing their stories on computers

itself. Ross and Roe (1990) suggest the following guidelines for using computers in the classroom:

1. Prepare a series of lessons to introduce students to the computer.
2. Demonstrate the use of the computer.
3. Establish rules for computer use and discuss them with the class. Post rules near the computer as a reminder.
4. Schedule time . . . for each student to use the computer during class hours. . . .
5. Let students sign up for nonclass times, such as before and after school.
6. Use the computer as motivation for practicing and reviewing concepts already learned in class.
7. Allow 2–4 students to work together on the computer.
8. Use short activities that students can complete within their scheduled time. (p. 418)

The Teacher's Role

The teacher must play an active and continuing role in children's use of the computer if the computer is to be used to help foster children's literacy development. Teachers who are familiar and comfortable with computers and the needs of individual children are able to promote an optimal match between computer and child (Nelson, Killian, and Byrd, 1988). Some computer literacy is necessary: the teacher needs to know how to operate the computer and how to run the programs. Other teacher roles are selecting and organizing hardware and software (see the next section for a discussion of selection criteria), setting goals and objectives for the children's use of the computer based on each child's needs and abilities, and organizing and scheduling the use of the computer. The teacher also needs to monitor the children's progress and interact with the children while they are using the computer even if they are able to use the software programs independently. The teacher can help the children by asking problem-solving questions, such as, "What can you do next? How do you think you could do that? or How did you do that?". The teacher can also provide positive feedback to the children and a positive social climate that encourages cooperative use and discovery of computers.

Selecting Equipment and Organizing Computer Use

The selection of a computer for classroom use involves the selection of both hardware and software.

Selecting hardware   Hardware includes the microcomputer itself, the keyboard, disk drives, monitors, printers, and cables. Ziajka (1983) suggests asking three questions in selecting computer hardware:

1. *Is the computer user friendly?* In other words, will it be easy for the teacher and children to operate? Some computers have the option of a simplified keyboard for the younger children, although many teachers and parents report that the young children can function quite well with a standard keyboard.

2. *Can the microcomputer system be expanded?* Can all the options that one wishes be done by the computer and does it have sufficient memory? Ziajka recommends that a system be at least 32K and be expandable to at least 64K.

3. *What kind of software can be used with this computer?* And what software is wanted? This is a critical question as some programs can be run only on one type of computer. The selection of hardware will limit the options for software.

It has been recommended that a minimum amount of hardware for a group of young children should include a computer with one disk drive and standard memory capacity and a color monitor (Hohmann, 1990).

Selecting software   The key component in effective computer use with young children is using a variety of high quality software programs. Every year, there are more and more of these programs on the market. Teachers should begin with specific learning goals in mind, look for a realistic number of programs, be realistic about what software can do (most educators' expectations for software are too high), and not expect the software to replace the teacher's role (Hohmann, 1990).

One useful set of criteria for software to be used in early childhood programs was developed by Haugland and Shade (1988):

- age appropriateness
- child control
- clear instructions
- expanding complexity
- independent exploration
- process orientation with the product being of secondary importance
- real world representation to which the children can relate
- technical features (e.g., colorful, realistic sound effects, fast enough speed to keep children interested, sturdy disks)
- trial and error (children can try alternative responses)
- visible transformations (children can affect the program; cause-and-effect relationships are used)

To assist the teacher in evaluating computer software, the High/Scope Educational Research Foundation produces an annual publication, *Survey of Early Childhood Software* (Buckleitner, 1989), which reviews and rates hundreds of programs. Several professional journals have regular columns or articles reviewing new computer software (e.g., *Childhood Education, The Reading Teacher,* and *Language Arts*).

Organizing the classroom computer center   Some classrooms have a computer center, and in others a computer is included in the literacy center. A table, cart, or stand for the computer and the chairs should permit the monitor to be at the child's eye level and the keyboard at elbow level. The monitor should be positioned so that there is no glare or reflection on the screen from electric lights or windows. The cables, cords, and plugs should be away from the children's reach. Nearby shelves are useful for storing materials; however, backup copies of programs should be stored elsewhere. Sufficient space in the computer center for two or more children can encourage cooperative use of the computer.

Potential Problems with Computers in the Classroom

Although software that is appropriate for young children is now available and computers have been shown to be effective with young children, there are potential misuses of the technology. One misuse occurs when computer work takes time away from other essential areas of the early childhood curriculum. Children need a variety of experiences in a variety of settings. A difficulty in effective computer use is that not all software advertised as suitable for young children is of good quality. The content of some software is inaccurate, misleading, or confusing to young children and does not provide a positive literacy experience. Software needs to be selected carefully and used to further the teacher's goals for the children; it should not be used because it is the latest trendy technological gimmick.

There are many classrooms in North America where the children do not have access to a computer. In many more classrooms, there is one computer for 20–30 children, so each child's experience with the computer is limited. The teacher also has time constraints. It takes time to select, organize, plan, and effectively use a computer with young children. The teacher must also be knowledgeable about what the computer can do and what is appropriate for the children. For example, "learning to use the computer does not automatically create authors and readers" (Heffron, 1986, p. 155). The use of computers in early childhood classrooms has not been universally successful (Schwartz, 1988). In summary, "we now know that computers are neither panacean nor pernicious" (Clements, 1987, p. 42). And if the computer "is used wisely, with the principles of early childhood development in mind, it can be a valuable addition to a developmental-based classroom. Although the computer has much to offer an early childhood classroom, its absence from the classroom will not be disastrous" (Davidson, 1989, p. 12).

How the classroom is organized, the use of the children's and teacher's time, and patterns of classroom instruction affect teaching and learning. And although there is no one best way to organize for teaching and learning, giving attention and thought to the points presented in this chapter is part of the teacher's role in helping to facilitate the development of children's literacy.

References

American Library Association, Children's Services Division, Games and Realia Evaluation Committee. (1977). Realia in the library. *Booklist, 73,* 671–674.
Anderson, R. C., Hiebert, E. H., Scott, J. A., & Wilkinson, I. A. G. (1985). *Becoming a nation of readers: The report of the Commission on Reading.* Washington, DC: The National Institute of Education.

Anselmo, S., & Zinck, R. A. (1987). Computers for young children? Perhaps. *Young Children, 42*(3), 22–27.

Arends, R. I. (1988). *Learning to teach.* New York: Random House.

Aukerman, R. C. (1981). *The basal reader approach to reading.* New York: Wiley.

Binkley, M. R. (1986). *Becoming a nation of readers: Implications for teachers.* Washington, DC: U.S. Department of Education, Office of Educational Research and Improvement.

Bredekamp, S (Ed.). (1987). *Developmentally appropriate practice in early childhood programs serving children from birth through age 8.* Washington, DC: National Association for the Education of Young Children.

Buckleitner, W. (1989). *Survey of early childhood software.* Ypsilanti, MI: High/Scope Educational Research Foundation.

Cambourne, B. (1988). *The whole story: Natural learning and the acquisition of literacy in the classroom.* Auckland, New Zealand: Ashton Scholastic.

Canadian Association of Toy Libraries. (1986). *Toy libraries: How to start and maintain a toy library in your community.* Toronto: The Canadian Association of Toy Libraries.

Cecil, N. L. (1987). *Teaching to the heart: An affective approach to reading instruction.* Salem, WI: Sheffield Publishing Company.

Clements, D. H. (1987). Computers and young children: A review of the research. *Young Children, 43*(1), 34–44.

Crouse, P., & Davey, M. (1989). Collaborative learning: Insights from our children. *Language Arts, 66*(7), 756–766.

Davidson, J. I. (1989). *Children and computers together in the eary childhood classroom.* Albany, NY: Delmar Publishers.

Durkin, D. (1989). *Teaching them to read* (5th ed.). Boston: Allyn & Bacon.

Ekwall, E. J., & Shanker, J. L. (1989). *Teaching reading in the elementary school* (2nd ed.). Columbus, OH: Merrill Publishing Company.

Fox, A. C. (1989). Basal reader insights for the teaching of reading. In R. A. Thompson (Ed.), *Classroom reading instruction* (pp. 13–27). Dubuque, IA: Kendall/Hunt.

Goodwin, L. D., Goodwin, W. L., Nansel, A., & Helm, C. P. (1986). Cognitive and affective effects of various types of microcomputer use by preschoolers. *American Educational Research Journal, 23*(3), 348–356.

Harp, B. (1989). What do we know now about ability grouping? *The Reading Teacher, 42*(6), 430–431.

Haugland, S. W., & Shade, D. D. (1988). Developmentally appropriate software for young children. *Young Children, 43*(4), 37–43.

Heffron, K. (1986). Literacy with the computer. *The Reading Teacher, 40*(2), 152–155.

Hiebert, E. H. (1983). An examination of ability grouping for reading instruction. *Reading Research Quarterly, 18*(4), 213–255.

Hohmann, C. (1990). *Young children and computers.* Ypsilanti, MI: High/Scope Educational Research Foundation.

Johnson, D. W., Johnson, R. R., Holubec, E. J., & Roy, P. (1984). *Circles of learning: Cooperation in the classroom.* Alexandria, VA: Association for Supervision and Curriculum Development.

Jongsma, E. (1985). Grouping for instruction. *The Reading Teacher, 38*(9), 918–920.

Katz, L. G., & Chard, S. C. (1989). *Engaging children's minds: The project approach.* Norwood, NJ: Ablex Publishing Corporation.

Katz, L. G., Evangelou, D., & Hartman, J. A. (1990). *The case for mixed-age grouping in early education.* Washington, DC: National Association for the Education of Young Children.

Kozey, L. M. (1989). Cooperative learning: An effective approach to reading instruction. In R. A. Thompson (Ed.), *Classroom reading instruction* (pp. 57-70). Dubuque, IA: Kendall/Hunt Publishing Company.

Labbo, L. D., & Teale, W. H. (1990). Cross-age reading: A strategy for helping poor readers. *The Reading Teacher, 43*(6), 362-369.

Logan, G. (1989). Computers in education. *CSSE News, 16*(7), 10.

Madden, L. (1988). Improve reading attitudes of poor readers through cooperative reading teams. *The Reading Teacher, 42*(3), 194-199.

Mason, J. M., & Au, K. H. (1990). *Reading instruction for today* (2nd ed.). Glenview, IL: Scott, Foresman.

Mayfield, M. I. (1988). Toy libraries in Canada: A research study. *Canadian Children, 13*(2), 1-9.

Moffett, J., & Wagner, B. J. (1976). *Student-centered language arts and reading, K-13: A handbook for teachers* (2nd ed.). Boston: Houghton Mifflin.

Morrow, L. M. (1989). *Literacy development in the early years.* Englewood Cliffs, NJ: Prentice Hall.

Moyer, J. (Ed.). (1986). *Selecting educational equipment and materials for school and home.* Wheaton, MD: Association for Childhood Education International.

National Council of Teachers of English, The Commission on Reading. (1989). Basal readers and the state of American reading instruction: A call for action. *Language Arts, 66*(8), 896-898.

National Toy Library Association. (1984). *Getting going: A guide to setting up and running a toy library.* Potters Bar, Herts.: Play Matters.

Nelson, J. N., Killian, J., & Byrd, D. (1988). A computer in the preschool: What happens? *Day Care and Early Education, 15*(4), 6-8.

Peterson, P.,. Wilkinson, L. C., & Hallinan, M. (Eds.). (1984). *The social context of instruction: Group organization and group processes.* Orlando, FL: Academic Press.

Petty, W. T., Petty, D. C., & Salzer, R. T. (1989). *Experiences in language: Tools and techniques for language arts methods* (5th ed.). Boston: Allyn & Bacon.

Ross, E. P., & Roe, B. D. (1990). *An introduction to teaching the language arts.* Fort Worth, TX: Holt, Rinehart and Winston.

Schickendanz, J. A., York, M. E., Stewart, I. S., & White, D. A. (1990). *Strategies for teaching young children* (3rd ed.). Englewood Cliffs, NJ: Prentice Hall.

Shannon, P. (1989). *Broken promises: Reading instruction in twentieth-century America.* Granby, MA: Bergin and Garvey Publishers.

Slavin, R. E. (1987). Ability grouping and student achievement in elementary schools: A best-evidence synthesis. *Review of Educational Research, 57*(3), 293-336.

Sorenson, A. B., & Hallinan, M. T. (1986). Effects of ability grouping in growth in academic achievement. *American Educational Research Journal, 23*(4), 519-542.

Spiegel, D. L. (1981). *Reading for pleasure: Guidelines.* Newark, DE: International Reading Association.

Stauffer, R. G. (1969). *Teaching reading as a thinking process.* New York: Harper & Row.

Taylor, B. J. (1989). *Early childhood program management.* Columbus, OH: Merrill Publishing Company.

Tompkins, G. E., & Hoskisson K. (1991). *Language arts: Content and teaching strategies* (2nd ed.). Columbus, OH: Merrill Publishing Company.

Topping, K. (1989). Peer tutoring and paired reading: Combining two powerful techniques. *The Reading Teacher, 42*(7), 488-494.

Unsworth, L. (1984). Meeting individual needs through flexible within-class grouping of pupils. *The Reading Teacher, 38*(3), 298-304.

Wilkinson, L. C. (1988). Grouping children for learning: Implications for kindergarten education. *Review of Research in Education, 15,* 203–223.

Woodhill, G. (1987). Critical issues in the use of microcomputers by young children. *International Journal of Early Childhood, 19*(1), 50–57.

Wrightstone, J. W. (1967). *Class organization for instruction.* Washington, DC: National Education Association.

Ziajka, A. (1983). Microcomputers in early childhood education? A first look. *Young Children, 38*(5), 61–67.

CHAPTER NINE

Evaluation of Language and Literacy

Advance Organizer

Teachers of young children use assessment to obtain information about children's literacy and language development. Assessment is also used to evaluate the effectiveness of their educational program through observations and review of samples of behavior. These purposes are achieved using measures that must be valid, reliable, practical, culturally sensitive, and congruent with the curriculum. Literacy in young children can be assessed by the process of reading and writing and by the resulting products. Reading is assessed by the way children interact with books, story retelling, print concepts, environmental print, recognition of decontextualized print, oral reading, and folders of evidence about a child's reading as well as by sound/letter knowledge and comprehension of the text. Similarly, writing is assessed by the process used in writing as well as by the mechanics of the written product. Oral language is assessed through evidence of communication competence, including oral expression and listening in actual social contexts. Assessment data are used to make instructional decisions and to evaluate programs.

Objectives

After studying this chapter, the reader should be able to —

- know the purposes of assessment for young children;
- understand the requirements of assessment;
- be familiar with the types of assessment, including observation and behavioral samples;
- be able to construct and use various types of assessment of reading, writing, and oral language;
- understand how to use assessment data.

Graphic Organizer

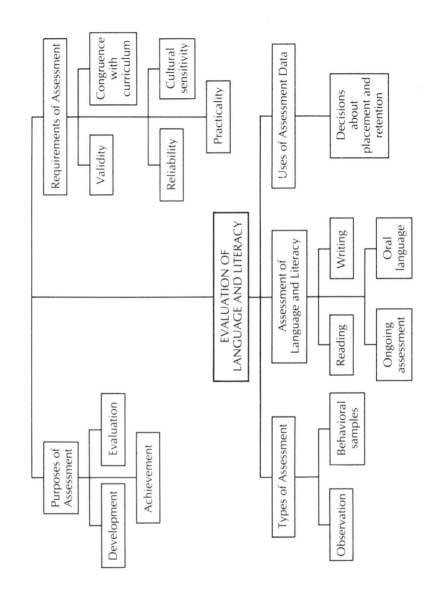

EVALUATION OF
LANGUAGE AND LITERACY

Purposes of Assessment
- Development
- Evaluation
- Achievement

Requirements of Assessment
- Congruence with curriculum
- Validity
- Cultural sensitivity
- Reliability
- Practicality

Uses of Assessment Data
- Decisions about placement and retention

Assessment of Language and Literacy
- Writing
- Oral language
- Reading
- Ongoing assessment

Types of Assessment
- Behavioral samples
- Observation

Introduction

"How is Maria doing in reading? Is Brian's oral language typical for a child of his age? Have the students in your class achieved what you expected in writing? Should I use a paper-and-pencil test with young children? What alternatives are there to testing?" These types of questions are frequently asked about the progress of young children in achieving fluency in oral language and literacy. This chapter will present ways to evaluate your language and literacy program and to assess young children's acquisition of language and literacy fluency. Current issues to be discussed in this chapter include the emphasis of many public school systems on standardized testing (accountability), the misuse of testing for promotion and retention decisions, the difference between developmental and achievement measures, and the need for new assessment procedures to assess an integrated language arts program.

Purposes of Assessment

The first step in developing an effective assessment program for young children is to determine the purpose or reason for doing the assessment. The three broad purposes of assessment that need to be considered are—

- to attain information about children's development,
- to attain information about children's achievement, and
- to evaluate the effectiveness of your program.

For any of these purposes, accurate assessment must be based on multiple observations or measures. Any one measure of the child's development or achievement provides only a partial view of that child's current level of functioning. To provide a complete picture of the child, several different appraisals must be made and decisions based upon the composite of the information obtained.

Assessment of Development

Developmental assessment measures compare the child's behavior to that of other children of the same chronological age. The developmental norm indicates the age at which that behavior is typically acquired: e.g., crawling—9 months. The development of infants and toddlers is best evaluated by comparing their present level of functioning to that of "typical" children of their chronological age. For example, a child's first word is to be expected at about 18 months of age, so the age norm for first word on a developmental oral language scale would be 1.5 years. Children being assessed with the developmental oral language scale would be compared to that expected age norm. Such age comparisons are very useful for physical development and behaviors largely determined by maturation. Typically children acquire these behaviors within a few months of the expected age (norm). A sizeable number of deviations may indicate a developmental delay and may put the child at risk for school failure.

Many behaviors are heavily influenced by the sociocultural context or environment in which the child is living and/or by direct instruction. For example, children's ability to tell about what they did on their summer vacation depends on their being in a family that takes summer vacations as well as their oral language memory and fluency. Similarly, labeling a triangle and counting from 1–5 both depend on instruction as well as maturation. In none of these three examples, then, is a developmental age scale the most appropriate assessment measure of the behavior.

Many developmental tests for young children are designed as developmental screening tests. They are designed to identify a certain segment of children who are at risk. Usually this means the lowest 20 percent of the population—those whose development is the most immature compared to other children of their chronological age. The purpose of this type of assessment is to identify the children in need of intervention programs or special educational services (Meisels, 1987). The implication is that without intervention the child is predicted to fail in school. Successful special programs (for example, a developmental language program for 3- and 4-year-olds) are designed to change that prediction.

Language development of a young child may be assessed by developmental screening tests, which compare the child's acquisition of language to that of other children of the same chronological age and identify a child whose language development is delayed, putting him or her at risk for school success. Because early intervention programs have been shown to be effective for young children, especially in language, use of developmental screening measures can be very important.

Assessment of Children's Achievement

Achievement measures compare the child's level of performance on a particular behavior at an expected level of performance (criterion). One objective of an instructional program may be for the children to retell a story, including placing the major events in sequence. The child's retelling of the story is scored by noting if the three events were retold in sequence, and if not, how many events were included. Scores may indicate whether the criterion was attained (yes/no) or the extent to which it was attained (100 percent, 67 percent, 33 percent, 0 percent).

Achievement measures include readiness tests for prekindergarten, kindergarten, and beginning first-grade children. These tests are measures of the children's current level of functioning (achievement) in particular areas related to academic success: for example, listening comprehension or language concepts. The purpose of readiness assessment is to determine where the child is at this point in time in order to plan instruction. Readiness tests are not designed to predict how the child will do at some future point in time.

Acquisition of language and literacy occurs continuously throughout the kindergarten and primary years — and indeed, throughout life. Achievement measures can be selected to determine where to begin instruction at any one time and how to plan future instruction for primary level pupils. This information allows the teacher to plan individualized, developmentally appropriate instruction for each student in the class.

Evaluation of Program Effectiveness

Teachers, principals, and other school personnel need to evaluate the effectiveness of instructional programs (curriculum, materials, and instruction) in addition to assessing the development and achievement of the children. Achievement tests provide norm-referenced data as well as criterion-referenced data. *Norm-referenced tests* are nationally standardized tests designed to compare students with other students at the same grade level across the country. *Criterion-referenced tests* provide an assessment of the students' mastery of specific objectives. These objectives may be derived from textbooks, such as the basal reading series, or from the curriculum of the state or local school system. By looking at group scores (class, school, system), educators may compare the effectiveness of their programs to those in other areas. As with all types of evaluation, more than one measure of effectiveness needs to be considered. For example, standardized test data need to be combined with classroom observations, interviews with teachers, and class performance by the pupils.

Before selecting the means of assessment to be used in your program, you must first determine the purpose for assessing your pupils. Usually teachers are primarily concerned with assessing achievement and/or development in language and literacy. Administrators, however, may also require assessment for the purpose of program evaluation. In many instances the information obtained can be used for both purposes.

Requirements of Assessment

All assessment instruments and all ongoing assessment (e.g., checklists, observations, portfolios) regardless of type or purpose must meet five basic requirements. They must be valid, reliable, practical, culturally sensitive, and congruent with the curriculum.

Validity

Measures are valid if they measure what they say they measure. If the test purports to be a measure of mathematical operations (e.g., addition and subtraction), it needs to measure that, not reading comprehension. Even nonverbal tests may present the test item verbally: for example, numerical word problems that require reading and verbal comprehension as well as mathematical operations. A student with limited reading or language proficiency will fail the mathematics test, not because of limited math skills but because of limited reading skills. Thus this type of test question is not a valid measure of mathematics. Similarly a tally kept of which students contribute to a group discussion after reading a storybook gives a measure of oral participation but not of oral fluency. Some children who did not contribute to the group discussion may simply be too shy to speak in a group or not aggressive enough to get a turn. The validity of a measure is important to be certain that you are assessing what you say you are.

Reliability

Every assessment technique must yield reliable data: that is, the same score or information each time the technique is applied. If a child's literacy behavior is being observed during free-choice time, the instrument used to record reading and writing behaviors must be reliable enough so that several observers would note the same behaviors when observing that child. Carefully defining the behaviors to be observed or rated improves reliability. For example, if time spent looking at books is to be recorded, is the behavior noted if it occurs only once that day or each time it occurs that day? Is the length of time spent looking at books to be recorded or just the frequency of the behavior? What constitutes looking at books—looking all the way through a book? looking at the pictures? flipping through several books? These questions need to be addressed in order for the observation instrument to be reliable. Reliability is essential to determine that the assessment is consistent across time, observations, and observers.

Practicality

In addition to being valid and reliable, assessment procedures and instruments must be practical. They must take a reasonable amount of time, be used easily by a classroom teacher, not be too expensive, be scored and summarized relatively quickly and easily by the classroom teacher, and include an efficient, clear way to report the results to parents.

A detailed running record of language and literacy behaviors kept every day about every child would provide a very rich record of the children's development and learning. However, no one could keep such records and still have time to teach. Nor can such detailed records be easily reported to parents. Therefore, such an assessment technique is not practical.

Cultural Sensitivity

Many assessment measures and techniques make assumptions about students that are incorrect: for example, they may assume that all students are from a middle socioeconomic level, are native English-speaking, and are white children from suburban, two-parent families. Because it is obvious that this description does not fit all children in North American schools, it is important to review assessment techniques for possible assumptions that might bias the results against some students. Several screening tests ask children to state their age and/or birthday and to tell about their most recent birthday party. These are both culturally relevant concepts — age is calculated differently in some Asian cultures and the concept and practice of birthday celebrations vary with the socioeconomic and cultural context of the family. A child's failure on items such as these tells nothing about the child. Rather it highlights the lack of cultural sensitivity of the instrument. Unfortunately, however, often low scores on such measures are recorded and follow the child for many years with attendant negative consequences.

Of particular concern are non-native, English-speaking children. Frequently they enter prekindergarten, kindergarten, or first grade with little or no oral English proficiency. They need time to interact with English-speaking children and adults in the class in order to acquire some proficiency in English. Assessment measures designed for native English speakers and especially those comparing their performance to that of native English speakers are not valid for these students. Even nonverbal and performance measures have verbal directions that create problems for limited English proficient students.

Tests and other assessment measures should be reviewed for items, illustrations, or content that might be unfamiliar to any particular group of young children. Vocabulary and dialect differences should be considered so that the child is not unfairly penalized by lack of familiarity with a particular concept or by a nonstandard home dialect. For example, a child might not pronounce the vowel sounds in *pen* and *pin* as two distinct sounds (a difference between Southern and Midwestern dialects in the United States) or might be familiar with zoo animals, but not farm animals. Attention to these cultural and linguistic issues is essential if each child's individual strengths and potential are to be recognized.

Congruence with Curriculum

Assessment instruments may meet the first four requirements discussed above and be acceptable assessment instruments for young children yet still be inappropriate for use in a particular setting. Assessment measures must share the same theoretical orientation as the classroom curriculum and instructional materials in order to be appropriate in a particular setting. If the assessment is to determine whether the instructional objectives have been attained, then the objectives measured by the assessment must be essentially the same as those taught by the curriculum. Such is not always the case. Durkin (1987) has noted the wide use of developmental screening tests assessing kindergarten children's development in motor and visual-motor skills in classes in which phonics instruction was given to the whole class regardless of developmental level. If the purpose of the developmental screening tests was to assess level of maturity and readiness for instruction, then the results should have been used to plan instruction. Some of the children might have been ready for phonics instruction, but others would not have been. If whole-group phonics instruction was to be given to all students in the class regardless of developmental level, there was no point in giving the developmental screening test. There needs to be a congruence between the underlying philosophy of the curriculum and the assessment measure if the assessment is to provide help in planning instruction or to be an evaluation of the effectiveness of the program.

Teachers who use an integrated language arts and literacy program realize that most published assessment measures of language and literacy are based on a skills approach to reading and writing. This means that children are being assessed on instruments that do not reflect the philosophy, goals, or purpose of their instructional program (Heald-Taylor, 1986; Samway, 1989; Strickland and Morrow, 1989; Teale, Hiebert, and Chittendon, 1987; Willert and Kamii, 1985). If literacy is to be taught as a process, it must be assessed as a process. There are many techniques that are appropriate for assessing the literacy of young children: for example, observation of behavior with books, understanding of print concepts, oral reading miscues, process scoring of writing, story retelling, and literacy portfolios. These techniques will be discussed in the next section of this chapter.

In 1988 the National Association for the Education of Young Children (NAEYC) published a position statement on testing of young children. They stressed the importance of following accepted testing standards in the development and use of all assessment with young children. NAEYC also emphasized the importance of developmentally appropriate instruction for both kindergarten and primary grade children (Bredekamp, 1987). Assessment must also be developmentally appropriate; that is, it must take into account the developmental levels of the young child in both the content and the format of the assessment. For example, if the curriculum emphasizes the total development of the child (social, emotional, sensory-motor, linguistic, and cognitive development), then all these areas must be assessed. If just academic knowledge is assessed even for primary grade children, there is a mismatch between the theoretical assumptions of the curriculum and the assessment instrument.

Types of Assessment

Two techniques are used to assess young children's language and literacy proficiency: (1) observing their behaviors as they use language and literacy and (2) collecting oral and written samples of language and literacy behavior. Both may be in natural settings (observing reading behavior in the library corner or collecting writing done by children on their paintings) or elicited through specially arranged activities (asking a child to retell a familiar story or giving a standardized test).

Observation

Teacher observations of students' language and literacy behavior may be recorded by checklists, rating scales, or anecdotal notes. Each will be described with examples of their use.

Checklists Checklists provide a listing of discrete behaviors to be observed with a place to record their occurrence. Each behavior must be carefully defined to be observable and discrete. Examples of literacy behaviors that might be assessed by a checklist are:

recognizes own name
"reads" story by retelling it from pictures
writes caption for picture phonemically

It is important that the behaviors be observable; e.g., "Chooses to read during free time" rather than "Loves to read." Each item on the checklist should be discrete and separate: e.g., "Follows two directions in sequence" rather than "Gives and follows directions." Most classroom teachers will choose to use a published checklist rather than to construct one of their own. Careful review of the checklist is necessary to make certain it meets the measurement criteria and that the behaviors are observable, discrete, and necessary to the acquisition of literacy. See Heald-Taylor (1986) for an example of such a checklist.

Responses to a checklist may be set up so that the teacher simply checks yes or no, tallies the frequency of the behavior (e.g., number of times it occurred that day or week), or tallies the behavior along a time or event grid. To do the latter, set up a grid with behaviors across the top and time or event units down one side; then tally within the blanks (see Figure 9-1). Time units might be weeks, days, hours; event units might be activities in the daily schedule, groupings of children (alone, pairs, small group, large group), teacher involvement (teacher-directed, independent). Use of a grid allows the teacher to assess the occurrence of the behavior within a time or event framework: e.g., writing occurs primarily in small groups or reading occurs primarily in pairs.

Rating scales Checklists tell of the presence or absence of behaviors but do not evaluate them. A rating scale lists behaviors and rates them against a predetermined standard. For example, a child's written expression might be rated along a continuum from scribbling to conventional writing, as follows:

Scribbling
Letterlike Symbols
Letters
Phonemic Spelling
Conventional Writing

Another example of the use of a rating scale would be to indicate that a child participated in group discussions frequently, most of the time, some of the time, or never.

FIGURE 9-1 • *Sample Time and Event Sampling Checklist*

Child's Name _____ Date _____

Age/Grade _____ Teacher _____

Tally each time child asks a question.

Event

Time	Socio-dramatic	Art Activities	Snack	Storytelling	Outdoor Play
8:30 A.M.					
8:45 A.M.					
9:00 A.M.					
9:15 A.M.					
9:30 A.M.					
9:45 A.M.					
10:00 A.M.					
10:15 A.M.					
10:30 A.M.					
10:45 A.M.					
11:00 A.M.					
11:15 A.M.					
11:30 A.M.					
11:45 A.M.					
12:00 P.M.					

Anecdotal notes   Instead of responding to a list of predetermined behaviors, teachers often prefer to keep notes on children's behavior. Notes about specific behaviors observed, behavior at a particular time or location, or behavior in different groups (with or without a teacher, small- or large-group) may be kept in a convenient format (note cards or individual folders). The anecdotal record should include the date, time period, setting, group size, others present, and activity observed. Behaviors observed should be separated from interpretations of that behavior by dividing the card or page into two sections. The observation section is an exact description of the behavior; the interpretation section is an evaluation or comment on the behavior. For example:

Observation: "Bradley is working at the word processor typing a story. He stops frequently to ask how to spell a word. When it is suggested he try to spell it himself, he writes the first sound(s) and goes on."

Interpretation: "Bradley seems to be unsure of how to guess at the spelling of words. He does not attempt phonemic spelling unless encouraged to do so by the teacher. He appears to only hear the initial sound in the word."

Behavioral Samples

Spontaneous and elicited samples of young children's language and literacy behavior provide another record of the children's emergent communication proficiency.

Products and processes Samples of children's language and literacy products may be collected to show their progress over time. Examples include paintings and art work, writing samples, photographs of language interactions, audiotapes of oral language, audiotapes of reading, videotapes of individual or interaction behavior, and any other appropriate samples. These samples may be spontaneously produced, as when a child writes a caption on a painting at the easel. They may also be elicited, as when the teacher asks a child to tell the story of "The Little Red Hen." A file of these products shows development over time in varying contexts. Each entry should be dated, and an indication given as to whether the behavior was spontaneous or elicited. Descriptions of the processes used in producing these products may also be recorded and kept with the products.

Tests Collections of standardized behavioral samples (i.e., a sample of the same behavior for all students collected under standard conditions) are also useful. These standardized samples of behavior are tests. Tests may be oral or written; they may require the student to produce the answer or to select the correct answer from several options. Performance on tests may be compared to a predetermined standard (criterion-referenced) or to the performance of others (norm-referenced). As indicated earlier, tests may be used to assess development or to measure achievement.

Standardized tests for children 4–7 years old usually assess the following:

language development,
vocabulary,
concepts,
listening comprehension,
mathematical concepts,
auditory and visual skills (discrimination and memory),
letter/sound correspondence,
letter/numeral recognition and naming.

For primary students standardized tests assess:

sentence and paragraph reading and comprehension,
word analysis,
word recognition,
vocabulary,
penmanship,
mathematical operations and problem solving.

Occasionally, the tests assess knowledge and information (social studies and science); spelling; language mechanics (grammar, punctuation, capitalization); and study skills. In the late 1980s, standardized reading tests were being developed to assess reading from the perspective of construction of meaning. These tests measure background knowledge of topics, comprehension of longer pieces of text, and concepts about how to read (Wixson, Peters, Weber, and Roeber, 1987). Most standardized tests provide both criterion-referenced and norm-referenced data to facilitate their use in planning instruction for individual children and to evaluate groups of children (class, school, system).

Multiple measures are always required to produce an accurate assessment of a student or an evaluation of a program. No one test can tell the complete story. Tests provide a standardized measure not available through observation and behavior samples, but decisions should never be made on the basis of one test score any more than they should be made on the basis of one observation or one language product. For example, a test score may indicate that a child's reading skills are average compared with other children in the country; however, records of the books read by the child and stories written over several months may indicate that the child's actual literacy functioning is above what is expected for that grade level.

Language and literacy tests measure certain language skills and behaviors in a particular setting, but they do not measure the actual use of language and literacy in real settings (Lindfors, 1987). Accurate assessment of a child or program requires both types of information. Teachers need to plan an assessment program that provides sufficient quantity and variety of data to meet their purposes for assessment. A common way to do so is to keep a portfolio on each child in which test data, work samples, reading records, writing over a period of time, and other data on the child's acquisition of literacy are kept. These portfolios permit a comprehensive review of the child's literacy development over a period of time.

Assessment of Language and Literacy

In keeping with the integrated language arts approach to language and literacy in this text, assessment techniques will be presented that are designed to assess reading, writing, and oral language use in actual situations. Procedures to be discussed include those designed to assess the processes an individual child uses, not just the products or results.

Reading

The reading behavior of 4–7-year-olds covers the span of emergent literacy behaviors from little or no concept of print or story to relatively fluent reading of beginning texts. Assessment techniques need to cover this span as well.

Book behavior   Observation of young children to determine their interest in books, time spent looking at books, and attention while books are read is one way to assess emerging literacy. When children select cassette recordings of books, do they look at the book while they listen? Do they follow the text or just look at the pictures? When given a familiar picture storybook, does the child retell the story turning the pages at the appropriate places in the text? During storytime does the child ask questions about the story, repeat phrases, or join in refrains? Does the child enjoy hearing stories read? Does the child respond to questions about the story or try to guess what might happen next? These behaviors indicate an interest in books and stories and a growing concept of story reading. They also indicate the child's understanding of reading as a communication task; that print represents meaning.

Story retelling   After hearing an interesting picture storybook read several times, most young children can retell the story by looking at the pictures in the book. Listening to their retelling allows the teacher to check to see what story elements they are including in the retelling. Woodley (1988) has noted that this task is easier when the text is predictable and uses patterned language such as *Brown Bear, Brown Bear, What Do You See?* (Martin, 1970). Does the story have a beginning? Are the characters named? Is the setting and time given? Are the author's conversation and description included? Are the major events and resolution of the plot presented in the author's sequence? Does the story have an ending? These same questions can be used to evaluate the oral retelling of a familiar story without the picture props.

Print concepts   Another measure of early literacy behaviors is the child's understanding of print concepts. These may be assessed by asking the child a series of questions about books and print or by using one of the standardized tests of print concepts. Concepts to be assessed include knowing how to hold a book, which part is to be read, the direction it is to be read, and the names of various aspects of print (letter, capital letter, word, period, question mark). An interview may be held with the child and a book in order to assess these concepts.

Reading environmental print and logos   One of the first written symbols young children read is the logo for familiar fast foods or soft drinks (e.g., Mc-Donald's or Coke). Gradually they associate the logo (e.g., the golden arch) with the printed name (McDonald's) and eventually are able to read the name in conventional print out of context. You can gain information about children's attempts to read logos and environmental print by observing their responses to print in their play; listening to their conversations when looking at magazines or newspapers and noticing their use of meaningful labels around the room. These behaviors give an indication of the child's understanding of the functions of written language (Teale, 1988).

Recognizing decontextualized words and phrases   As literacy continues to develop, the child begins to recognize decontextualized words and phrases (i.e., words and phrases not in their natural environmental context). For example, the child initially might recognize *Corduroy* on the cover of the familiar storybook; later *corduroy* might be recognized in a different context, such as a sign on the display table labeling different materials and their textures. Teachers can keep records of examples of words and phrases a child can read over time to give another assessment of the child's developing literacy. Many standardized reading tests often measure word recognition out of context; that is, they present a picture and ask the child to mark which of four words goes with that picture.

Hearing children read   Listening to children read books aloud gives an assessment of the child's growing ability to read text. By using stories and "real" texts (picture storybooks, for example), you can observe their ability to use illustrations, the structure of the story, and the print context to figure out words. The use of a systematic technique for recording observations while listening to an oral reading of real texts storybooks and reading instructional texts allows the teacher to determine what strategies the children are using in reading. The most common technique is *miscue analysis* (Goodman, Watson, and Burke, 1987). Each word that is read differently from the printed text is noted as a miscue (e.g., in the sentence, "The trucks rolled down the road" the child reads "The trucks went down the road"). The substitution is studied to determine if it alters the meaning of the passage or the sentence. In the example given, substituting *went* for *rolled* does not change the meaning of the passage. The substitution can also be studied for grammatical, visual, and/or phonemic similarity to the word replaced. Using the above example, *rolled* and *went* are the same grammatically (both are past tense verbs) so the grammatical sense of the passage also remains unchanged. This substitution, however, was visually and phonetically dissimilar to the word in the text. The child who read this sentence was using semantic and grammatical information in reading the text, but not graphophonic (visual and phonemic) information. Since the emphasis of an integrated language program is on encouraging children to read a text so that they understand it rather than calling or saying each word exactly, this miscue would be noted but would not cause undue concern to the teacher. It is often helpful to note miscues when a child reads a text and then rereads it. The second (or third) reading may more accurately reflect the child's understanding of the passage.

An Informal Reading Inventory (IRI) is also used to assess a child's oral reading by having a passage read aloud and the errors coded. Oral reading is usually followed by comprehension questions over the passage. Because an IRI focuses on errors in exact reading of the passage without attention to whether the error changes the meaning of the passage, it is less useful than a miscue analysis of a child's oral reading of the same passage. Using a miscue analysis while hearing children read is a particularly effective way to assess reading of primary grade students whose oral reading would be expected to reflect both comprehension and fluency.

Assessing sound/letter knowledge In an integrated language and literacy program, instruction begins with real language in natural settings and with actual texts, not with isolated symbols. Thus, literacy instruction for young children does not revolve around a phonics program. In order to be a fluent reader, however, the concept of sound/letter correspondences must be developed and children should be able to apply this knowledge to figuring out words in the text. Many children who are exposed to a rich language and literacy program will develop the concept of sound/letter correspondence from their interactions with oral language and written texts. They will begin to use this knowledge of sound/letter correspondences in their writing: for example, using phonemic spelling (*kt* for *cat*). Other children, however, will need more direct instruction and practice in hearing the sounds and connecting them to the corresponding letters. As a teacher, you need information about young children's concept of sound/letter correspondences and their skill in using this information in reading and writing (Teale, 1988).

Children who have difficulty separating the initial sound in a word from the rest of the word (phoneme segmentation) may have difficulty with sound/letter correspondence. Continued opportunity for language play with rhymes and jingles, exposure to attempting to read texts, and opportunities to attempt to write will help most children acquire phoneme segmentation. Most standardized readiness or beginning reading tests include a measure of letter/sound correspondence. Many basal reading series have criterion-referenced tests that measure this knowledge also.

Understanding the text Asking questions and discussing a story is a technique used to assess children's comprehension of stories read aloud to them. These same techniques can be used for stories they read. Especially useful are questions where children predict what comes next, project the feelings of the characters, explain why something happened or didn't happen, or retell the sequence of events in the story. These open-ended questions require the child to use thinking processes rather than just remember specific information as in *yes/no* or *who, what, when, where* questions. *How, why,* and "What do you think" questions give a clearer picture of the child's understanding of the text.

Both standardized tests and criterion-referenced tests designed to accompany a reading series include reading passages and comprehension questions. Usually these tests use a multiple-choice format so the child selects the "best" answer to the question. There are several other assessment techniques that require the child to produce language indicating understanding of the text. The *Cloze procedure* has been recommended as a way to assess student's comprehension of the whole passage (Lee and Rubin, 1979). This technique uses reading passages in which every fifth word has been replaced by a blank. The student is asked to write in the missing words (or, in a modified Cloze technique, to select the missing words from a list of four possible words). Scoring is similar to the miscue analysis by looking for semantic and grammatical acceptability. Recently there have been criticisms of this technique, suggesting that it depends heavily on prior knowledge of syntax and the topic (Farr and Carey, 1986).

A technique for assessing comprehension frequently suggested for primary grade pupils is having the child retell a story. By recording the child's retelling (on tape or in writing), the teacher has a record of the child's version of the story and can review it to determine what the child has included in the retelling. The same elements used to assess oral storytelling are considered: the story beginning, setting (place and time), characters, events, sequence, description, conversation, statement of the problem(s), climax and resolution, and the story ending. Often children will add information that was implied in the story but not explicitly stated or add relevant background information. Comprehension of the story is heavily affected by the child's background knowledge and prior experiences with the topic. Failure to understand the text may not indicate a lack of reading comprehension skills but rather a lack of context for the story. It is important to estimate the influence of background knowledge and cultural experience on a child's comprehension of text.

Reading folders   Assessment of actual reading done by the young child requires both observation of reading behavior and systematic record keeping. How often does the child actually read texts (books, magazines, directions, newspapers, signs and labels)? What does the child read? Reading folders kept for each child provide an opportunity for the teacher to record this information. The reading folders might contain a list of the books the child has read, book reports in which the child has drawn picture(s) of the story and written caption(s) for these illustrations, notes on discussions or interviews the teacher has had with the child about books read (reading conferences), a survey of the child's reading interests, anecdotal notes kept by the teacher about the child's reading, and audiotapes of samples of the child's reading (Samway, 1989). Records need to be kept throughout the year.

Writing

Children's writing begins with their early scribbling attempts. When the child tells the story recorded by the scribbling (and does so consistently over time and setting), there is strong indication that the child understands the purposes of writing to communicate ideas with others. Several studies have documented young children's development of stages of written expression (Nurss, 1988). These include scribbling, pictures, letterlike symbols incorporating the elements of the written language in the child's environment (Clay, 1986; Harste, Woodward, and Burke, 1984), letters and numerals, phonemic (invented) spelling, and traditional spelling. A checklist of these stages allows the teacher to note the child's concepts of writing as written expression emerges.

Dictation   Use of the language experience approach to reading gives children the opportunity to engage in narrative and expository writing through dictation. These attempts may be assessed in terms of quantity of dictation (length of the piece), clarity of ideas, sequence of events, descriptive language, and cohesiveness. Scales developed to assess process writing (see Box 9-1) may also be used to assess dictation. Samples of children's dictation copied by the children or written or typed by the teacher provide a measure of the child's emergent writing without the interference of penmanship (fine motor skills).

BOX 9-1   •   *Process Writing Scoring Guide*

6	Ideas are very well developed and expressed.
	The writing has fully developed structure.
	The ideas are connected logically and are well organized.
	Sentence variety and expression are good.
5	Ideas are fairly well developed and expressed.
	The writing has a discernible structure.
	The ideas are connected logically, but they are not so fully developed or so well organized as score 6 papers.
4	Ideas are only loosely connected or not developed.
	The structure may be disjointed, but what is provided is clearly more than a list.
	The ideas are relevant but are not developed or expressed well.
	The sentence structure may be repetitive.
3	Ideas lack development.
	The writing often merely lists ideas.
	The phrasing and sentence structure are repetitious.
2	Ideas have little or no relationship to the topic.
	An idea or a list is provided that is not connected logically to the topic.
1	Lack of ideas.
	All that is presented is a restatement of the question or topic to be addressed.
UN	Undecipherable
BL	Blank

Source: Adapted from M. R. Zurn (1987). *A comparison of kindergarteners' handwritten and word processor generated writing.* Unpublished doctoral dissertation, Georgia State University, Atlanta. *Dissertation Abstracts International, 49,* 427-A. (University Microfilms No. 88-08112).

Assessment of the writing process   Early writing attempts by young children reflect their understanding of writing as an expression of ideas even though they may not have mastered conventional handwriting (penmanship), spelling, or other writing mechanics (capitalization, punctuation). Assessment of the child's acquisition of written expression centers around the writing process, not the resulting product. This process approach to writing includes teacher/student interaction in the form of conferences and interviews. Writing samples are kept in individual writing folders. Writing portfolios (Samway, 1989) are a systematic way to keep samples of writing (works in progress as well as completed works) over time. Portfolios can also contain anecdotal notes about the child's writing, records of writing conferences in which the child reads writing samples to the teacher and they discuss these works, and interviews with the child about writing. Questions of interest include: "Who initiated the writing? Was the topic assigned or self-selected? How much writing has been produced? What behaviors — oral language, interaction with others, body language — were noted during writing? Is there evidence of rereading and revising? Does the child have a clear audience for writing?" (Rhodes and Dudley-Marling, 1988).

Several scales have been developed to assess the quality of children's written expression. One of these is the Process Writing Scoring Guide developed by Zurn (1987) to assess kindergarten children's compositions produced in a writing-to-read program (see Box 9-1). These are particularly useful for primary grade students' writing.

Writing mechanics   The emphasis in assessing written expression of young children is on the process of writing, not the written language mechanics. Thus, penmanship, spelling, punctuation, capitalization, and grammar are considered secondary to the expression of ideas. Children are encouraged to reread and revise their work. In the process of revising, many children begin to edit their work for mechanics as well. Frequently they ask questions about how to spell a word or what mark to put to indicate that the passage is to be read with enthusiasm and excitement. Thus, the child's early acquisition of writing mechanics will be reflected in the samples of their work in their writing folders and in the teacher's notes observing their writing behaviors. When works are prepared for publication, editing draws attention to the mechanics of writing. The child's proficiency in this process may be noted on a checklist or with a scale assessing the spelling from prephonemic to transitional to correct (Temple, Nathan, Burris, and Temple, 1988).

Ongoing Assessment

The setting for the literacy event (place, time, persons present, materials, purpose, child- vs. teacher-initiated activity) will have an influence on the child's behavior. Thus, assessment needs to be done in a variety of settings to give a comprehensive picture of the child's literacy development. It has been noted (Rhodes and Dudley-Marling, 1988) that teacher behavior also affects the child's literacy behavior. Assessment that is designed to reveal underlying processes, not just external evidence, requires the teacher to ask questions and follow up student responses. Teacher questions provide important information about why the child is or is not behaving in a particular way, but may also influence the child's behavior. Thus, it is important to record both the teacher's and the student's questions, comments, and actions.

Literacy needs to be assessed over time, not just at the end of the unit, book, or school year. A developmental record of reading and writing behaviors over several years (e.g., prekindergarten through the early primary grades) affords an opportunity to view the child's emerging literacy over time in a variety of contexts (Rhodes and Dudley-Marling, 1988; Teale, Hiebert, and Chittenden, 1987).

Reflecting on these suggestions for assessment of children's emerging literacy, you may be wondering how teachers have time to do all this assessment and still teach. Assessment should be integrated with instruction, not separated from it. By so doing, the teacher can observe the children's behaviors while reading and writing, making notes to be summarized later in the day (Teale, 1988). For example, teachers can observe children while they are engaged in silent reading, making notes about the children's silent reading behaviors, such as the ease with which the child is distracted, the time involved in reading, whether the child asks for assistance, responses (e.g., smiling or laughing) to the story (Fields and Lee, 1987).

Clearly, information recorded about children's literacy development needs to be summarized and analyzed in order to be useful. If the purpose for assessment is to plan future instruction for the child, the teacher needs to reflect upon information recorded in order to use that information for planning and instruction (Marek et al., 1984). Reading and writing interviews allow the teacher to obtain information about the children's perceptions of their reading and writing behavior (Rhodes and Dudley-Marling, 1988; Woodley, 1988).

Oral Language

Typically 4–7-year-old children have already acquired proficiency in speaking and listening. They are able to use language to make their needs and desires known, express their feelings, and communicate thoughts to others. They have made great strides toward developing adult forms of articulation and grammatical usage. They are also able to comprehend the language of others. Their oral language continues to develop as they become more sophisticated in expressing their thoughts orally and develop listening comprehension skills needed to understand stories, follow directions, and remember information. Assessment of oral language, like assessment of written language, needs to consider both speaking and listening in the context of "real-world" language use.

Communicative competence   Assessment of a child's communicative competence considers not only acquisition of oral language, but also acquisition of the functions of language and the sociocultural context in which language is used. Observation of children's use of oral language in various classroom settings (sociodramatic play, blocks, art, storytime, outdoor play, routines) is an effective way to assess communicative competence (Genishi and Dyson, 1984). Anecdotal records and both audio- and videotapes provide good records of language use over time; however, they can be very time-consuming and may not meet the assessment criterion of practicality. The focus of such observations might be the effectiveness of the child's communication, the clarity of expression, the appropriateness of the language for the situation, the richness of the vocabulary, and variety of functions with which language is used. As with written expression, the purpose is communication, not articulation of isolated sounds or assessment of grammatical knowledge. Observation of oral language interchanges allows the teacher to note the child's use of turn taking (a social device important to oral communication) and nonverbal expression (facial expression, body language, gestures) used to supplement verbal expression.

An effective way to assess communication competence using anecdotal notes or a checklist is to arrange small-group interaction activities in which children must use oral language. Examples include a card game in which one child must ask the other for the card needed to make a pair; a feely box in which children must describe the item felt and name it; a cooking activity; roleplaying a situation such as a fast-food restaurant; or acting out a favorite story. The checklist can include items such as clarity of expression, accuracy of vocabulary, understanding of concepts, richness of description, turn taking, and quantity of language (Jewell and Zintz, 1986).

Language variation   Because children acquire their language from the models in their environment, they learn both the language and the specific dialect of that language spoken in their home and community. This language and dialect may be different from what they encounter in school. Assessment of oral language needs to consider the environment in which the child acquired language. Language variation reflects these sociocultural differences, not errors or mistakes. Both the limited English proficient and the nonstandard dialect speaker demonstrate the present level of their language acquisition. Increased exposure to a rich language environment in which they have constant opportunities to interact with native, standard dialect speakers as active users of language will result in a continuation of their development of oral language fluency in standard English. Assessment of these children's language should note their progress in becoming bidialectal or bilingual but should not penalize them for the variety of their linguistic expression.

Listening   Listening comprehension is easily assessed in a story reading situation. As with reading comprehension, asking open-ended questions to foster thinking and discussion is both an instructional and an assessment device. It exposes the children's understanding of the story and, with support from the adult, can provide the framework for increasing vocabulary and comprehension (Genishi and Dyson, 1984). Listening can also be assessed by observation of the child following oral directions in games or projects. Reading sentences aloud with the final word or phrase omitted and asking the child to complete the sentence with a word or phrase that makes sense assesses the child's skills in using oral context to create meaning.

Uses of Assessment Data

Assessment must always be for a specific purpose. There is no point in collecting assessment data unless it is to be used in the instructional program and unless it affects language and literacy instruction for the children. For this reason, good records are essential. Unless the data are readily available to the teacher, they will not be used in planning. Record keeping need not be complex. It can consist of folders (i.e., folders of work samples, reading folders, writing portfolios), checklists, summarized anecdotal notes, test scores, and tapes.

In order to be valid and reliable, decisions based upon assessment must always include multiple assessment measures. Decisions should not be made on one test score or one observation. By using multiple evidence, the teacher can present a clear picture of a child over time (Pellegrini, Dresden, and Glickman, 1988).

Assessment data about young children's achievement in language and literacy should also be reported to parents. Parent/teacher conferences are the most effective means of reporting using a portfolio or case-study methodology. In preparing the case study, the teacher assembles a portfolio by collecting over time a broad sample of data about the child — work samples, audiotapes of oral language and reading, reading and writing folders, checklists and anecdotal notes over the school year, and test scores. The teacher reviews all the information and prepares highlights of the child's progress. By emphasizing the processes the child is using in acquiring language and literacy proficiency as well as the developmental sequence to date, the teacher and parents can plan future instruction for the child.

Decisions about Placement and Retention of Young Children

In the late 1980s, new questions were raised about the use of tests to determine a child's placement in school. Practices such as using a standardized test score to determine a child's promotion into first grade were widely criticized (Bredekamp and Shepard, 1989; Charlesworth, 1989; Shepard and Smith,

1988; Smith and Shepard, 1987, 1988). In many instances retention policies and the provision of transition classes were heavily based on —

developmental screening tests assessing the child's maturation (visual and auditory discrimination, fine motor skills, attention span);
language development (oral vocabulary, fluency, listening skills);
concept development (knowledge of colors, shapes, and body parts);
cultural information (families, weather, seasons, holidays, animals, transportation);
social skills (working in a group, completing a task, caring for one's own property).

In some instances, the child's knowledge of the alphabet, rote counting, letter/sound correspondence, and penmanship (letter formation) is also assessed. If a child's performance indicates that the child is immature, at risk, or not ready for the language and literacy demands of first grade, the recommendation is made that the child be retained in kindergarten or placed in a transitional class. Concerns have been raised about the appropriateness of such recommendations. Research by Shepard and Smith (1988) and Smith and Shepard (1987, 1988) suggests that in the long-term retention may result in no real academic advantage, possible negative emotional effects, and lack of equity in educational opportunity (boys and minorities are more likely to be retained than girls and nonminorities). Furthermore, children who repeat kindergarten are likely to simply repeat the same experiences and activities as they had the prior year. That is, the curriculum is not adjusted to meet their individual levels of attainment and needs. Even transition classes often provide limited opportunities for language and literacy, thus guaranteeing that the child must move into first grade rather than having the option of moving into second grade.

Expectations of homogeneity at any grade level result in whole-group instruction rather than individualized instruction. However, assessment data can be used to plan developmentally appropriate instruction by determining what the child has learned to date and planning for what comes next. In this way, the language and literacy curriculum is adapted to the individual child rather than expecting the child to fit into a predetermined curriculum. The integrated approach to language and literacy instruction is particularly well suited to making these adaptations. Within the group activities of the classroom, each child is using language and exploring reading and writing individually. The integrated approach makes available activities over a wide range of difficulty. By using assessment data from more than one source (teacher observation, developmental screening tests, local school checklists, or standardized readiness tests) the teacher can match the child to the appropriate activity, moving the child along in acquisition of language and literacy rather than forcing all children into the same activity, boring some and frustrating others. No matter what chronological age span or range of maturational levels is present in the class, there will be a range of levels of language and literacy acquisition. Comprehensive assessment data stored in a concise format assists the teacher in providing appropriate activities to meet all children's needs within an integrated curriculum. Instruction can still be in groups with each child participating at her or his own level.

Conclusion

Assessment of the language and literacy program for young children requires the teacher to collect multiple indicators of the children's progress. Teacher observation, checklists of language and literacy behaviors, samples of oral language and writing, records of reading progress, and tests (criterion-referenced and norm-referenced) provide a variety of means of assessment. Whatever instruments are used, they must be reliable, valid, practical, culturally sensitive, and congruent with the curriculum. Assessment of an integrated language and literacy program requires use of measures of language and literacy in actual situations (i.e., real-life reading, writing, speaking, and listening). Such continuous assessment should be a part of the instructional program, not a one-time, single measure. Used in this way assessment becomes a part of the planning process and gives information about which objectives have been attained and what type of instruction is needed next.

References

Bredekamp, S. (Ed.). (1987). *Developmentally appropriate practice in early childhood programs serving children from birth through age 8* (expanded ed.). Washington, DC: National Association for the Education of Young Children.

Bredekamp, S., & Shepard, L. (1989). How best to protect children from inappropriate school expectations, practices, and policies. *Young Children, 44,* 14–24.

Charlesworth, R. (1989). "Behind" before they start? Deciding how to deal with the rest of kindergarten "failure." *Young Children, 44,* 5–13.

Clay, M. (1986). *The early detection of reading difficulties* (3rd ed.). Portsmouth, NH: Heinemann Educational.

Durkin, D. (1987). Testing in the kindergarten. *The Reading Teacher, 40,* 766–770.

Farr, R., & Carey, R. F. (1986). *Reading: What can be measured?* (2nd ed.). Newark, DE: International Reading Association.

Fields, M. V., & Lee, D. (1987). *Let's begin reading right. A developmental approach to beginning literacy.* Columbus, OH: Merrill Publishing Co.

Genishi, C., & Dyson, A. H. (1984). *Language assessment in the early years.* Norwood, NJ: Ablex Publishing.

Goodman, Y. M., Watson, D. J., & Burke, C. L. (1987). *Reading miscue inventory: Alternative procedures.* New York: Richard Owen.

Harste, J., Woodward, V., & Burke, C. (1984). *Language stories and literacy lessons.* Portsmouth, NH: Heinemann Educational.

Heald-Taylor, G. (1986). *Whole language strategies for ESL primary students.* Toronto: Ontario Institute for Studies in Education.

Jewell, M. G., & Zintz, M. V. (1986). *Learning to read naturally.* Dubuque, IA: Kendall/Hunt Publishing Co.

Lee, D. M., & Rubin, J. B. (1979). *Children and language: Reading and writing, talking and listening.* Belmont, CA: Wadsworth Publishing.

Lindfors, J. W. (1987). *Children's language and learning* (2nd ed.). Englewood Cliffs, NJ: Prentice Hall.

Marek, A., Howard, D., Disinger, J., Jacobson, D., Earle, N., Goodman, Y., Hood, W., Woodley, C., Woodley, J., Wortman, J., & Wortman, R. (1984). *A kid-watching guide: Evaluation for whole language classrooms.* Occasional Papers, Program in Language and Literacy, College of Education, University of Arizona.

Tucson, AZ: University of Arizona. (ERIC Document Reproduction Service No. ED 277 978).

Martin, B. Jr. (1970). *Brown bear, brown bear, what do you see?* New York: Holt, Rinehart & Winston.

Meisels, S. J. (1987). Uses and abuses of developmental screening and school readiness testing. *Young Children, 42,* 4–6, 68–73.

National Association for the Education of Young Children. (1988). Position statement on testing of young children 3–8 years of age. *Young Children, 43,* 42–47.

Nurss, J. R. (1988). Development of written communication in Norwegian kindergarten children. *Scandinavian Journal of Educational Research, 32,* 33–48.

Pellegrini, A. D., Dresden, J., & Glickman, C. D. (1988). A not so new look at the assessment of kindergarten children. *Georgia Journal of Reading, 14,* 17–20.

Rhodes, L. K., & Dudley-Marling, C. (1988). *Readers and writers with a difference: A holistic approach to teaching learning disabled and remedial students.* Portsmouth, NH: Heinemann Educational.

Samway, K. D. (1989). I'm a whole language teacher . . . but the tests aren't. *Elementary ESOL Education News, 12,* 6–7.

Shepard, L. A., & Smith, M. L. (1988). Escalating academic demand in kindergarten: Some nonsolutions. *Elementary School Journal, 89,* 135–146.

Smith, M. L., & Shepard, L. A. (1987). What doesn't work: Explaining policies of retention in early grades. *Phi Delta KAPPAN, 69,* 129–134.

Smith, M. L., & Shepard, L. A. (1988). Kindergarten readiness and retention: A qualitative study of teachers' beliefs and practices. *American Educational Research Journal, 25,* 307–333.

Strickland, D., & Morrow, L. M. (1989). Emerging readers and writers: Assessment and early literacy. *The Reading Teacher, 42,* 634–635.

Teale, W. H. (1988). Developmentally appropriate assessment of reading and writing in the early childhood classroom. *Elementary School Journal, 89,* 173–183.

Teale, W. H., Hiebert, E. H., & Chittendon, E. A. (1987). Assessing young children's literacy development. *The Reading Teacher, 40,* 772–777.

Temple, C., Nathan, R., Burris, N., & Temple, F. (1988). *The beginnings of writing* (2nd ed.). Boston: Allyn & Bacon.

Willert, M. K., & Kamii, C. (1985). Reading in kindergarten: Direct vs. indirect teaching. *Young Children, 40,* 3–9.

Wixson, K. K., Peters, C. W., Weber, E. M., & Roeber, E. D. (1987). New directions in statewide reading assessment. *The Reading Teacher, 40,* 749–754.

Woodley, J. M. (1988). *Reading assessment from a whole language perspective.* Denton, TX: University of North Texas. (ERIC Document Reproduction Service No. ED 296 309).

Zurn, M. R. (1987). *A comparison of kindergartners' handwritten and word processor generated writing.* Unpublished doctoral dissertation, Georgia State University, Atlanta. *Dissertation Abstracts International, 49,* 428-A. (University Microfilms No. 88-08112).

CHAPTER TEN

Parents and Teachers: Partners in Emerging Literacy

Advance Organizer

Young children who have good oral language, listening, reading, and writing skills tend to come from homes in which literacy is valued and plays an important role in the daily life of the family. In this chapter, we discuss parental involvement in the literacy development of preschoolers, kindergarten, and primary grade children. In the first part, we describe how parents can create an atmosphere where literacy can grow and flourish and give suggestions for developing a print-filled, literacy-rich environment. We discuss a variety of methods and techniques and show through a number of examples how parents can involve their children in literacy activities by playing a guiding, supportive, and extending role, letting their children take the initiative and then following this lead. The second part of this chapter focuses on the parent/teacher partnership and how parents can be informed about the school literacy program, how they can participate in literacy activities in the classroom, and how they can work with their children on literacy activities at home. Examples of appropriate activities, programs, and guidelines for implementation are provided.

Objectives

After studying this chapter, the reader should be able to —

- state what effective behaviors parents exhibit in helping their children develop literacy;
- describe parental values, attitudes, and expectations that help develop literacy learners;
- explain how modeling is effective in helping children learn literacy behaviors;

Graphic Organizer

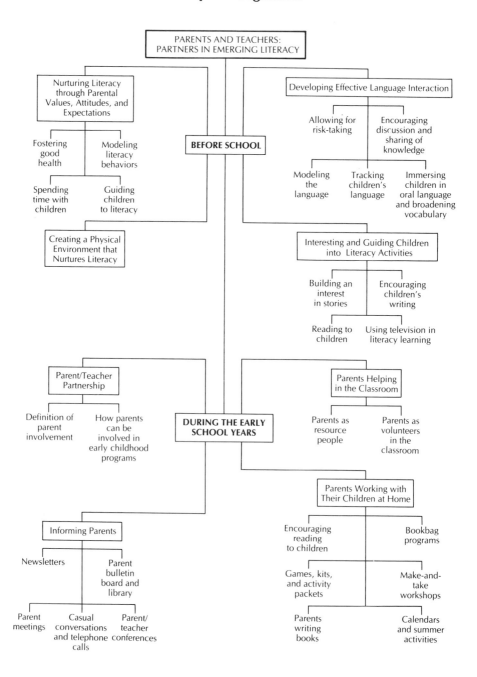

PARENTS AND TEACHERS:
PARTNERS IN EMERGING LITERACY

Nurturing Literacy through Parental Values, Attitudes, and Expectations

BEFORE SCHOOL

Developing Effective Language Interaction

Fostering good health

Modeling literacy behaviors

Allowing for risk-taking

Encouraging discussion and sharing of knowledge

Spending time with children

Guiding children to literacy

Modeling the language

Tracking children's language

Immersing children in oral language and broadening vocabulary

Creating a Physical Environment that Nurtures Literacy

Interesting and Guiding Children into Literacy Activities

Building an interest in stories

Encouraging children's writing

Reading to children

Using television in literacy learning

Parent/Teacher Partnership

DURING THE EARLY SCHOOL YEARS

Parents Helping in the Classroom

Definition of parent involvement

How parents can be involved in early childhood programs

Parents as resource people

Parents as volunteers in the classroom

Parents Working with Their Children at Home

Informing Parents

Encouraging reading to children

Bookbag programs

Newsletters

Parent bulletin board and library

Games, kits, and activity packets

Make-and-take workshops

Parent meetings

Casual conversations and telephone calls

Parent/ teacher conferences

Parents writing books

Calendars and summer activities

- describe ways in which parents can encourage and motivate their children to develop (a) oral language skills, (b) emerging reading skills, and (c) beginning writing skills;
- list a number of effective techniques in reading stories to children;
- describe how to set up a home physical environment that nurtures literacy;
- discuss the role of television in literacy learning;
- describe the importance of the parent/teacher partnership and the role of the teacher in developing this;
- define *parent involvement* and give several examples of it;
- describe six ways of informing parents about the school literacy program;
- describe how parents helping in the classroom as resource people and volunteers can help foster young children's early literacy development;
- describe six ways a parent involvement program can assist parents in working with their children on literacy activities at home.

PARENT INVOLVEMENT BEFORE SCHOOL

Parents are key players in their children's literacy development although they often do not fully realize their strong personal influence. The effects of parent involvement can range from richly enhancing literacy learning to stunting its growth. Parents' influence on their children's intellectual, social, and emotional growth has been widely documented. It can also be studied informally by watching parents interact with their children.

Parents are the child's first teachers. When children first enter preschool or kindergarten, you can observe a wide range of levels of development and background knowledge from one child to the next, traceable in part to the parents' prior influence. At one end of the spectrum are children who begin school socially confident and verbally adept. They are able to recite stories from memory, print a number of alphabet letters, or know how to read and write. At the other extreme are children who have poor language development, lack social and emotional maturity, and have little knowledge of print materials and their functions. A few children do not understand the concept of a book or what it means to read. Most beginning school children fall somewhere between these two extremes in terms of literacy development. Much of the discrepancy in development between children is a result of the home environment and parental involvement.

The effects of parent involvement continue as the child progresses through school. Parents' involvement is reflected in the child's attitude toward school and teachers, willingness and ability to attend to instruction, complete homework, and add to school lessons by bringing resource books from home. Even

the level of attendance at school can reflect the parents' involvement, cooperation, and support of the school program. Parents of preschool, kindergarten,
and primary children can involve themselves in their children's literacy learning. They can make a difference. This chapter details many of the ways parents
can be involved productively and enhance their children's development in literacy.

Nurturing Literacy through Parental Values, Attitudes, and Expectations

Children are watchful observers. They sense how their parents feel about many
things: e.g., about spending time with them, about discussing different things,
about expectations for their learning, about books and writing. Parents are creating images and impressions about learning that stay with their children and
subconsciously and consciously influence the way they look at the world. Parents are also fostering the way children see themselves as individuals. This parent power is tremendous. Henderson (1988), in a review of parent involvement
research, found a number of studies demonstrating that in homes conducive to
learning the parents had high expectations for their children and helped foster
positive attitudes towards learning. These homes had a positive measurable effect on children's achievement in school. Durkin (1966) looked at factors contributing to children learning to read before elementary school and reported
that the parents played a critical role in acting as role models, sharing and discussing experiences with children, and providing print materials. Some of these
forms of parent involvement are expanded upon below.

Fostering Good Health

Basic to a child's success in learning and well-being is the parent's good
physical care of the child. Vision and hearing checks provide evidence of the
child's ability to perform beginning literacy tasks successfully. Good nutrition
and reasonable sleep patterns help maintain the good health needed for children to be able to learn well.

Spending Time with Children

Parents who spend time with their children discussing the day's events, participating in their play, providing a number of stimulating experiences, and
working together on family projects are building a foundation of learning experiences. Underlying messages that build feelings of self-worth are sent to the
child. Children from these homes feel that what they have to say is important to
the parent, and this encourages self-expression. By being included in a variety
of activities, children feel that their presence is important and that they can

contribute too. Today most parents work outside the home and have less time to spend with their children. These parents can take a special effort to prioritize their time so they can meet the needs of their children and spend time in discussions and activities on a regular basis.

Modeling Literacy Behaviors

Young children imitate their parents so they will be more like them. As they grow older, they may continue to imitate an activity their parents engage in if it has a purpose for them or provides enjoyment in itself. If children see their parents as regular readers getting enjoyment out of books, magazines, and newspapers, they may also want to learn to read. If they see their parents using maps, reading recipes, or following diagrams to build a project, they will learn that reading is functional and can help them learn. If they see their parents writing letters, lists, or greeting cards, they may see the value of writing and want to write also.

Modeling literacy activities also shows children what is involved in doing the activity. For instance, children develop concepts about writing as their mothers use pencil and paper to write something down. If the mother occasionally explains what she is doing as she writes, the children develop a further understanding of writing.

Guiding Children to Literacy

Parents can guide children towards literacy in any number of ways. They can provide a variety of materials (e.g., books, magazines, paper, pencils) for their children to use. They can promote print awareness by pointing out signs and print in the environment and discuss the messages with their children. They can demonstrate their use of print by modeling. They can encourage their children's attempts at some literacy activity by genuine interaction. Rewarding children as a way to motivate their literacy development is important. There are many ways to motivate them: warm words, buying new books, special trips (including a trip to the library), recognition by showing a child's efforts to others. The list of motivational rewards is only limited by parents' imagination and their knowledge of what appeals to their children. In his discussion of children who develop literacy early, Holdaway (1979) lists motivation first among the factors involved in establishing early literacy in the child. He states, "Predominant is the personal joy and motivational strength displayed in the behavior [literacy]" (p. 52).

Parents can tell or read stories to their children. However, we caution them not to push or pressure their children into learning to read or write. Some children love to do these type of activities and will show rapid progress. Others will find these activities too sedentary and would rather be involved in active play. Forcing children to sit down and read just doesn't work. It results in frustrated

Father telling a story to his baby

parents and unhappy children. Becher (1985) underscores this warning: "In contrast, however, children whose parents exerted excessive pressure for reading achievement and who punished them for not reading well exhibited significantly less positive attitudes and lower achievement scores" (p. 48). Instead, parents must take cues from their children, point out print activities, develop interesting opportunities with reading and writing, and encourage any interest and initiative in that direction. Using this approach, children develop as literacy learners as much as possible and enjoy the experience.

Creating a Physical Environment that Nurtures Literacy

In studies of early readers (Clark, 1976; Clay, 1980; Durkin, 1966; Taylor, 1983) prominent characteristics of their homes were accessibility of many books and other print materials, as well as availability to the child of writing materials including pens, pencils, crayons, and paper. Both research and common sense suggest that parents who wish to nurture literacy learning should organize a physical setting that includes many forms of print materials. In the child's room, for example, parents could include bookshelves filled with children's books. There are a variety of sources of books, not all of which are expensive: e.g., paperback books, books purchased secondhand from garage sales or bazaars, and library books. Children's magazines, other picture-filled magazines, and advertisements, can also be stacked in the bookshelves for cutting, browsing, and copying activities. A comfortable chair with good lighting in the room can become a warm memorable place where parents can share stories with children in a quiet atmosphere. There are many imaginative ways a parent can create a print-filled environment, such as colorful posters with print, a calendar with a child's significant events marked down, or labels on objects like "Toy Box" on the toy box. Children can have their own desk in their room. However, many preschoolers would rather work close to their parents as they do various activities. A kitchen drawer set aside for children filled with writing and drawing materials is a convenient spot. The kitchen table may be a good place to draw, write, or read.

Children should see print all around them, have its use modeled for them, and be able to handle and use it. Just having bookcases filled with books, piles of magazines, stacks of paper, and drawers filled with crayons, pencils, and markers does not necessarily ensure that children will use these materials. And even if a child scribbles on the paper or flips through a book, he or she may not learn as much about writing and reading as a child whose parents involve themselves in these activities with their child. Some experiences with print are far more meaningful than others. Parents can make the difference by sharing a book, showing how to form letters when their children ask, and pointing out *In* and *Out* on the supermarket doors.

Developing Effective Language Interaction

Using language and learning about language are social activities. The verbal interaction between parents and children is basic in fostering an environment of literacy in the home. In recent years educators have learned much about how children acquire language, and we will discuss some of these findings.

Allowing for Risk Taking

Effective language learning is done in an atmosphere of warm acceptance and support from parents. As children learn to speak and develop better facility in a language, they necessarily try out new concepts and strategies. Some prove successful; however, errors are frequent and inherent in language acquisition. Risk taking is an important element to developing facility in speech. Parents should be aware of this and support attempts in language learning, rather than expecting immediate "good" language, sharply correcting or ignoring poor language usage, or, at worst, ridiculing the child's attempts.

Modeling the Language

Effective interaction between parents and young children includes modeling of the language by the parents (Wells, 1985). Parents model the communicative function of language. They show such things as how wishes are made known, how language can explain directions, and how approval or disapproval can be expressed without resorting to physical actions. Parents also model correct language usage. They do not support children's errors by mimicking a child's mistakes or using "baby talk" when speaking to their child.

Encouraging Discussion and Sharing of Knowledge

Parents who are effective in helping their children learn language provide an environment that encourages frequent discussions and the sharing of ideas and knowledge. In fact, Halliday (1975) speculated that a child's initial use of language can be traced to infancy when he or she begins to express stable vocalizations. By interpreting these as meaningful communication (although often meaningful only to the family), parents encourage and support this form of social interaction. Gradually, the young child proceeds from one word vocalizations to phrases to complete sentences as parents discuss and share knowledge and ideas. They are building on the child's language and language learning.

Larrick (1988) points out that a child coming from a home with lots of verbal interaction may enter school with a vocabulary as large as 32,000 words. A child with such a large vocabulary learns to read and write easily and can advance more rapidly than a child with limited language experience.

A child coming from a home with little verbal interaction, however, may begin school with a vocabulary of only 4,000 words. The children who have limited experience with verbal interaction begin school with limited oral language skills—in short, they begin school with a handicap. Larrick (1988) pointed out specific language skills that these children did not possess:

1. They did not feel comfortable asking questions.
2. They couldn't hold their own in the give-and-take of group conversations.
3. They had such limited vocabularies that they could not speak of many things or many ideas.
4. They had not learned to observe details or to note differences and similarities.
5. They did not question cause-and-effect.
6. They had not heard stories told or read aloud, so they had little experience with the sequence of events basic to a story.
7. They had difficulty recalling or anticipating the events of even the simplest story. (pp. 3–4)

In studying the home environments of young fluent readers, Clark (1976) found that the mothers in the study spent a lot of time with their children and "welcomed rather than rebuffed attempts at verbal interaction by the children" (p. 42). These parents were often encouraging and took the time to play with their children, even at the expense of delaying their other activities. Taylor (1983) found effective parents of literacy learners stressed the importance of talking and listening to their children as they began to read.

Tracking Children's Language

Researchers have identified several characteristics of verbal interaction between parent and child that seem to help children develop language and listening skills. According to Wells (1980), an adult's skill in tracking a young child's vocalizations is critical to the smooth flow of conversation between the adult and the child. Parents talk to their children with the idea of communicating with them rather than teaching them to talk. Parents interpret what their child is saying by sizing up the situation, knowing their child's previous facility with speech, and understanding the wants, needs, and interests of their child. Effective parents let children take the initiative in language, then support and add to the conversation.

Using semantic contingency   One method of tracking a child's language is called *semantic contingency.* The child begins a topic and the parent continues it, answering questions and providing new information (Snow, 1983). For example, when a parent and child share a book, the parent answers questions about the pictures or text. The child and parent might discuss events or characters that interest the child, or the parent might read aloud on request (Thomas, 1985).

Using scaffolding   Another effective practice in tracking children's language is called *scaffolding.* Here the difficulty of the language is reduced by structuring the discussion so that children will have an easier time understanding the meaning, following the directions, or completing the task (Snow, 1983). For example, a mother and her toddler see a black cat on the backyard fence. The child says, "Me-ow." The mother replies, "That's right, that's a cat. He says 'Me-ow.' " The mother points and says, "Look at what the cat is doing now." The child responds, "It jumping." "Yes," answers the mother, "The cat is jumping from the fence. He's coming to our door." "In," commands the child. The mother responds, "Do you want me to open the door and let the cat come in the house?" In this segment of conversation, parental tracking is evident. The mother did not correct the child's grammar directly, but modeled the correct structure in her reply. She wisely interprets, clarifies, and extends the child's ideas, and gives the child feedback on what he has said. This is effective parental involvement in a child's language development.

Immersing Children in Oral Language and Broadening Vocabulary

Again, effective parental involvement in language learning requires parents to set aside time to be with their children and welcome opportunities for discussion. Frequent verbal interaction is important. Parents need to provide opportunities for children to become involved in oral language by singing and talking to their children from birth. For example, parents can encourage their children to chime in on the repeated words or chorus of a story or folksong, and they can make comments and raise questions to sharpen their children's observational skills.

Parents can also help broaden their children's vocabulary through providing a rich variety of stimulating experiences. Stimulating experiences do not necessarily have to cost much money: e.g., going shopping, visiting a pet shop, spending a day at the park, discussing a television program they are watching, and cooking and cleaning up together. A broad variety of experiences increases children's knowledge of the world and expands their vocabulary as they discuss their experiences with their parents.

Interesting and Guiding Children into Literacy Activities

Providing a broad background of experiences not only helps children with oral language development, it will also help them develop the ability to read and write. Larrick (1988) contends that parents must understand that reading is a two-way process, with the reader bringing his or her experience to extend the meaning of the printed page. And as Dolores Durkin (1966) puts it, "The more we know before we read, the more we know after we read" (p. 12).

Building an Interest in Stories

Parents can involve their children in literacy by building their children's interest in stories. These stories can include old folktales that parents or grandparents have heard in their childhood or newly improvised stories. Besides parents telling stories, they can encourage their young children to tell their own stories. Describing a visit to the zoo, the parent might say, "First we drove our car and parked in the zoo parking lot." Then ask a question, "What did we do next?" The child may have to be prompted, but he or she gradually develops the ability to put incidents in order. This type of activity develops the skill of sequencing, which will help the child as he or she reads and writes.

Reading to Children

Reading aloud to children on a regular basis is one of the best things parents can do to help their children develop literacy skills. Researchers (Clay, 1979; Doake, 1982; Holdaway, 1979) found early readers were read to often and enjoyed this experience with their parents. Becher (1985) reported that studies show that children should be read to at least 8–10 minutes a day. The children in these and other studies (Rasinski and Fredericks, 1990) who had been read to on a regular basis exhibited more positive attitudes toward literacy and higher achievement levels in reading than children who had not been read to regularly.

As children are read to, they build the connection between oral language and print. They learn to listen and focus attention for a period of time — two basic skills of learning. By sitting next to the parent or on the parent's lap as they read, children learn to associate books with warm feelings. Also, they can follow the text as the parent reads. They learn concepts about handling books, such as left-to-right and top-down progressions. They learn literary conventions and story structure — the book language that will assist them in learning to read.

Too often parents expect children to "sit quietly and listen" when they read stories to them. However, researchers (Becher, 1985; Teale, 1984) maintain that reading aloud can be enhanced if parents interact with the child as they read. Parents can discuss the story and extend it by stopping in the reading to remark about events, characters, and simple details of a picture. These conversations should help the children to understand the story structure and answer a variety of different types of questions (e.g., detail, predictive, inferential, evaluative) about the story. Becher reports that studies of interaction during reading aloud to children revealed that "children who had higher performance scores on reading tasks were those who talked more about the story and asked more questions during the reading process than those children who did not" (p. 46).

Encouraging Children's Writing

Many young children have an interest in writing and begin writing before reading (Chomsky, 1971; Clay, 1976; Durkin, 1966; Haley-James, 1982). Parents can encourage children's writing by making pads of paper, pencils, crayons, and markers accessible in the home and by helping their children when they start experimenting with writing and drawing letters (Strickland and Morrow, 1989). Parents can model their writing for their children as they do such daily activities as write letters, make lists, and print reminders. For example, when a parent writes a letter to his or her parent, the child can be given paper and pencil to make their own letter to grandmother or grandfather. Parents are likely to observe scribbling, copying, and invented spellings as they watch their children become writers (see Chapter 5). This early experimentation should be encouraged. Having unrealistically high expectations for well-formed handwriting, correct spelling and punctuation, grammatically correct sentences, and capitalization will inhibit or at worse stop a child's progress in learning to write. Rather, parents should accept whatever writings their children produce, respond to these communications, and answer any questions about writing (Coe, 1988). Parents should also point out and discuss specific features of writing to increase the child's awareness of writing and what is involved when people write. This can help develop such concepts as sound/letter relationships, holding a pencil correctly, and letter formation.

There are a number of specific suggestions for parents as they encourage their young children's writing. Providing convenient models of writing for children to copy is helpful. Many young children take extreme pleasure in being able to print their name, and parents can help them with this. The power of being able to reply to a written message is a real motivator for many young children. Including children's attempts in parent's letters can encourage children to write. Writing messages such as "Don't touch!" and "Keep out!", which other family members read and follow, demonstrates some of the power of writing for children. Helping parents to put together family scrapbooks provides an opportunity for children to dictate to their parents appropriate captions for photos, draw pictures, or help co-author a journal of events on a family trip. Even when children are too young to hold a pencil, parents can provide them with such devices as magnetic boards and letters to help them learn about letters and words (Anderson, Hiebert, Scott, and Wilkinson, 1985).

Using Television in Literacy Learning

Many young children spend many hours a day watching television. For some parents, TV is a convenient babysitter while they busily complete their household chores, relax, enjoy hobbies, and so on. Young children who watch excessive amounts of TV, however, run the risk of becoming passive listeners. When a lot of their time is spent watching television, the development of their imaginations can be inhibited, and experiences in play where children learn to interact with others and solve problems are more limited. However, television can be an effective and positive tool in helping children become literacy learners if parents monitor both the amount of TV children watch and the choice of programs. Parents can encourage their children to watch TV programs of educational value, and they can watch these with their children. Television programs that teach about reading and language can have a positive effect on children's learning. When watching some programs with their children, parents can ask questions about shows, focus attention on information, and relate what children see to other situations.

PARENT INVOLVEMENT DURING THE EARLY SCHOOL YEARS

Parental involvement in the development of literacy in their young children does not need to stop at their own front door. Indeed, many of the literacy activities that occur in the classroom are similar to those the children may have experienced in the home (e.g., drawing a picture and then writing or dictating a caption or story to accompany the drawing). Ideally, there should be continuity in the development of literacy between the home and the school program. Hall (1987) has identified "three aspects that are critical if the emergence of literacy is to be continuous. There must be an environment where literacy has a high profile status; there must be access to valid demonstrations of literacy; and opportunity to engage in purposeful literacy acts which are acknowledged as valid literacy behavior" (p. 82). Both the child's home environment and the school environment should share these characteristics.

Parent/Teacher Partnership

Although parents and teachers share many similar behaviors related to teaching and learning (Ispa, Gray, and Thornburg, 1988), their roles in fostering early literacy are not the same (Sulzby, Teale, and Kamberelis, 1989). Teachers have different responsibilities and relate to larger groups of children in a school setting.

Early childhood educators traditionally have recognized, valued, and tried to include the family in the young child's education. What happens in school influences the family, just as what happens in the family influences what happens in school. Thus, there is a triadic relationship of the child, the parents/family, and the teacher/school. The teacher/school need to plan and establish ways in which this relationship can be fostered and used to support the child's development. One way in which this can be done is to encourage and provide for parents' involvement in their children's early school experiences.

The teacher is "the key to actualizing positive parental involvement in early childhood education programs" (Swick and McKnight, 1989, p. 19). According to the Office of Educational Research and Improvement (1986), "parental involvement helps children learn more effectively. Teachers who are successful at involving parents in their children's schoolwork are successful because they work at it" (p. 19).

Definition of Parent Involvement

Parent involvement is a catch-all term that has come to mean a variety of things to a variety of people. For some, it means parents working in the classroom or assisting on class fieldtrips; for others, it means helping children at home with their homework; for still others, it means being part of the PTA or running a fund-raising school lunch or bake sale. It can be all of these and more. *Parent involvement* can be defined broadly as "a process of helping parents use their abilities to benefit themselves, their children, and the early childhood program" (Morrison, 1988, p. 322). (We consider *parent* in this definition to include all family members such as siblings, grandparents, extended family members, family friends, and so forth.) The focus of the following sections is on how parents can participate in early childhood programs to help foster their children's early literacy development.

How Parents Can Be Involved in Early Childhood Programs

There is a variety of ways that parents can be involved in an early childhood program. In fact, variety is desirable and effective in meeting the needs of children, teachers, and the parents themselves. Not everyone can or is able to participate in the same way. For example, it is very difficult for working parents to find time during their workday to participate in classroom activities; on the other hand, they are usually willing to do activities with their children at home in the evenings. A parent who works evenings might be available during the day to assist in the classroom or go on a fieldtrip but unable to read to their child in the evenings. The recognition and accommodation of the need for parental choice and options is important. According to Harste (1989), "effective programs of reading treat parents as participants and partners in learning who are permitted options, choices, involvement, and information about the instructional alternatives available to students" (p. 54).

Informing Parents about the Early Literacy Program

Some parents may be reluctant to help their children with literacy tasks because they are afraid of doing something "wrong," which will interfere with their child's learning (Tovey and Kerber, 1986). Parents have told us, "I'd love to work with my child or help in the classroom, but I don't know anything about teaching." First of all, they *do* know quite a bit about teaching their children and have been doing it for years. Secondly, one does not always need to be a trained teacher to assist young children with literacy activities at home or in the classroom. However, this common misperception of parents does point out the need for informing parents about literacy and what they can do. We will discuss next some ways in which teachers can help parents to be more informed about young children's literacy learning.

Newsletters

One effective method of informing parents about the literacy program and how they can help their children is through a weekly or monthly newsletter. Each newsletter could contain a brief description of one or more aspects of the literacy program: e.g., how we teach reading, what is phonics. (These topics always seem to be a concern of parent groups we speak to, whether their children are 3 or 13.) A newsletter is also a way to respond to parental concerns throughout the year (e.g., "Why doesn't my child spell words correctly in the daily journal writing? Do the children have handwriting lessons every day?").

Some other topics for inclusion in a newsletter are —

- titles of children's books related to a current class theme or project that parents and children might read together;
- an upcoming television program or movie that would be appropriate for and of interest to the children;
- a list of games or books for possible birthday or holiday gift-giving;
- activities that the family can do together in the evening or on weekends;
- appropriate magazines for young children and subscription information;
- special events in the community;
- brief reviews of books on early literacy or child development that might be of interest to the parents;
- copies of the children's favorite songs;
- a new finger play;
- interesting programs for children in the community (e.g., recreation programs, toy libraries, or storytimes at the local public library);
- samples of stories or riddles the children have written or dictated.

As discussed in Chapter 8, the children can and should do some of the illustrating and writing or dictating of the newsletter (see Figure 10-1). In the newsletter, it is important to clarify terms that parents, who are not educators, might not understand: for example, *emerging writing, language experience, buddy programs.*

Some teachers may write a quick note to individual parents at the bottom of a child's newsletter. Informal notes to parents can be used as needed to inform the parents of particular happenings during the day: e.g., "Timmy finished his book today!" or "Josie drew this picture for you because she said you are ill. Hope you feel better soon."

In some families, the parents may not be able to read the newsletters because they are not English-speaking or they cannot read. Sometimes there is an older child or close family friend who can assist these parents. Many schools with non-English speaking families translate materials sent home into one or more languages. This translation can be done by the school staff, the children, school aides, volunteers, or other parents. In families where illiteracy is a problem, an older child or neighbor can assist the parents in reading the newsletters. Another way to convey information to these families is by video- or audiotapes. For some parents who are illiterate, the importance of their child

FIGURE 10-1   •   *Excerpts from Grade 1 Newsletters*

Grade one News from Mrs. LeBoeuf's Room

Dear Parents;
During the first part of the school year the class has co-operated in writing class stories. Each day the class decides on the topic and I will print the story on chart paper for them. The students help with the spelling whenever possible. For example: They supply all the beginning sounds for me and any other letter sounds that they hear. We

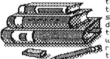

then read the story together. I do not expect that all children will be able to recognize all of the words but it is important that the children see that talk is just words print down on paper. We use these stories to practise and reinforce what phonics and vocabulary skills that the children have been taught at school. Sometimes I will ask the students to find words that I know they shoud know, sometimes I ask them to find words that begin with a certain beginning sound that has been taught. I will be sending these stories home periodically and asking you to read these stories with your child. I will also ask you to help your child locate certain words to reinforce the skills taught at school. This will be a perfect opportunity for you to share school news with your child as well as reinforcing skills taught at school. Hope this news and your child have fun with this news letter

PARENT HELPERS:
Each year I ask parents if they wish to help out in the classroom. Some typical jobs that I've had help with in the past are: colouring, cutting, putting up displays, cooking listening to the children read, checking work. Please let me know if you wish to help.   Mrs. LeBoeuf

Sept. 11, 1990
We are starting school. We are in grade one. Our **teacher is Mrs. LeBoeuf.** Ask your child to find the word "we", "are", "is".

Sept. 14, 1990

We are in grade one. We will learn to read, and print and paint in school. We are happy. Ask your child to find a word that begins like "wish", "run", "snake". Can you tell me what these words say?

Sept. 17, 1990

It was Sarah's birthday. She is six years old. She is happy. Ask your child to find a word that begins like "ball", "supper". Have them frame the word "is".

Oct. 2, 1990   **A fireman came to the school He told us about fire safety. We went into the fire house.** (begins like "fun", "hop".

learning to read and their desire to be part of this process is motivation for them to attend adult literacy classes. One type of adult literacy program uses children's books to teach the parents to read so that they can then read those books to their children. These classes assist "parents to help their own children as they themselves become more literate" (Nickse, 1990, p. 13).

Parent Bulletin Board and Library

A parent bulletin board and parent library shelf are useful for providing parents with information about literacy and other topics. The bulletin board, conveniently located where parents drop off or pick up their children, can display the following types of information:

- notices of upcoming events in the school and community,
- an extra copy of the latest newsletter,
- articles cut or photocopied from magazines or professional journals,
- examples of the children's work,
- cartoons and funny stories, copies of recipes from classroom cooking activities,
- a monthly or term calendar,
- brochures and pamphlets on a range of topics relevant to literacy and young children.

These brochures and pamphlets are often published by professional organizations, such as the International Reading Association and the National Association for the Education of Young Children, as well as by local organizations, state or provincial government agencies, and the federal government. Some early childhood classrooms have a shelf of books, magazines, and tapes that parents may borrow; and some schools have a schoolwide parent library. This is a quick and convenient method for parents to access information on a particular topic of interest or concern.

Parent Meetings

Parent meetings can be organized for a wide variety of purposes. The most frequent type seems to be the group meeting. Group meetings include orientation meetings, parents' evenings, or open houses. The *orientation meeting,* as the name implies, is held at the beginning of the year so the teacher can explain the program, the curriculum, and answer parents' questions. When we were teaching in the classroom, we used videotapes of a "typical day," slides of the children's activities, samples of their work, and handouts to assist in explaining what they would be doing in the coming year in our classrooms. It is helpful to a parent to have something in print to take home to show and discuss with a spouse who had to babysit or work.

At a *parents' evening,* a guest speaker may present information on one topic. Ideally, the parents have been surveyed to discover which topics they would like more information about during the coming months. Some literacy topics we have presented at parents' meetings include:

- how to read with your child
- encouraging your child to read
- your child's writing development
- good books for young children
- storytelling

- toys to make at home
- selecting toys and books for the holidays

An *open house* is typically a schoolwide event when parents can visit the various classrooms and talk with the school staff. Each teacher greets parents in his or her classroom and may make a formal presentation to the group and/or chat informally to each parent. An open house does not take the place of a parent/teacher conference but gives parents a chance to meet the school staff, see the child's classroom, and examine some samples of the children's work.

Parent meetings can be scheduled in the evening, on a weekday, or on a weekend. Meetings may be held at different times throughout the year to try and provide opportunities for all parents who wish to participate. Some preschools and elementary schools plan Saturday sessions once or twice a year—sometimes for children and fathers only and sometimes for the whole family.

At these meetings it is important to emphasize the valuable role that parents play in their children's early literacy development. Teachers can provide parents with suggestions for what they can do to help (e.g., read to their children every day, talk to their children about what they're doing in school); show them that their interest and assistance are appreciated; and inform them that the staff are available to answer questions and discuss their concerns. Parents should be invited to observe in the classroom and be made aware of the option for individual conferences with the teacher. The loan of photographs or videotapes of classroom literacy activities and special events are much appreciated by parents who cannot or do not come to the school. Some schools have improved parent attendance at meetings by providing babysitting or combining meetings with events for the whole family, such as potluck suppers.

Casual Conversations and Telephone Calls

One of the most frequent types of parent/teacher contact occurs at the beginning and end of the school day when the parent drops off or picks up the child. The parent may relay current information about the child, news of the family, concerns, or ask a question. Often these concerns and questions can be responded to in a few minutes and can be addressed immediately. Sometimes the question or concern raised is more complex, requires more consultation, or is of a confidential nature. In this case, it may be best for the teacher and parent to set a mutually convenient time to meet and discuss the issue later.

Many teachers we know use telephone calls to keep in touch with parents they do not see frequently. These informal contacts can be an excellent way to maintain regular, ongoing contact with parents in a nonthreatening way. If teachers initiate these calls early in the school year, parents realize that teachers do not only want to talk to them when there is a problem. This is particularly important for parents who may not have had positive experiences with school in the past and do not normally attend school functions.

Parent/Teacher Conferences

Most early childhood programs schedule 2–4 parent/teacher conferences a year. (This is not to say that parents and teachers should not arrange additional conferences at other times if the need arises.) The purpose of these conferences is to share information with the parents about their children's development and progress, to seek their input and ideas, to provide an opportunity for both the parents and teacher to ask questions, to plan future instruction for each child, and to develop further a working relationship with the parents. Information on children's literacy development needed for a parent/teacher conference is gathered over time before the conference using methods described in Chapter 9. Some guidelines to consider in conducting the conference are to —

- choose an informal but private location;
- start the conference with a positive, sincere comment about the child;
- convey the impression that this is a two-way conference and that you want the parents' input;
- allow parents to talk about their concerns and to ask questions (listen carefully);
- document your comments by showing the parents samples of the children's work or cite specific examples of behaviors;
- focus on the most important points you wish to discuss and involve the parents in planning possible follow-up activities, including some ideas they can do at home with their child;
- share information about any relevant community resources or referral agencies that might be appropriate;
- summarize the conference for the parent and end it on a positive note.

For parents who cannot or do not choose to attend parents conferences, you will need to try alternatives. Perhaps the parent cannot attend because there is a younger child or elderly parent at home who requires care or perhaps the parent works shifts. Some alternatives would be to schedule the conference at another time of day, talk to the parent on the telephone, make a home visit, or provide a translator if language is the problem. Some parents need more encouragement to come to school for parent conferences than do other parents; it is important for the teacher to be understanding and to suggest alternatives.

Parents Helping in the Classroom

There are many different ways that parents can help in the classroom depending on their interests, abilities, time available, needs of the children, and the teacher's plans. In many early childhood programs, such as parent-cooperative preschools, parent participation is essential for the operation for the program. Parents can participate either in paid positions, such as teacher aides, or as unpaid volunteers. Other family members besides parents can also participate in classroom programs: older siblings can be tutors or buddies to the younger children (see Chapter 8), senior citizens (whether related to the children or not) can also assist in the classroom. Some corporations in North America encourage and facilitate their employees' participation as volunteers in the schools.

Parents as Resource People

Parents are excellent resource people because "any group of parents represents a considerable collection of knowledge, skill and experience; there are many things that parents know and can do that stem from their backgrounds, their work, their leisure pursuits, and, above all, their experiences of life" (Atkins and Bastiani, 1988, p. 65). Parents as resource people can provide information to the children on a wide variety of topics related to the children's interests and what they are currently studying. In programs we are familiar with, parents have done the following activities with the children: told stories from another culture or country, staged puppet shows, made puppets, cooked ethnic food, discussed illustrating and authoring children's books, demonstrated photography and then used photos to help the children illustrate a class story, played a musical instrument, and organized a creative drama/movement activity. Using parents as resource people can help children make the connection more easily between the school and their home and community.

Parents as Volunteers in the Classroom

Parents can also assist in the classroom as volunteers or aides. Some literacy activities they may do with the children include —

- reading to one child or a small group of children;
- listening to the children read;
- playing board games with the children that are designed to teach or reinforce literacy skills, such as matching letters, sound/symbol correspondence, rhyming words, initial consonant sounds, and spelling;
- assisting the children with their writing by serving as scribes for the younger children or helping the older children with editing or using the computer;
- making instructional materials and games;
- bookmaking;
- assisting on fieldtrips (for example, walks to the local public library);
- assisting in the classroom or school library;
- tutoring individual children;
- assisting children to correct their work;
- doing displays or bulletin boards to promote and encourage reading;
- organizing and supervising a bookbag program or games lending program (see the description later in this chapter);
- inviting and serving as guest readers in the classroom (we like the idea of asking the principal and the school board members to come and read to the children at least once a year);
- taping stories and poetry for use in the listening center;
- organizing and supervising a monthly lunchtime book swap where children can bring

books and exchange these for other books brought by the children or contributed by adults.

Using parent or other adult volunteers in the classroom requires planning and monitoring. A good volunteer program does not happen automatically. A teacher must recruit parents and plan for a variety of possible tasks to accommodate parental interests, abilities, and time commitments. An orientation session or workshop for parent volunteers will help increase the effectiveness of parent volunteers. Such a workshop enables teachers to communicate their expectations, specify duties and responsibilities, explain classroom routines and their classroom management techniques, provide information on resources available and their location in the classroom and school, answer questions and concerns, and explain the options available for their participation. Volunteers appreciate being thanked after each session and periodically receiving a little "extra special" recognition from the teacher, the children, and the school. Parent volunteers can and do contribute much to enrich and expand classroom literacy programs. As Fredericks and Rasinski (1990b) concluded: "Volunteers can be a vital part of any reading program. . . . Aggressively seeking the partnership of parents in an active volunteer effort can be of inestimable worth in the reading development of children" (p. 521).

Parents Working with their Children at Home

In our experience, parents are willing and eager to help their children with literacy activities in the home. However, they may not always be certain what they can and should be doing or may need extra encouragement from the teacher. As mentioned earlier, ideas for family literacy activities can also be included in the regular newsletters to the parents. Brochures and booklets from professional organizations (such as the International Reading Association) can be shared with the parents: e.g., "Helping Your Child Become a Reader," "You Can Help Your Young Child With Writing," "Your Home is Your Child's First School," and "Summer Reading is Important."

A handout of ideas to promote literacy could be developed by the school staff and distributed to the parents. Some possible ideas might include—

- reading books to each other;
- talking about books the family has read;
- giving books and magazine subscriptions as gifts;
- visiting the local public library as a family;
- visiting a bookstore and helping the child to select a book to buy;
- using television programs and videos to foster reading;
- encouraging children to write and illustrate stories, journals, or letters;
- visiting local sites and discussing these;
- finding out about possible travel destinations and reading travel brochures;
- taking books on family outings or whenever a wait is likely (e.g., the doctor's or dentist's office, train or plane trips, etc.).

Encouraging Parents to Read to their Children

The most frequently suggested literacy activity for parents to do with their children at home is to read to them (Vukelich, 1984). In families where the parents are unable to read to their children, other family members, family friends, neighbors, or an older "buddy" at school can read to the children. Innovative programs have recruited senior citizens to read to children who attend after-school programs that are housed in public libraries and senior citizen centers.

Although telling parents to read to their children is an easy and straightforward suggestion for teachers to make, parents may appreciate some guidance. Some teachers do workshops for parents where they model the techniques for reading aloud to one or two children in a home setting (i.e., lap reading), review the criteria for selecting good books for young children, and provide a wide variety of good children's books for the parents to examine. Teachers and schools may also assist parents in reading to their children at home by helping to provide books and materials. Many schools encourage parents to borrow books from the school or classroom libraries, and some schools operate bookbag programs.

Bookbag Programs

In a *bookbag program,* the children take home books and other reading materials to be read by, with, or to their parents or other family members. Parents may not be able to easily provide an ongoing and varied supply of books for their children (Hart-Hewins and Wells, 1988). In some programs, the children can exchange the bookbags whenever they wish; in other programs there are specific exchange days. In one program, a bookbag contained four or five books on a specific theme or author, such as the Robert Munsch bag, the Clifford bag, the space bag, and the dinosaur bag. In addition, a book with a tape was included if "the taped story would provide a good oral reading model for both parents and children" (Baskwill, 1989, p. 36). In another program, the bookbag contained one book and an exercise book for the teacher and parents to jot down comments about the book, the child's responses to it, how the child read the book, and any questions or problems (Davis and Stubbs, 1988). Encouraging the parents to write comments on the materials and the child's response to them can develop into a dialog journal between the parents and teacher about that child's reading.

Games, Kits and Activity Packets

Children's literacy skills can be improved when teacher-developed materials are provided for use in the home by parents and young children during the school year and over the summer. Examples of the materials include games (Poy, 1985); kits (Baskwill, 1989); activity sheets (Probst, 1986); board games (Cooknell, 1985); and activity packets (Children First, 1980). These materials typically have a page outlining the activity: e.g., sorting, classifying, and matching pictures cut out from a magazine or the instructions to a game: e.g., rhyming picture lotto or word bingo. In addition, materials necessary to do the activity are included unless they are readily available in the typical home. There is also a feedback sheet. The writing suitcase/briefcase described in Chapter 7 can also be used in the home by the parents and children.

Make-and-take Workshops

Another way to assist parents in providing literacy materials for their children is to help them make these materials. The teacher, or a group of teachers, can present a workshop for parents after school or in the evening where the parents can make educational materials such as games, books, puzzles, and other materials suitable for their children, receive instruction on why and how these materials can be used, role play the use of the materials, and participate in informal discussions (Vukelich, 1978).

Parents Writing Books

A project in an inner-city area of London encouraged parents to write down stories for their children in their own language. These stories were usually about the children in the family, the parents' childhood, or experiences of the family (Bloom, 1987). A goal of the program was to "acknowledge and use this linguistic richness and also to involve its parents, bringing home and school closer" (p. 112). The family, with the assistance of the teachers, would edit and retype the story. Illustrations, a photograph of the child for whom the story was written, and an autobiographical note about the author were added. The story was assembled as a book with a cloth cover (see Appendix B for instructions on bookmaking).

Calendars and Summer Activities

Parents can also be encouraged to engage their children in literacy activities during holidays and in the summer. One way to facilitate this is to provide a list of suggested activities that tie in with the family's summer activities. This can be done using a calendar format with a suggested activity for each day or two. As the teacher knows the child well by the end of the school year, he or she can suggest books that would be both of interest to the child and appropriate for that child's level of literacy development. Games and other activities can be suggested to help reinforce and further develop the child's skills and reading abilities. Some possible activities are —

* making lists for a picnic supper,
* reading about a place the family plans to visit,
* magazines with articles about outdoor activities or sports,

- informational materials about pets and their care,
- making grocery lists and then helping find the items on the grocery shelf,
- helping read a recipe while cooking or baking,
- writing postcards to friends who are away or while the child is on a trip,
- keeping a diary of the summer happenings,
- special summer activities at the local library or museum.

These activity calendars should not pressure parents or children to do all of the activities; they are *suggestions* or reminders of *possible* activities (see Figure 10-2).

Parent involvement programs can be effective tools in fostering young chil-

FIGURE 10-2 • *Summer Calendar of Literacy Activities*

AUGUST						
Sun.	Mon.	Tues.	Wed.	Thurs.	Fri.	Sat.
						1 Read Rosie's Walk, then go for a walk.
2 Write a letter to Grandma or a friend faraway.	3 Make a puppet - or 2 or 3! Do a puppet play with a friend.	4 Visit the public library for the storytelling hour.	5 Draw or make models of your favorite storybook characters.	6 Plan a picnic menu. Design the menu. Make a grocery list.	7 Do the grocery shopping. Cross each item off the grocery list.	8 Fix some of the food for the picnic. (Read the recipes.)
9 Picnic! Write or draw about it in your Summer journal.	10 Tell a friend all about the picnic or tape-record your story and send it to a friend.	11 Write or tell the text to a book without words e.g., Frog Goes to Dinner.	12 Visit the public library and take out some new books.	13 Read Sylvester and the Magic Pebble. Look for interesting rocks.	14 Read or tell a story to a friend or a younger child.	15 Ask Mommy and Daddy to tell you about their favorite book when they were young.
16 Look for insects or birds in the garden or park. Identify them in a nature guide.	17 Read The Gingerbread Boy and then make gingerbread.	18 Pretend you are a favorite storybook character.	19 Make fingerpaint and have fun painting.	20 Make up a tongue twister. Practice until you can say it really fast.	21 Read a number book. make one yourself.	22 Help make pancakes for breakfast. Read the recipe.

dren's literacy development; however, "it is important to keep in mind that such outcomes are not guaranteed. . . . Good parent involvement requires much thought and effort to best meet the needs and goals of the children, the parents, and the program" (Mayfield, 1990, p. 243). Also, parent involvement programs require persistence and follow-through. It may not be sufficient to simply send home a notice of a meeting, activity, or request for classroom volunteers. Repeated invitations may be necessary because "one-shot publicity campaigns are not sufficient to provide parents with the information they need to become involved and stay involved in the reading program" (Fredericks and Rasinski, 1990a, p. 424). However, we have found that encouraging and involving parents in their young children's literacy development is well worth the time and effort and is valuable for the children, the parents, and the teachers.

References

Anderson, R. C., Hiebert, E. H., Scott, J. A., & Wilkinson, I. A. G. (1985). *Becoming a nation of readers: The report of the Commission on Reading.* Washington, DC: The National Institute of Education.

Atkin, J., & Bastiani, J. (1988). *Listening to parents: An approach to the improvement of home/school relations.* London: Croom Helm.

Baskwill, J. (1989). *Parents and teachers: Partners in learning.* Toronto: Scholastic.

Becher, R. (1985). Parent involvement and reading achievement: A review of research and implications for practice. *Childhood Education, 62*(1), 44–50.

Bloom, W. (1987). *Partnership with parents in reading.* Sevenoaks, United Kingdom: Hodder and Stoughton.

Children First. (1980). *Promising practices for administrators in pre-elementary right-to-read programs.* Washington, DC: U.S. Department of Education.

Chomsky, C. (1971). Write first, read later. *Childhood Education, 47,* 296–299.

Clark, M. (1976). *Young fluent readers.* London: Heinemann Educational Books.

Clay, M. (1976). *What did I write?* London: Heinemann Educational Books.

Clay, M. (1979). *Reading: The patterning of complex behavior.* Auckland, New Zealand: Heinemann Educational Books.

Clay, M. (1980). Learning and teaching writing: A developmental perspective. *Language Arts, 57,* 735–741.

Coe, D. E. (1988, April 6). *Emergent writing behavior of young children: Taking the task of writing to task.* Paper presented at the annual meeting of American Educational Research Association, New Orleans, LA.

Cooknell, T. (1985). An inner-city home reading project. In K. Topping, & S. Wolfendale (Eds.), *Parental involvement in children's reading,* (pp. 246–254). London: Croom Helm.

Davis, C., & Stubbs, R. (1988). *Shared reading in practice.* Milton Keynes, United Kingdom: Open University Press.

Doake, D. B. (1982). Learning to read: A developmental view. *Elements, 137,* 4–6.

Durkin, D. (1966). *Children who read early.* New York: Teachers College Press.

Fredericks, A. D., & Rasinski, T. V. (1990a). Involving the uninvolved. *The Reading Teacher, 43*(6), 424–425.

Fredericks, A. D., & Rasinski, T. V. (1990b). Lending a (reading) hand. *The Reading Teacher, 43*(7), 520–521.

Haley-James, S. M. (1982). When children are ready to write. *Language Arts, 59,* 458–463.

Hall, N. (1987). *The emergence of literacy.* Portsmouth, NH: Heinemann Educational Books.

Halliday, M. A. K. (1975). *Learning how to mean.* New York: Elsevier North-Holland, Inc.

Harste, J. C. (1989). *New policy guidelines for reading: Connecting research and practice.* Urbana, IL: National Council of Teachers of English.

Hart-Hewins, L., & Wells, J. (1988). *Borrow-a-book: Your classroom library goes home.* Toronto: Scholastic-TAB Publications.

Henderson, A. T. (1988). Parents are a school's best friends. *Phi Delta Kappan, 70,* 148–153.

Holdaway, D. (1979). *The foundations of literacy.* Sydney, Australia: Ashton Scholastic.

Ispa, J. M., Gray, M. M., & Thornburg, K. R. (1988). Parents, teachers, and daycare children: Patterns of interconnection. *Journal of Research in Childhood Education, 3*(1), 76–84.

Larrick, N. (1988). Literacy begins at home. *Claremont Reading Conference,* fifty-second yearbook, 1–17.

Mayfield, M. I. (1990). Parent involvement in early childhood programs. In I. Doxey (Ed.), *Childcare and education: Canadian dimensions* (pp. 240–253). Toronto: Nelson Canada.

Morrison, G. S. (1988). *Education and development of infants, toddlers, and preschoolers.* Glenview, IL: Scott, Foresman.

Nickse, R. (1990). Family literacy and community education: Prospects for the nineties. *Community Education, 8*(2), 12–18.

Office of Educational Research and Improvement. (1986). *What works.* Washington, DC: U.S. Department of Education. (ERIC Document Reproduction Service No. ED 263 299).

Poy, C. A. (1985). *The effects of a parent-child game program on readiness of kindergarten children.* Unpublished master's thesis, University of Victoria, Victoria, British Columbia.

Probst, A. M. (1986). *The effects of parent involvement on the learning of kindergarten children.* Unpublished master's thesis, University of Victoria, Victoria, British Columbia.

Rasinski, T. V., & Fredericks, A. D. (1990). Working with parents: The best reading advice for parents. *The Reading Teacher, 43*(4), 344–345.

Snow, C. E. (1983). Literacy and language: Relationships during the preschool years. *Harvard Educational Review, 53,* 165–189.

Strickland, D. S., & Morrow, L. M. (1989). Emerging readers and writers: Family literacy and young children. *The Reading Teacher, 42*(7), 530–531.

Sulzby, E., Teale, W. H., & Kamberelis, G. (1989). Emergent writing in the classroom: Home and school connections. In D. S. Strickland & L. M. Morrow (Eds.), *Emerging literacy: Young children learn to read and write* (pp. 63–79). Newark, DE: International Reading Association.

Swick, K. J., & McKnight, S. (1989). Characteristics of kindergarten teachers who promote parent involvement. *Early Childhood Research Quarterly, 4*(1), 19–29.

Taylor, D. (1983). *Family literacy: Young children learning to read and write.* Exeter, NH: Heinemann Educational Books.

Teale, W. H. (1984). Reading to young children: Its significance for literacy development. In H. Goelman, A. A. Oberg, & F. Smith (Eds.), *Awakening to literacy* (pp. 110–121). London: Heinemann Educational Books.

Thomas, K. F. (1985). Early reading as a social interaction process. *Language Arts, 62*(5), 469–475.

Tovey, D. R., & Kerber, J. E. (Eds.). (1986). *Roles in literacy learning: A new perspective.* Newark, DE: International Reading Association.

Vukelich, C. (1978). Parents are teachers: A beginning reading program. *The Reading Teacher, 31*(5), 524–527.

Vukelich, C. (1984). Parents' role in the reading process: A review of practical suggestions and ways to communicate with parents. *The Reading Teacher, 37*(5), 472–477.

Wells, G. (1980). *Learning through interaction.* Cambridge, England: Cambridge University Press.

Wells, G. (1985). *Language development in the preschool years.* Cambridge, England: Cambridge University Press.

Summary Statement

The integration and interrelatedness of oral and written language, the incorporation of written language across the curriculum, the increased use of literature and other real texts, and the reconceptualization of beginning reading and writing as a process of emerging literacy have dramatically changed the way young children are experiencing literacy in the schools. These changes have meant a shift to a meaning-based approach to written language communication and away from a heavily skill-based approach to reading and writing instruction.

In our book, *Emerging Literacy: Preschool, Kindergarten, and Primary Grades,* we have attempted to span current preschool to primary practices in emerging literacy. We have blended research with many practical ideas and concrete examples to help each teacher build that vital foundation of literacy necessary for children's future growth and success in school. We have deliberately presented and discussed a variety of strategies for use with young children. This was done because we know that every community of young learners is diverse and unique. The teacher must be adaptable and have available a variety of means and strategies to promote emerging literacy.

Finally, we would like to encourage all readers of this book to remember the importance of fostering children's positive attitudes towards literacy. We want children not only to be proficient in and use their literacy skills, but to enjoy their learning along the way. We want these children to emerge ultimately as life-long literacy learners.

Example of a Thematic Unit: The Gingerbread Boy

Introduction

Read Paul Galdone's *The Gingerbread Boy* to the class using the interactive story techniques described in Chapter 6. Begin with a discussion of gingerbread cookies, pointing to the illustrations to establish the concept for LEP students. While you are reading, point to the appropriate pictures to identify the characters. Some characters/objects will be familiar, while others will have to be explained and/or demonstrated. Ask questions to help predict what will happen next, especially as each character tries to catch the boy. At the end, discuss whether the predictions were accurate. Reread the story emphasizing the cumulative refrain and encouraging the children to join in.

Story of the Week

Use *The Gingerbread Boy* as a story of the week. Read the story every day doing a different follow-up activity each day.

Monday: Read story as described in introduction. Make construction paper gingerbread people. Cut out shape from brown paper after tracing with a template *or* cut out parts, traced on oak tag and colored with markers (body, head, two arms, two legs) and attach with paper brads. Decorate by pasting on cut-out eyes, nose, mouth, buttons, or by drawing these on with markers. Display on bulletin board with title *The Gingerbread Boy* and each child's name beneath it.

Tuesday: Reread story. Dramatize story by selecting children to pantomime each part. Teacher gives narration and class chants refrain. Repeat to give all an opportunity to play a part.

Wednesday: Reread story. Make gingerbread cookies using a printed recipe and directions. Emphasize oral language and write language experience story (see Box 6-2).

Thursday: Reread story. Divide class into groups to make pictures of story – a different group illustrates each section. For example:

man and woman making cookie Gingerbread Boy
Gingerbread Boy running away from each character
Gingerbread Boy being eaten by fox and others at end

Put pictures on bulletin board with appropriate caption and refrain.

Friday: Children read story using bulletin board illustrations and captions. Repeat several times so individual children have a turn to read caption while group chants refrain. Discuss feelings of each character. Put book on library table for repeated readings.

Additional Activities

- Read additional cumulative tales (*Mr. Gumpy's Outing, Henny Penny, This Is The House That Jack Built*).
- Read related food tales (*Hansel and Gretel, Little Red Hen*).
- Read other national variants of *Gingerbread Boy* (Norway: *The Pancake,* England: *Johnny Cake*).
- Make pancakes or gingerbread cookies.
- Do gingerbread people lacing cards.
- Retell the story in sequence.
- Use the refrain as a choral reading.
- Illustrate a class or individual book of the story.
- Use puppets or flannelboard to dramatize story.
- Rewrite story (dictation) as a news article about the "Escape of A Gingerbread Boy." See Huck, C. S., Hepler, S., and Hickman, J. (1987). *Children's literature in the elementary school,* (4th ed.). New York: Holt, Rinehart & Winston.
- Make a mural of the story with captions.
- Label the body parts.
- Use sensory descriptive words (touch, smell, taste, sight) for gingerbread boy.
- Farm vocabulary—actions, products of threshers and mowers.
- Learn gingerbread song.
- Discuss and dictate story about changes in dough during mixing, rising, baking.
- Count number of raisins on each gingerbread cookie.
- Make a graph of favorite kind of cookies.
- Do movements in story—knead and roll dough, pop out of oven, run away, snap of fox's mouth.

Gingerbread Center

- Turn the housekeeping kitchen into a gingerbread bakery.
- Put up a chart with the "recipe" for gingerbread; label the "ingredients" (use empty containers).
- Have utensils for mixing, kneading, rolling, baking.
- Have cut-out felt or tagboard gingerbread people wrapped in plastic wrap ready for "sale."
- Add price tags, a chart of prices, cash register.
- Children roleplay making, selling, and buying gingerbread people.

APPENDIX B

Bookmaking

FIGURE B-1 • *Examples of Teacher-/Child-made Books*

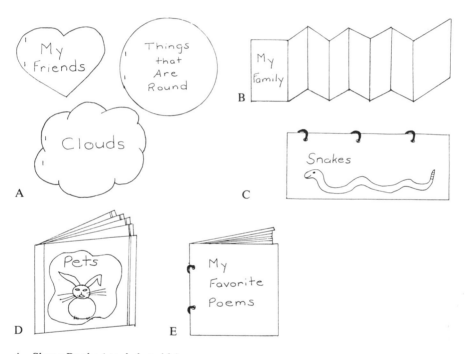

A. Shape Books (stapled at side)

B. Folding Book (Accordion Book)

C. Ring Book

D. Plastic Bag Book (Take several sealable plastic bags. Staple together at non-opening end. Cover staples with colored tape. Children insert their drawings or writing, then seal the bags.)

E. Wooden Book Covers (2 pieces of thin plywood with holes drilled for rings or ribbon/yarn ties)

FIGURE B-2 • *Bookbinding*

1. Fold papers in half to make the pages. Insert pages inside each other.

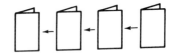

2. Sew down the fold by hand or machine.

3. Cut 2 pieces of cardboard a bit larger than the pages. Leave space in the middle so the book will fold.

4. Covers can be made from fabric, contact paper/mactac, or wallpaper (prepasted does not need glue). Cut the cover about one inch (3 cm.) larger on each side of the pages.

5. Place the cardboard on the wrong side of the cover.

   If using contact paper/mactac or prepasted wallpaper, fold in the corners, then the top and bottom edges. Press down to set. (Go to step 7.)

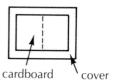

cardboard   cover

6. If cover is fabric, cut a piece of dry mount tissue (available at photo supply stores) a bit smaller than the cover but larger than the cardboard.

   Press the surface of the cardboard with an iron. Fold in the corners, then fold the top and bottom edges. Iron.

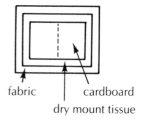

fabric   cardboard

dry mount tissue

7. To attach the pages to the cover, the endpapers can be glued to the covers *or* a piece of dry mount tissue the same size as the pages can be placed between the cardboard and the endpapers and then the endpapers ironed.

Magazines for Children

Canadian Geographic
39 McArthur Ave.
Vanier, Ontario K1L 8L7

Chickadee Magazines
Suite 304, 56 The Esplanade
Toronto, Ontario M5E 1A7

Cricket, the Magazine for Children
Carus Publishing Company
315 Fifth St.
Peru, IL 61354

Highlights for Children
2300 W. Fifth Ave.
P.O. Box 269
Columbus, OH 43216

Owl Magazine
Suite 304, 56 The Esplanade
Toronto, Ontario M5E 1A7

National Geographic World
P.O. Box 2174
Washington, DC 20013

Ranger Rick
National Wildlife Federation
8925 Leesburg Pike
Vienna, VA 22184-0001

More information on magazines for children: Stole, D. R. (Ed.). 1990. *Magazines for Children*. International Reading Association and Educational Press Association of America, Newark, DE.

APPENDIX D

Professional Journals and Organizations

Booklist
American Library Association
50 E. Huron St.
Chicago, IL 60611

Child Education
Scholastic Publications
Marlborough House
Holly Walk
Leamington Spa
Warwickshire, England CV32 41S

Canadian Children: Journal of Canadian Association for Young Children
CAYC Publishing & Printing Service
36 - Bessermer Court,
Unit 3
Concord, Ontario L4K 3C9

Childhood Education
Association for Childhood Education International
11141 Georgia Avenue
Suite 200
Wheaton, MD 20902

Children's Literature
The Children's Literature Foundation
Box 370
Windham Center
Storrs, CT 06268

Children's Literature in Education
Exeter University Institute of Education
Gandy St.
Exeter, EX 4 3QL

Day Care and Early Education
Human Science Press Inc.
72 5th Ave.
New York, NY 10011

Educational Leadership
Association for Supervision and Curriculum Development
1250 N. Pitt St.
Alexandria, VA 22314-1403

The Elementary School Journal
University of Chicago Press
P.O. Box 37005
Chicago, IL 60637

Instructor
P.O. Box 3018
Southeastern, PA 19398-3018

Language Arts
The National Council of Teachers of English
1111 Kenyon Rd.
Urbana, IL 61801

Infant Projects
Subscriptions Dept.
Scholastic Publication Ltd.
Westfield Road
Southam, Leamington
Warwickshire, CV33 OJH England

Learning
P.O. Box 2580
Boulder, CO 80322

The Lion and the Unicorn
The Johns Hopkins University Press
Journals Division
701 W. 40th Street
Suite 275
Baltimore, MD 21211

The New Advocate
Christopher-Gordon Publishing, Inc.
P.O. Box 809
Needham Heights, MA 02194-0006

Parents
Parents Magazine Enterprises Inc.
New Bridge Rd.
Bergenfield, NJ 07621

The Reading Teacher
International Reading Association
800 Barksdale Road
P.O. Box 8139
Newark, DE 19714-8139

The School Librarian
The School Librarian Association
Liden Library
Barrington Close
Liden, Swindon SN3 6HF
England

Teaching Pre.K-8
Early Years
P.O. Box 218
Knoxville, IA 50198

Young Children
National Association for the Education of Young Children
1834 Connecticut Ave. NW
Washington, DC 20009

For good reference materials, contact these associations:

Canadian Children's Book Centre
35 Spadina Rd.
Toronto, Ontario M5R 2S9

Children's Book Council, Inc.
67 Irving Place
New York, NY 10003

See also:

State, provincial and local educational and professional organizations. For example, local chapters of I.R.A., A.C.E.I., and N.A.E.Y.C.

Index

Emerging literacy